Telling the Truth

Telling the Truth

*Preaching about Sexual
and Domestic Violence*

Edited by
John S. McClure and Nancy J. Ramsay

United Church Press
Cleveland, Ohio

United Church Press, Cleveland, Ohio 44115
© 1998 by John S. McClure and Nancy J. Ramsay

Library of Congress Cataloging-in-Publication Data

Telling the truth : preaching about sexual and domestic violence /
edited by John S. McClure and Nancy J. Ramsay.
    p.   cm.
    Papers from the Consultation on Preaching and Sexual and Domestic
Violence, held at the Presbyterian Center in Louisville, Kentucky,
Feb. 28–Mar. 2, 1997.
    Includes bibliographical references.
    ISBN 0-8298-1282-2 (paper : alk. paper)
    1. Preaching.   2. Sexual abuse—Religious aspects—Christianity.
3. Family violence—Religious aspects—Christianity.   I. McClure,
John S., 1952–   .   II. Ramsay, Nancy J. (Nancy Jean), 1949–   .
III. Consultation on Preaching and Sexual and Domestic Violence
(1997 : Presbyterian Center, Louisville, Ky.)
BV4221.T45   1998
261.8'327—dc21   98-36258
                                                                         CIP

For Marian
—JSM

*For J. Mark Barnes and Barbara Z. Barnes, pastors whose
preaching about sexual and domestic violence is a faithful
witness to God's fierce and tender love*
—NJR

Contents

Part 4: Model Sermons

Acknowledgments

In November 1995 we began to brainstorm how to better train homileticians to re-source preachers so that they could tell the truth about sexual and domestic violence. This brainstorming involved many persons, including clergy, faculty, and Presbyterian denominational staff. In the spring of 1996 we found a home for our concern in the Societal Violence Initiative Team of the National Ministry Division of the Presbyterian Church USA. The Societal Violence Initiative Team offered to sponsor a Consultation on Preaching and Sexual and Domestic Violence. The consultation would include scholars representing constructive, biblical, and practical theological perspectives and representative homileticians from Presbyterian and Presbyterian-related seminaries.

The Consultation on Preaching and Sexual and Domestic Violence was held at the Presbyterian Center in Louisville, Kentucky, from February 28 to March 2, 1997. It was jointly funded by grants from the Trull Foundation, Independent Presbyterian Church (PCUSA) in Birmingham, Alabama, Health Ministries, National Ministries Division (PCUSA), and the Societal Violence Initiative Team, National Ministries Division (PCUSA). The essays collected in this book are the fruits of this consultation.

We could not have held this consultation or pieced together this book without significant assistance. We wish to thank Marian McClure, who helped us raise the grant money that would make the consultation a possibility. Jeannine Frenzel, staff person for the Societal Violence Initiative Team, spent endless hours assisting with organizational details and correspondence. In the final hours before the consultation, Annie Wu King, then acting associate for the Women's Ministries Unit, provided invaluable support and troubleshooting expertise. We appreciate the ongoing counsel provided by the Societal Violence Initiative Team, whose members were Kristine K. Thompson, James Poling, Earnest (Camp) Edwards Jr., Thelma Burgonio-Watson, Jinny Miller, Maria Yee, Loretta Bradley, and Peggy Barnett. In particular we are grateful for the careful attention to the consultation provided by James Poling, the official liaison between the team and the consultation. We are indebted to David Zuverink and Health Ministries, USA, the Trull Foundation, and Felix Yarboro and the session of Independent Presbyterian Church for financial support. We also appreciate the moral support and coordination among theological schools provided by Dottie Hedgepeth from Theological Education, Congregational Ministries Division (PCUSA). The message of the consultation was deepened and brought home in worship services led by Alexa Smith and Marian McClure. Secretarial assistance provided by Tonya Vickery and Melisa Scarlott smoothed out many organizational wrinkles along the way, and the preparation of the final manuscript of the book by Melissa Nebelsick brought an often disheveled stack of papers and floppy disks into coherent order and consistent style.

Special thanks are due the homileticians who attended the consultation and gave a weekend of their time to providing feedback to the presenters and discussing this topic. These homileticians were Charles Campbell from Columbia Theological Seminary, Jana Childers from San Francisco Theological Seminary, Pamela Moeller from Emmanuel College, Toronto, Richard Oman from Pittsburgh Theological Seminary, Beverly Zink Sawyer from Union Theological Seminary in Richmond, Teresa Stricklen from Vanderbilt Divinity School, and Leonora Tubbs Tisdale from Princeton Theological Seminary.

Introduction: Poured Out like Water

> I am poured out like water,
>   and all my bones are out of joint;
> my heart is like wax
> my mouth is dried up like a potsherd. (Ps. 22:14–15)
>
> Every night I flood my bed with tears:
> I drench my couch with my weeping. (Ps. 6:6)
>
> My tears have been my food day and night. (Ps. 42:3; Isa. 16:9)
>
> My enemies trample upon me all day long. (Ps. 56:2)
>
> I lie down among lions. (Ps. 57:4)
>
> Rise up, O [God], confront them,
>   overthrow them!
>
> By your sword deliver my life
>   from the wicked. (Ps. 17:13)

These psalms are the words of our tradition, words spoken and prayed in worship. They are laments and petitions uttered by victims of radical evil, pain, and violence. These whispers, cries, and prayers are not only to be spoken by victims or survivors of violence. The people of God have spoken these words *together* across time, as if to say, "We, the congregation, will not keep silent" in the face of such violence. "We will name both the pain and the enemy." "We will hear and hold the victim and survivor." "We will confront the perpetrator and insist on retribution. For our God is a God of compassion and justice."

It is the task of preaching to bring focus, direction, and purpose to these biblical words in each generation. Who are the victims? Who are the perpetrators? What is the name and the nature of this evil? Where is God? What is our hope? What can the church do to help? What must be changed in our society in order to stop the violence?

Statistics tell us that sexual and domestic violence have escalated in recent years. Certainly our awareness of such violence has increased, even though less than 10 percent of sexual assaults are reported to the police. We know that one in three American girls below the age of eighteen and one in seven boys are sexually abused. According to estimates, every six minutes a woman is raped in the United States. Woman-battering is one of the major causes of serious injury to women and is a primary cause of much of the homelessness of women and children. Sexual harassment is as common in the workplace as is salary inequity between men and women. Date rape and marital rape are mirror images of what many women can expect to confront in their quest to find meaningful relationships with men.[1]

It is likely that in most churches on any Sunday morning, there are batterers or child abusers and many victims of sexual or domestic violence. In a 1989 survey of various denominations, the 105 respondents "reported that they had encountered a total of 885 cases within the prior year, an average of over eight per minister or priest."[2] The problem is pervasive and insidious.

And yet, the usual course of action in most congregations is silence. The truth about sexual and domestic violence is not told. In some instances, the reason for this silence is an almost willful disbelief that these dreadful things could be occurring in our midst. In other instances, it seems expedient to protect the pastor's or the congregation's reputation, especially in an age of declining membership. Pastors wonder if their image in the community will become "dirty" because they talk about topics such as incest, rape, or battering. Sometimes inaction stems from a misplaced desire to protect the private realm from public scrutiny. At other times, inaction stems from lack of awareness, education, and preparedness; or it may be that pastors are overextended already and don't need another item to occupy their busy schedules. Whatever the reasons, the silence is profound.

The silence, however, is not really silent. It sends a clear "hands-off" message to victims, perpetrators, and bystanders. At the very least, this silence communicates to victims that they are alone with their suffering. To perpetrators it says that the church does not hold them accountable for their evil actions. To bystanders it says that it is okay to remain on the sidelines of a brutal and sometimes deadly game.

This book began with our desire to help pastors break the silence and tell the truth about sexual and domestic violence in their congregations. As editors, we believe that preaching is crucial to the task of speaking out about injustice, pain, and suffering in the church. We do not see preaching in isolation from other aspects of ministry. Preaching is deeply related to the worshiping, caring, educating, and serving ministries of congregations. We remain committed to the work of attending to particular instances of domestic violence through intervention, pastoral care, and counseling.

We hope that congregations will offer educational classes on sexual and domestic violence and will get involved in outreach to individuals in the community. And yet, we also believe that preaching is closely connected to these ministries of pastoral care, education, and justice. Preaching extends and broadens the pastoral care ministry of the church. Preaching is at the center of the larger educational ministry of the congregation and plays a vital role in interpreting what the church believes. Preaching is also proclamatory and missional—challenging congregations to take a communal and public stand, inviting response and involvement, and welcoming victims and survivors as full members of the community.

THEOLOGICAL AND BIBLICAL PERSPECTIVES

These chapters represent a range of perspectives and emphases. Wendy Farley encourages preachers who speak about sexual and domestic violence to think carefully about theological issues such as radical evil, God's judgment, forgiveness, and grace. According to Farley, preachers should preach that human beings are not only mired in sin but are victims, and sometimes perpetrators, of radical forms of evil and suffering. Violence against another should be interpreted by the preacher as privation, as an "undoing" of the other person that has as its goal the destruction of what God has done in the act of creation. She asks, "What kind of power can begin to rebuild what has been undone?" She answers that compassion can be preached as a form of power that helps to resist violence, "undo" perpetrators, and re-create what violence has "decreased."

Johanna van Wijk-Bos asserts that preachers must assure congregations that the God of the Bible is not a God of violence. She assesses the word "violence" as it is used throughout the Bible and concludes that it is a word used principally for those who are opposed to God's righteous, loving, and redemptive intentions for the world. She reminds us that violence is not only personal, but also social and systemic throughout the Bible. It can be seen in various forms of exploitation and in a lack of hospitality to women, children, the elderly, and strangers.

M. Shawn Copeland asserts that violence has wounded African American culture and religious imagination. The pervasive violence against women in rap and hip-hop music, print and visual media, films, MTV, and video games has left the African American community "wounded culturally." In this context, the sermon becomes a central tool for the "healing of distorted imagination."

PASTORAL RESOURCES FOR TELLING THE TRUTH

Marie Fortune challenges preachers to be attentive to how they preach the standard doctrines of the Christian faith so that they won't be tacitly approving sexual or domestic violence. In particular, she helps preachers rethink the theme of forgiveness. She provides a way to preach forgiveness so that it cannot be turned into a form of "cheap grace" by perpetrators or a reinforcement of the guilt and shame of victims and survivors.

Nancy Ramsay turns the preacher's attention to the task of preaching to survivors of childhood sexual abuse. She invites preachers to help their congregations rethink the human condition as tragically structured: shaped by vulnerability, fear, shame, and sometimes hopelessness, yet remarkably resilient and resourceful. She identifies several theological issues that shape the content of preaching truthfully about sexual abuse: the nature of God's power and love, love for self, confusion about forgiveness, the nature of freedom and accountability, and the complicity of the church in the level of violence perpetrated against women and children. She encourages preachers to view their sermon preparation through two "hermeneutical lenses": (1) compassion and resistance, and (2) love as the context for power.

Jim Poling considers how to preach to perpetrators of sexual and domestic violence. He invites preachers to use a "hermeneutics of suspicion" that exposes the history of domination in which the church is enmeshed, a history rooted in years of slavery, the property rights of men, and the spiritualization of the gospel. This suspicion in the pulpit is supplemented by a "hermeneutics of confession" that accesses the present power of Jesus' spirit in the face of evil and injustice. According to Poling, the messages heard in pastoral care to victims and perpetrators critique the gospel that has been preached for many years. Based on this critique, he provides guidelines for confronting and challenging perpetrators in worship and preaching.

David Goatley challenges preachers to "step up to the plate" and to preach relevant sermons that challenge the violence in their communities. He examines violence in African American life and notably the recent emergence of gang violence, pointing to patterns of domination and exploitation inherited from a past of brutal slavery and a present situation of morally bereft corporate capitalism. He urges experiential, event-oriented preaching that will engage this violence head-on in a way that can "birth something new."

TRANSFORMING HOMILETIC PRACTICE

Preachers cannot simply read a few books and begin to preach "about" sexual and domestic violence. According to Barbara Patterson, the best way to learn how to preach these subjects is to enter into a process of formation that requires engagement, repentance, and a new commitment. Preachers should find ways to become existentially involved with victims and perpetrators in order to discern the incarnate Christ in the lives of violated women. She suggests a set of practices as a means of learning experientially what can and cannot be preached and how to make preaching a ministry that incarnates the continuing presence of Christ in the church and the world.

Preaching about sexual and domestic violence raises a host of homiletic questions. John McClure answers several of these: What role should the experience of the preacher and the stories of victims or survivors play in preaching? What topics could a long-range preaching plan include? What does it mean to preach a nonviolent theology? What do preachers need to be aware of when illustrating sermons? How should preachers conceptualize their sermons when they are addressing different audiences: victims and survivors, perpetrators, and bystanders? What commentaries will be most helpful? What kinds of logic and language will work best? What kind of delivery should the preacher use?

CHAPTER THEMES

Throughout these nine chapters, several common themes sound forth over and again. The first is the theme of radical evil. Such evil must be recognized for what it is, rightly named in public worship, and resisted by the church in every way possible. A second theme is the concern to empower victims and survivors. Instead of silencing, avoiding, or blaming victims, they are to be welcomed, supported through solidarity and resistance, and learned from as preachers engage in theological and spiritual reflection. A third theme is the systemic nature of violence. The invasive violence manifest in sexual and domestic violence is endemic to a patriarchal society in which power is coercive, relationships are instrumental, and exploitation and betrayal of trust have become entrenched patterns of behavior. To address sexual and domestic violence is also to confront systemic violence. A fourth theme is the conviction that one cannot remain aloof or detached if one wants to be a partner in healing sexual and domestic violence in our churches and in our culture. If one really embarks on this journey, one is truly risking personal and spiritual transformation. A fifth theme is that preaching about sexual and domestic violence is both difficult and an absolute necessity if the church is to faithfully proclaim God's Word. It is in preaching, more than anywhere else, that the Word of truth must be spoken. Martin Luther made it clear to his generation that when the Word is spoken in preaching, both the gates of hell and the portals of heaven swing open. If it is done well, preaching exposes evil for what it is and discloses God's judgment and grace. If it fails to do this, preaching becomes vain triviality, and no Word at all will be heard in the church.

While preaching about sexual and domestic violence is not the entirety of the truth that must be told from the pulpit, it is, in some ways, a test case for the willingness of preachers to relate their preaching ministry to truth-telling in the contemporary American context. We now know that this problem is pervasive both in society and in the church, and many persons in our congregations also know this; therefore, to avoid it is like missing the proverbial snake that is about to bite us. Clearly people need to know what their church has to say about sexual and domestic violence. It is time for the truth to be told. These pages are a resource for preachers who are willing to take this challenge.

MODEL SERMONS

As we imagined the flow of these nine chapters, it seemed well to seek out sermons that demonstrate contemporary efforts to preach truthfully about sexual and domestic violence. We inquired among our colleagues around the country to find persons whom we could ask to share their sermons with us. Our search confirmed our hunch that effective preaching on this topic is being done, as these sermons demonstrate. However, our experience also suggests that such sermons are rare. From the sermons we gathered, we have chosen six. Many of these were preached in congregations as a part of regular Sunday services; two of them were preached at conferences.

Although the sermons gathered here represent diverse approaches, in every case they tell the truth about sexual and domestic violence. In "Whoever Looks Lustfully," Mark Barnes, a Presbyterian pastor, draws on Matthew 5:27–37 to explore cultural distortions of the gift of sexuality. He rightly defines "lust" as the will to possess or control another in various destructive and abusive ways.

Marie Fortune, a United Church of Christ minister and director of the Center for the Prevention of Sexual and Domestic Violence, the author of chapter 4 of this book, draws in her sermon on psalms of lament and a powerful image in Revelation; these allow her to name rightly the destructiveness of domestic violence and the healing power of God's love and justice.

Karen Brau, a Lutheran pastor in Baltimore, and W. Eugene March, a Presbyterian and dean of Louisville Presbyterian Seminary, both develop their sermons from 2 Samuel 13:1–22, the rape of Tamar. Their approaches to the text differ, but each finds in it resources for naming the sin of violence, for the promise of God's healing love, and for the challenge to empower victims of violence.

Anne Marie Hunter, a United Methodist pastor, draws on Exodus 16–17 as well as Psalm 105 to confront forthrightly the sin of domestic violence and to describe the sustaining and liberating love of God which congregations are called to embody with survivors of such violence.

Aubra Love, a Baptist pastor on the staff of the Center for the Prevention of Sexual and Domestic Violence, takes Genesis 21:8–20 as her text. She looks at the experience of Hagar through the lens of domestic violence in a way that affirms the power of God's love and the importance of our commitment to victims of violence as agents of God's love.

The themes identified in the first nine chapters emerge often in the sermons. Radical evil, for example, is directly addressed in Anne Marie Hunter's sermon when she describes the controlling, "soul-shriveling oppression" of domestic violence. Mark Barnes's reflections on lust also name the sin of objectifying and seeking to possess another to satisfy one's own needs. Aubra Love describes the sin of rejecting the image of God in one another.

Empowerment is a prominent theme in many of these sermons. Gene March's reflections on "Amnon's Folly" describe the importance of crying out for justice and the empowerment that comes when voices of victims are heard. Aubra Love draws on the experience of Hagar to remind us of ways God speaks through victims who are able to say "no" to the objectification of abuse.

The systemic nature of violence emerges in these sermons as the preachers acknowledge the church's complicity in silence and tolerance, and name the pervasive consequences of sexism in economic, legal, and relational spheres as well. Marie Fortune helpfully describes the limiting effects of fear which pervades women's lives and is intensified for victims. She painfully describes the failure of the justice system for some victims of violence. Anne Marie Hunter shares her own experience of a priest challenging her faithfulness when she would not return to an abusive husband.

While many of these sermons note the impossibility of remaining aloof from the experience of victims if we begin to acknowledge the truth of the violence they have endured, Karen Brau and Anne Marie Hunter in particular call us to recognize our solidarity with survivors of violence. When one suffers such abuse, the fabric of the human community as a whole is affected. Brau rightly notes that when we hold perpetrators accountable, our witness is a sign of hope.

The theme of hope that arises through a partnership with victims and congregations is present throughout these sermons. Mark Barnes, for example, directly challenges members of his congregation to understand themselves as resources for truthful and healing action. Anne Marie Hunter develops the poetic image of the congregation's presence with survivors as manna in the wilderness of fear and disorientation, suffering, and difficult questions.

Virtually every sermon here claims the necessity of faithful and compassionate resistance to sexual and domestic violence as a witness to God's love which is just and tender. Truthful preaching about sexual and domestic violence will seek to create a safe and empowering environment for victims who long for God's *shalom* in every sphere of their lives. It will hold perpetrators accountable and invite them toward the freedom that comes through repentance and new life. It will confront bystanders in congregations to give up the comfort of self-deception and acknowledge complicity in violence if they are not resisting it.

We hope that in reading these sermons you will come to share our conviction that in partnership, we can make a difference in resisting the tragedy wrought by sexual and domestic violence. We invite you to join with these preachers and the other contributors to this book to embark on your journey toward preaching truthfully about such violence. We are confident that you will find it a journey that transforms you as well as those you seek to help, as together you experience the empowering love of God.

PROSPECTS

We are strongly encouraged by the groundswell of interest in and commitment to issues related to sexual and domestic violence in many seminaries and churches today. The journey, however, has only just begun. There are many aspects of seminary teaching and congregational life and ministry that still require transformation if we are to meet this issue squarely and forcefully. It is our hope that teachers of preaching will find in this book adequate resourcing to teach preachers to preach about sexual and domestic violence. We also hope that preachers will find in this book enough material to sustain a vital pulpit ministry that confronts sexual and domestic violence. With the reader's help, more preachers and congregations can become strong witnesses against sexual and domestic violence and learn how to extend hospitality to victims and survivors. We are convinced that in partnership with one another, we can make a difference.

Part 1

Theological and Biblical Perspectives

1

Evil, Violence, and the Practice of Theodicy

Wendy Farley

I am often troubled about my role as a theologian, a theorist of religion. The violence in our society does not require a correct theory, but rather praxis: preaching, counseling, comforting, lobbying. It requires the practical work of compassionate action. But I re-membered an anecdote a friend related to me about Mother Teresa which served for me as a sort of metaphor for the role of theology. Mother Teresa's community was given an extravagantly expensive silver chalice for communion. When someone suggested that there was something inappropriate about these riches in the midst of their poverty, she disagreed. They must be nourished for their work, and the ridiculous, unseemly beauty of the chalice was entirely appropriate to the gift of Christ's presence which it mediated.

CONSEQUENCES OF EVIL AS SEXUAL AND DOMESTIC VIOLENCE

Compassion must be nourished if it is to face the scathing reality of violence. One of the things that can nourish compassion—even as it can undermine it—is theology. There are practical and immediate ways we can respond to violence against women: a sermon, a liturgy, an ongoing relationship with a shelter for battered women. But what we do and refrain from (or avoid) doing will be deeply and fundamentally shaped by our experi-ence of God. This experience is partly present in what we say about God, about for-giveness, about women, about sin. Theology is, most superficially, just that: what we say about God. But what we say about God has to do with lived experience. Theology is more properly *wisdom* about God, a tasting of the reality of God.

Sister Chan Khong, a Buddhist nun who practiced compassion in Viet Nam during our war there, quotes a friend who told her that doing social work without enlightenment is "like holding a knife by the blade . . . [it] can destroy you."[1] If we try to extend our sympathies beyond our knowledge of God, beyond the empowerment for compassion that is rooted in God, we are likely to harm ourselves and perhaps others as well. The-ology is one of the spiritual disciplines available to Christians through which our knowl-edge and experience of God can be deepened.

Theology may not itself be a social praxis, but is a nourishment without which praxis can burn itself out too quickly.[2] Preachers have a particular opportunity to convey this empowering presence through sermon and liturgy. By conjoining work on behalf of women who have been battered or sexually abused with experiences of divine compassion, preachers can both inspire and empower their listeners to participate in this work.

Preaching occurs, however, in situations where we do not always see or recognize the suffering that is present. What we say and do when we are not even thinking about sexual violence or battered women can be as important as our explicit words about domestic violence. One of the best preachers I have ever heard gave a terrible sermon about forgiveness. Taken on its merits, it was a reasonably insightful articulation of this central theme of Christian ethics. But I happened to be sitting next to a friend who had suffered a mind-bendingly violent childhood. She was fuming and deeply hurt by the end of the sermon. While we cannot be omniscient when we speak or act, if we engage in theologies and practices that remind us of the omnipresence of suffering, our understanding of who God is, who we are, forgiveness—and all the other ideas central to Christianity—might be modified in helpful ways.

We encounter victims and practitioners of violence all the time without being aware of it. It may be that the bulk of our responses to violence occur without our even knowing it. Our theology must prepare us to preach well about violence, even when we do not know that is what we are talking about. My remarks here are concerned primarily with sexual and domestic violence against women, but the compassion of God and the beauty of the human soul are there all the time. If our theology and action are rooted in the deep knowledge of this compassion and beauty, we are more likely to act well even when the violence around us is invisible.

After twenty or so years of feminist theology, Christianity continues to imagine God's power as more like the power of sovereignty than anything else. Feminist theology is right to criticize this image, and I am going to add one additional reason for criticizing it: this image makes the problem of evil virtually insoluble; and, in the presence of abused women, traditional theodicy is worse than insoluble—it is blasphemy.

Theodicy is usually the intellectual effort to jerry-rig three mutually exclusive terms into harmony: divine power, goodness, and the experiences of evil. This is most often done by denying or undermining the reality of one of the three terms. As long as the image of the sovereign remains intact, it is suffering which must be reduced to unreality.

We can only hope to know anything truly about God if we are fearlessly realistic about the world; I am therefore going to begin with the assertion that violence against women—or anyone—is really evil. What I mean by "evil" is something very traditionally Christian. I mean that violence deprives women of something essential and proper to them. My graduate students are often grumpy and dissatisfied by Christian philosophers' interpretation of evil as privation. But I cannot think what could be more scathingly evil than to be deprived of something that is essential to one's very existence.

Evil is something that defrauds us of some aspect of the goodness appropriate to the kind of being we are. Violence does this in the most obvious way. At one extreme, it deprives someone of life itself. But, as Simone Weil points out:

> The might that kills outright is an elementary and coarse form of might. How much more
> varied in its devices; how much more astonishing in its effects is that other which does not

kill; or which delays killing. . . . This above all procedures turns a [person] to stone. From the power to transform [a person] into a thing by killing him [or her] there proceeds another power, and much more prodigious, that which makes a thing of [a person who] still lives. He [or she] lives, . . . has a soul, and strange the state of that soul. Who knows how often during each instant it must torture and destroy itself in order to conform? The soul was not made to dwell in a thing; and when forced to it, there is no part of that soul but suffers violence.[3]

The effect of violence is privation: it is privation of personhood, of spirit. It is an obscuration of the image of God; and this violence is, above all else, evil. The Hebrew prophets were clear and consistent in their condemnation of violence. Violence, especially against the most helpless, was one of the things that most fundamentally alienated people from God. Against the optimism of stoicism, it is necessary to understand this extreme vulnerability to which the human being is subject.

The evil of violence is not only the pain it causes, it is the power of violence to deface the human spirit. Again, as Weil writes:

The great enigma of life is not suffering but affliction. It is not surprising that the innocent are killed, tortured, driven from their country, made destitute or reduced to slavery . . . since there are criminals to perform such actions. . . . But it is surprising that God should have given affliction the power to seize the very souls of the innocent and to possess them as sovereign master. At the very best, [one] who is branded by affliction will only keep half his [or her] soul.[4]

This description of the effect of affliction is especially pertinent to women who have suffered from sexual and domestic violence, especially at the hands of someone close to them. It is characteristic of victims of incest or rape, for example, to conceive of themselves as worthless and despicable. "Evil dwells in the heart of the criminal without being felt there. It is felt in the heart of the [woman] who is afflicted and innocent. Everything happens as though the state of the soul appropriate for criminals had been separated from crime and attached to affliction."[5]

The statistics on violence against women are both shocking and numbing: violent attacks by men constitute the primary health risk to women; every eighteen seconds, a women is beaten; one-third of women will be assaulted by a partner; every hour, sixteen women confront rapists; every ten minutes, in the United States, a girl is molested; every thirty minutes, a daughter is molested by her father.[6] In my own completely informal and anecdotal calculations, at least one-half of the women I know have been attacked by a rapist.

If we reflect on these statistics with the help of Simone Weil, what becomes clear is not only the scope of the problem but its intensity. Violence has the effect of transforming persons into things. Violence is the excruciating transformation created when a person—an imago Dei—is treated as if she were a stone. This treatment produces something stonelike in a person. Such a transformation should not be possible if the world were created by a good, powerful, loving God. Human beings should not have the power to take a soul made by God and stamp it with undeserved self-loathing.

Examining the statistics from the other direction—that of scope—forces us to accept the reality that this unmaking is not a rare accident like contracting some horrible but very unusual disease. It, in a certain way, constitutes women's lives. Few women escape the fact of violence or the fear of violence. This means that there is not just a strange quirk in an otherwise good fabric of creation, but a violence and unmaking woven throughout. This unmaking all the more clearly constitutes human life if we remember the scope of suffering: sickness, poverty, torture, war, hunger, and, as Ivan Karamazov puts it, "the tears with which our earth is soaked from crust to core."[7]

That we are subject not only to suffering but to a defacing of our spirit that sears away even the capacities that make redemption possible is a fact so deeply unfair that it seems to point to some absurdity at the heart of the cosmos. Evil as privation names this radical sense in which creation is subject to decreation, to an unmaking that is more radical than death. Acknowledging the extent and depth and undeservedness of violence against women makes it difficult to understand how to relate God to a world in which these things are present. If we think of divine power as all-controlling, it seems we must blame God for the perverse violence of human beings.

A TRAGIC THEOLOGY OF SUFFERING

I propose we make another kind of beginning. Rather than assume God must be all powerful and then jerry-rig the other terms into conformity with that assumption, I am going to begin with the facticity of unjust suffering. Further, I remind us that unjust suffering has the power not only to make us uncomfortable or even miserable but to actually decreate us and that this decreation is not an anomaly but, to varying degrees, a characteristic feature of the human condition.[8]

In conceiving of the power of God in light of affliction, it is the ubiquity of decreative suffering that, paradoxically, gives us a clue about who God is and the kind of power God represents. With Weil, we can say that it is not surprising that there are rapes and beatings and murders, since there are people to perform these acts. And, with Weil, we can be pained by the fact that violence can exercise such incredibly destructive power.

But the next step is to ask, with Ezekiel, can these bones live? If we are to find God in the kind of world in which destructive suffering is a characteristic of our existence, we must seek a God with power to make a valley of dry bones into living, beautiful, enfleshed persons. But what kind of power can finger a soul that has taken on the reality of a thing back into a spirit? What power is it that can resurrect a dead rag of a soul, humiliated beyond recognition as human, and return to this degraded nothing the shining, golden image of God? The power to spin out a cosmos with shooting stars and glow-fish at the bottom of the sea, with the outrageous beauty of a giraffe and the song of a thrush, is certainly nothing to sneeze at. But a soul that has been humiliated and violated must not only be created but recreated. To draw beauty from nothing is surely a light thing compared to giving a woman back to herself when her very self has been stolen by violence.

Part of the difficulty is that although nothingness is passive, a soul—even a decreated one—is by its nature active. It is free, at least formally; it cannot be worked on like a stone or clay. It is precisely the work of violence to attempt the transformation of freedom into inertness. Redemption must give the soul back to itself, to free freedom. The great paradox of salvation is that it must make the soul capable of receiving its own beauty, and yet must do this in a way that ignites freedom rather than bypasses it.

THE POWER OF COMPASSION

The name for this paradoxical, infinitely varied, infinitely patient power is "compassion." Compassion is the power that ignites the beauty of a soul after suffering has snuffed it out. Compassion is the kind of power that works on spirit and not on matter. It is not an impotent emotion of pity or even sympathy. It is not only companionship in misery. It is the name of the kind of power—the only kind of power—that redeems.

When we think of the destructiveness of violence, the importance of conceiving of compassion as the most definitive attribute or characteristic of God becomes clearer. I do not mean that theology is psychology or even ethical pragmatism. I do not mean that because victims of violence need a compassionate God, theologians should be glad to provide that model along with all the others. I mean that compassion names more directly than most other terms the way God's power is manifest.

Compassion is not one of the moods of our moody cosmic parent. It is not a feeling God has about sufferers. It is the kind of power that God exercises toward the world. The power of compassion is the most real thing in the world, the signature of ultimate reality, and the name that truth bears in its active aspect. If we understand this—not in our heads but in our very bones—we will talk about God differently, interpret our scriptures differently, and relate to victims and perpetrators of violence differently. Compassion vitiates neat divisions between theory and practice, transforming theology into a practice of compassion even as it demands that all practice be rooted in the wisdom that discerns compassion as the signature of reality.

It is the nature of God to be compassionate in all things, but here I will in particular focus on the implications of that for a theodicy that is attentive to sexual and domestic violence against women. Perhaps the most basic thing this means is that the suffering we experience from others has no connection at all with the will of God. The decreation of human beings is never the desire of God. God created us for love and out of love; there is nothing of violence or unmaking in this desire for love.

Every syllable that comes out of the pulpit, every word mouthed by religious people, every scripture quotation, every form of ostensible comfort that implies that the suffering of women at the hands of men in any way conforms to the will or the permission of God is a violation of the third commandment, in which we are commanded not to make wrongful use of the name of God (Exod. 20:7). God makes us for love and urges us, commands us, begs us, to choose life. Those acts that violate life are separated from God as far as the East is separated from the West. Any theodicy that implies that suffering is deserved, is pedagogical, is just, because we deserve whatever we receive from the hand of God (which, it turns out, is the same as the hand of those who commit violence), is likewise a violation of the third commandment.

Conversely, suffering is one of the places where God is most intimately present. The incarnation and crucifixion tell us something deeply important about who God is and where God chooses to appear. It is in those places furthest from prosperity, fullness, beauty, honor, and power that Christians have had God revealed most distinctively to them. God, source of all reality, split the heavens to come to us in a cow shed so that God could be *with* us. And, as if the ridiculousness of being born in a manger weren't enough, God dies on a cross—as loathsome, humiliating, cruel, and helpless a death as imaginable—just in case we didn't get it. As Paul says, nothing can separate us from the love of God.

To make sure we can see that the most abject poverty and homelessness are not enough to separate us from God and that the most severe violence human beings can invent cannot separate us from God—God embodies Godself in precisely these places. These are the places we are most in need of God, and God does not tell us about the divine presence in these places; God enacts this presence as histrionically as possible. It is necessary to do this partly because human beings love gorgeous displays of power and are sorely tempted to imagine God to be just like a monarch or emperor or—best of all—the most powerful sorcerer and sultan in the world. It's hard to imagine a clearer correction of this view than a birth in a stable and a death on a cross.

Another reason for the embodiment of God in these places of misery is that the power of suffering over us is very great. Stoicism is wrong: it is not a normal human capacity to suffer affliction, humiliating violence, or long pain, and not feel our humanity chiseled away. The terrible thing about mortal beings is that we are mortal (that is, vulnerable) according to the kind of beings we are. We are persons, and it is as persons—and not only minds or bodies—that we can be harmed. Affliction in a deep and substantive way unmakes us. Paradoxically, suffering can damage the very capacities we need to be comforted and healed. Women who have suffered violence can feel plenty of pain, but too often the capacity to feel God's love is damaged. Women can feel as if they are far too worthless even to pray to God. Bad theology can deepen this and make women feel as if God somehow willed their suffering and that, as divinely ordained, worthlessness is their true name.

It is as if God is intimately present to those who have been blinded; and yet, because we are blind, we cannot see that. And, in fact, in our blindness, we imagine almost the direct opposite to be the case. We imagine that God was the one that blinded us, that God is punishing us for sins known or unknown, that it is God's will that we suffer this way.

The events of Christ's life teach us the exact opposite. God is near us, tenderly like a lover, cooing like a mother over a sick child. We learn that God violated the most basic laws of reason and reality by transforming that which is utterly and radically beyond all finite expression into a particular person. We learn that God violated the most basic rules of human value and embodied Godself in the body of a homeless baby who grew up to be a torture victim. The embodiment of divine power in these places of suffering brings transforming power where it is most needed. This story is so outrageous that even Christians don't believe it.

But it is this story that victims of violence need to hear; it is this reality that victims of violence need to encounter. God is the power of compassion and will engage in the most outrageous behavior to us—to give us that power and to make us understand who God is. To the extent that the church is more than a historical and cultural artifact, it is a preacher's role to mediate healing power to the afflicted.

Preaching should offer to women who have suffered from violence a pure drink of the living water which is God's own compassionate presence. Sermons can do this in part by being an antidote to such women's self-loathing. Only the truth can redeem us. Women who have known violence, more desperately than others, have need of truth. The lie of their worthlessness has been branded onto their souls through their bodies. This is a stamp burned into them which defaces the beauty of the image of God in them. It is a real burn, a real branding, not something superficial or psychological. Effective preaching brings salve to that burn and counters it with the truth of who this person is. To these women who feel that their name is "Not my people," the church's preaching and teaching must convey with passion and clarity that their name is "My people" (see Hos. 3:23). The church must, in the thousand concrete ways demanded in any particular situation, help to enable this person to taste her own beauty and power again.

One of the relatively few theological categories the church has to work with in situations of wrongdoing is forgiveness. This is a very important theological category; but as a response to violence, it too often becomes empty and destructive. Like all true words of power, "forgiveness" is not one to toss around as if it were harmless or trivial. It is a true redemptive word only when employed skillfully, with wisdom and compassion. As a Tibetan monk with whom I work said, forgiveness is something that can only come from someone who is very strong. Forgiveness is not the first word to the afflicted; if it comes at all, it comes very late. The condition of possibility of forgiveness is strength. This is the very last thing the afflicted have. One does not ask the afflicted to forgive. An antidote to humiliation must first be offered.

The miracle of redemption even from affliction can be hoped for because we can hope and act in God, the power of infinite compassion. But it is as we experience the power of *compassion* that we trust in God. God's power is not mechanical, like that of a billiard ball striking another to push it where it should be. It is not the power of a ruler who has the military and economic resources to make a situation match his or her will. It is the power appropriate to spirit.

Recreating spirit occurs within the conditions of finitude, within the psychosomatic, social complexity of personhood. This transformation is long and slow. The power of compassion can wash the rock of a heart for many decades before the heart softens and the effect may be discerned. The work of compassion takes on every form that human action takes: pastoral counseling, support groups, legislative action, sanctuary, the intimacy and fun of friendship.

Theology's role in this is to be the water of true words that work every day, in every song, in every prayer, in every sermon, to bring the compassionate power of God into view so that it can become part of experience. Every anonymous victim of violence who worships should hear over and over again about the intimate, delicious kindness and goodness of God. Every woman trying to live a human life when her image of herself is as a worthless worm should hear about the beauty of her soul, made by God, loved for its own unique and irreplaceable strength and loveliness.

Theology's distinctive work is to bring nearer the true and living God while casting down the idols and impostures we all carry with us. Doing that work all the time, every day, will be a practice of theodicy for those known and unknown among us whom God is calling tenderly and sweetly back to Godself, calling them, at the same time, back to themselves.

THE COMPASSIONATE WORK OF WRATH

There is another face of violence besides that of the victim. There are those, of course, who carry out violence, and some of them are in the pews right next to their victims. Compassion has a wrathful form. This wrath is not a psychological response to suffering, any more than compassion itself is a psychological feeling within the mind of God.

To speak even analogically about the divine wrath as God's hatred of evil is perhaps not very helpful. We can, in our deep and passionate love for justice, believe that hatred of perpetrators of violence is the obvious and even necessary counterpart. By this view, it is neither possible nor desirable to feel anything but condemnation for those who commit violence. Victims need to hear the church condemn violence and violent people in unequivocal terms. Employing the image of divine wrath is a theological version of that.

I myself think that the condemnation of violence that victims, and all Christians, need to hear might have a somewhat different tone to it. The condemnation of crime does not arise only from the psychological need of a victim to be vindicated (although victims do need to be vindicated, and hearing violence condemned is part of that vindication). It arises out of compassion. The divine wrath arises out of compassion—not as the mirror of God's love for victims, but out of God's love for all human beings, even those unmade by their own evil.

It can be relatively easy to feel pity, if not real compassion, for victims of violence. But feeling pity for those who accomplish the defacement of personhood is more difficult. Evil can provoke hatred. But criminals are human, too; and Paul's beautiful phrase that nothing separates us from the love of God is true for them, too. Compassion wishes happiness for all beings; the universality of compassion is not stopped by crime. Crime does present a different kind of problem to compassion, though.

Affliction sears away in the sufferer the capacity to feel again the love of God. It is very difficult to recreate this capacity. It happens very slowly and may not be finished even in the span of an entire lifetime.[9] But the problem of restoring the image of God to the afflicted is, by comparison with restoring the image of God to a criminal, an easy and straightforward matter. The afflicted must be lured out of undeserved self-contempt.

The criminal must first be driven to self-contempt. The criminal's soul must first have the capacity to see—with perfect clarity and immediacy—the horror of what he or she did. To get to this place, the criminal's soul must first be unmade. This decreation is not strictly penal; it is not a balancing of wrong with some penalty or fine. The apparent symmetry between the decreation of the victim by violence and the criminal by punishment has nothing to do with a restoration of harmony.

Nothing that could be extracted from a criminal would undo or balance the suffering caused. Even an eye for an eye, humiliation for humiliation, pain for pain, cannot match the wrong, because it is the suffering of punishment rather than the gratuitous unraveling of an innocent life.[10] There is no match between wrongdoing and punishment. This lack of a match is part of the unbearable horror of the recognition of one's own wrongdoing.[11] It is the recognition of the damage one has accomplished that nothing in all eternity can undo, that no suffering one undergoes oneself can atone for.

The compassionate work of wrath is to move the soul of the criminal toward this recognition.[12] Just as "forgiveness" is not the first word to one who suffers violence, neither is it the first word to one who performs violence. Forgiveness is the fruit of transformation, not its seed. When these are reversed, the power of forgiveness becomes poisoned and inverted. It is more likely to contribute to the chaos of violence. Forgiveness is necessary because restitution is impossible. But forgiveness is not, in Bonhoeffer's words, "cheap grace." The longing of compassion is for happiness. A forgiveness that precedes transformation does not create happiness, it only justifies evil, vindicating the wrong rather than the wronged.

Compassion must first put forth wrathful power to create in the criminal the capacity to thirst for the good and therefore to be tortured by evil, all the more deeply when the evil is his or her own. When this capacity emerges, the pain of knowing the suffering one has caused is like a fire burning in the soul, and this fire cleans the soul so it can be prepared for real love. At this point, forgiveness is possible.

Withholding forgiveness and the offer of forgiveness are equally works of compassion. Forgiveness is the presence of real love to a soul that is becoming capable of receiving it. It is the fruition of a long and difficult work of redemption that moves someone into the love of God. It is this transformation of evil into good that alone restores harmony to creation. Punishment and suffering are always negations of life. A cosmos in which punishment could last forever is one in which redemption is a ghost but not a reality. Evil is redeemed by becoming good; the afflicted and the criminal approach this from opposite directions, but they both must get there eventually.

Preachers are in the difficult position of having to speak words of comfort and wrath to the same population, without knowing the full experiences of their listeners. The skillful means required for this might come more easily as one stretches roots deeply into the infinite compassion of God. Facile words about forgiveness might come less quickly. A capacity to see a woman who has been raped with the eyes through which God sees her might develop and with it the ability to convey to her how lovely she is and how dear she is to God.

It might be less difficult to find words of challenge to those well-known and respected members of a congregation who have been discovered to be abusive to their families. Nourished by holy compassion, preachers can feel the urgency of the demand to address the destruction to God's holy temples that violence against women causes. In ways suited to the particular needs of their congregations, they can participate in the work of recreation.

In speaking words of redemption to humanity, torn by violence and populated both by criminals and the afflicted, the church must learn to manifest the compassion of God as a chord rather than as a single note. Compassion comforts and protects the afflicted, and it brings criminals to consciousness of their guilt. Through a long journey in the wilderness in which both of these are practiced, we can hope for a spring of clear water, where forgiveness can be drunk, and at the end of things, if not at the beginning, the beauty of every soul may shine again.

COMPASSION AS VOCATION

The vocation of every human being is to embody the compassionate power of God: that is what the image of God in us is. It requires what the Buddhists call "skillful means" to know how to do this in concrete situations: toward victims of violence, each with unique needs; toward perpetrators of violence, who simultaneously deface and possess the image of God; toward local communities, which are inhabited by both, those anonymous and those known to us.

As a theologian, I cannot go far in recommending particular strategies, in part because these strategies must arise out of concrete situations and do not translate directly from situation to situation. But I can remind us that all of our particular work is a practice of our theology. It seems extravagant and irrelevant to engage in theoretical work when the suffering of peoples presses on us with such urgency. But it can be one of the ways in which the living waters of divine beauty flow to us and nourish us, quenching our thirst for God as we continue our work in the desert to bring healing to this world.

2

Violence and the Bible

Johanna W. H. van Wijk-Bos

> In the age of Auschwitz and Trident, to ignore the darkness is to surrender
> to its forces. Walking more deeply into our darkness is our only hope.
>
> James W. Douglass, *The Nonviolent Coming of God*

Preachers who address the subject of violence will be faced with a number of assumptions on the part of their listeners about the Bible and this topic. Many of these biases, firmly embedded in the Christian community, are for the most part unexamined and will not be erased by a sermon or two. Yet preachers will do well to take into account some of the stereotypes that live in the imagination of their audience. When old and false images are exposed and discarded, surprising truths may emerge from a text that many consider to be permeated with violence.

For many Christians, the Old Testament is an especially violent part of the biblical heritage, filled with stories of violent aggression on the part of God's people. Moreover, many assume that the God of biblical faith as reflected in the Old Testament firmly supported and authorized such human violence. As is often the case with stereotypes, there is a partial truth hidden in this bias. For hermeneutical and homiletic purposes, we need to take seriously the fact that most of the backdrop of the Bible consists of the violent upheaval and destruction brought about by war and by its aftermath—foreign occupation with its concomitant burden of physical and economic violence. During most of the biblical period, ancient Israel was on the receiving end of this violence.[1] In terms of the Old Testament, periods of political and social tranquillity for the ancient Israelites were few and far between.[2]

Naturally, this reality of upheaval and lack of stability found its reflection in the biblical text. Economic, social, and political violence were known factors for the folk who told biblical stories, who recorded the laws, the songs, the sayings, and the prophetic words that eventually found their place in the Bible. It interests us then to review biblical perspectives on violence in light of such a context.

It is not my intent to examine in detail a few texts that depict hostilities between the ancient Israelite community and its neighbors as sanctioned by divine fiat.[3] Rather, I intend to sketch a general perspective on violence that may be called "biblical." My focus will be on the Hebrew Bible, the Christian Old Testament, rather than the New Testament. But I seek to uncover a perspective on violence that is thematically consistent with the New Testament.

While we recognize the importance of the biblical context, it is also essential to articulate a context for the contemporary interpreter. Every preacher will need to outline such a context for his or her own interaction with the biblical text.[4] In order to clarify the personal context that informs this essay, let me briefly delineate my own place and perspectives.

I approach the subject of violence as a Christian feminist. Both my Christianity and my feminism were born in the crucible of the Second World War and especially the Holocaust/Shoah. My Christianity formed itself initially in the bosom of postwar Calvinist Holland, as a Bible-oriented faith that verified the propensity of humanity for violence/evil and redeemed this propensity at the same time. Biblical folk no less than my own community were presented to me as ordinary people with a special talent for mayhem. As my friend and former colleague George R. Edwards phrases it, "Even a superficial acquaintance with the Bible leads us to see that the real story is the deliverance of humanity from the pit by the God of the Bible."[5] It was not difficult for one of my generation and geographical location to observe how close we were to the pit.[6] It was profoundly appropriate for me to come to believe that it was and is precisely with such as these and for such as these that God is engaged in the work of liberation. Early on, I located the truth and authority of the Bible in its power to address a situation of oppression and to speak a liberative word to this situation.

During the war years, Dutch communities, including the small town where I was born, suffered all types of deprivation, fear, and loss; yet there was among us no group as clearly singled out for special suffering as the Jewish community. The awareness of the shape and extent of this particular oppression provided me in time with a paradigm for recognizing relations of oppression elsewhere. While there is a particular character to the persecution of the Jews with a specific connection to Christian collaboration in this persecution, it can be shown that the character of oppression is similar whenever a group suffers from domination by another.

When, much later in my life, I adopted a feminist perspective, I articulated this in a framework of concern for the earth's marginalized and vulnerable peoples. Today I identify the earth's poor, the victims of war and other violence, the homeless, and the hungry, all those without means to take care of themselves and their dependents, foremost as women and their children. I understand patriarchy in Elisabeth Schüssler Fiorenza's terms as a *pyramid of multiplicative oppressions.*[7]

Setting my personal experience in a broad contemporary context, it is clearer today than ever how women, together with their children, are victimized by the violence that accompanies patriarchal practices and ideologies. This violence is so widespread and takes place in such a variety of contexts that even a partial list would be outside the scope of this essay. One passage may sum up adequately the reality of the situation: "Violence against women constitutes the heart of kyriarchal oppression. It is sustained by multiplicative structures of control, exploitation and dehumanization: the oppressive powers of hetero-sexism are multiplied by racism, poverty, cultural imperialism, war, militarist colonialism, homophobia and religious fundamentalism."[8]

The question before us, then, is how the Bible speaks a word of verification and liberation to the victimization of women in situations of sexual and domestic violence. The wider framework for this discussion will be a biblical perspective on violence in general, as it is a part of the human scene. First, I look at texts that reflect overt forms of violence, acts of aggression on an individual and communal level. Second, I consider less-direct forms of violence, such as poverty and other types of discrimination that occur as a result of societal structuring. Next, I focus on the identity of those who are the principal recipients of the practices of violence. Last, I bring to bear the ramifications of this general biblical perspective on violence as it specifically affects women in the biblical text. At each point, I address the question of God's response to human violence in the Bible as well as that of human responsibility.

THE VOICE OF YOUR BROTHER'S BLOOD

> Let's assume that God is not a sadist.
>
> Dorothee Soelle,
> *The Strength of the Weak:*
> *Toward a Feminist Christian Identity*

From its stories of beginnings, the Bible presents a clear view of human interaction as full of the potential for violence and of the actual execution of it. In the myths that describe the construction of human society as told in the first ten chapters of Genesis, the emphasis in terms of violence is on overt destructive action.

Sin as Violence

The first time that the biblical word "sin" occurs in these chapters is in the story of the kin-slaughter of Abel by Cain. Sin is not introduced, contrary to many believers' presuppositions, in Genesis 2 and 3, the story of the garden. There, the humans were disobedient to the instructions laid down for them by God and faced the consequences of what they had done. In general, these consequences may be classified as alienation: humanity will henceforth live an alienated existence in terms of the entire created world: animal, natural and human (Gen. 3:14–19). This alienation is described as an ongoing process of deterioration in Genesis 4–10, until "God saw that the evil of humanity was great on earth and that all the devisings of its mind were only evil all the day" (Gen. 6:5). To emphasize the state of affairs, the text reiterates the situation in verse 11 as follows: "Now the earth was a ruin before God and the earth was filled with violence." The latter phrase is repeated once more, when God announces to Noah the divine plan to wipe out most of the creation and to make a new beginning for the human family with Noah (Gen. 6:13).

Literally, the phrasing of Genesis 6:5 locates evil in the imagination: "every form of the planning of their heart was only evil all the day." Violence is the result of planned evil, the "heart" in Hebrew being the location for the intelligence and will as well the emotions. Violence does not happen accidentally. Or, if it takes place by accident, it is not of the same category as the violence that "fills" the earth in the Genesis stories. Because we may find the idea of a God who plans to destroy humanity repugnant or "primitive," the profundity of the observations about evil and violence in this account may escape us. Yet it is clear from this text that the biblical writers viewed violence as directly opposed to God's intentions for the creation.

The text presents the first occasion of individual violence as one between brothers, motivated by envy. In Genesis 4, as in chapter 6, the mental posture of the one who contemplates violence is emphasized. In God's interaction with Cain, the word "sin" occurs for the first time in these stories, when God asks Cain why his face is downcast and warns him that *sin* crouches at the door but that he can rule it (Gen. 4:7). When Cain has perpetrated his violent act, God exclaims, "What have you done? Listen! The voice of the blood of your brother cries to me from the ground" (Gen. 4:10). In other words, the violence done to Abel demands God's specific attention. That God is not pleased with the turn of events appears from the sequel. Human violence is a matter for divine attention and punishment.

The people who composed the Bible had no illusions about human nature, it appears. Historically, as I noted earlier, the faith community that created the biblical text was overly familiar with violence in terms of overt acts of aggression. Ancient Israel was located at the crossroads where empires met in their violent attempts to achieve dominion over that part of the world. When Israel finally succumbed to the militarism of the reigning power of Babylon in the sixth century B.C.E., it was not to establish itself again as an independent country until the latter part of the twentieth century C.E. Intimate acquaintance with life as a victim of aggression was the mark of the faith community in ancient times. For many preachers today, especially in the context of the United States, such an acquaintance is not directly accessible. To gain access to this reality, it is essential not only to acquire basic information about biblical times but to exercise the imagination.

God's "Knowledge" of Victims of Violence

The beginnings of ancient Israel were marked by violence, and its creation as a covenant community took place in a framework of oppression. In the context of the suffering of the slaves in Egypt, the text observes God noticing the violence done to Israel's children. The text notes that God "saw," and "heard," and "knew" the woes of the people before the Egyptian slave drivers (Exod. 3:7). The verb "to know" significantly adds to the two verbs of observation, "seeing" and "hearing." To know (*yadá* in Hebrew) is to have intimate familiarity, to know from the inside out. God's knowledge of the violence that the slaves in Egypt underwent means that God not only has observed and is informed about, but that God knows their misery from the inside. God's motivation for the rescue through the agency of Moses lies in this identification of the Divine Liberator with the human community that suffers from oppression. In their turn, the people, once they have been established as a community in covenant with their God, are to find the point of their identity in their suffering, in the violence done to them. This identification will then serve as the motivation to refrain from the same type of violence and to engage in acts of liberation for those who suffer from violence. Therefore, the directive in the Torah stipulates: "A stranger you must not oppress; you yourselves know the heart of the stranger, for you were strangers in the land of Egypt" (Exod. 23:9).

Aggression Is Not Model Behavior

The entry into the land of the promise by Israel's children is told in the Bible as a violent affair. A disturbing note in the accounts of the so-called conquest is that the community viewed its actions as willed by God (Josh. 3:9–10; 8:1–2; 10:40, for example).

Yet the accounts of the military actions involved in the conquest served as stories about ancient Israel's history rather than as motivating tales of renewed violence. Ancient Israel had no concept of holy war, and was most often victim rather than perpetrator of the violence that constitutes war. Today we may consign the acts of aggression that are depicted in the book of Joshua to ancient stories—part history, part fiction—embellished like all such nationalistic accounts but not designed as models for future aggression.

God's reaction to overt human violence is generally depicted in the Bible as negative, and the Bible assumes that God intends *shalom,* peace or wholeness, for the human family. In the prophetic vision of the restored creation, the reality of war is a thing of the past; swords and spears are turned into plowshares and pruning hooks, tools that prevail in peacetime; no energy of imagination and mental process will be devoted to the study of war in that ideal time (Isa. 2:4). In Isaiah 11:4–9, the prophet provides a picture of the healing of hostility between creature and creature and an end to evil-doing and ruin: "they will not do evil and create ruin on all my holy mountain." In the latter passage, too, in explicit counterpoint to Genesis 6:11 and 6:14, the earth "will be filled with the knowledge of God" rather than with the violence recorded in the preamble to the flood story.

The word that most comprehensively and explicitly refers to human overt violence is "*hamas*" in Hebrew. This kind of violence is said to be "in the hands," to indicate its physical nature. Hands deal out *hamas,* so that it can be tantamount to slaughter. Physical violence and brutality are certainly a part of *hamas.* In the third chapter of Jonah, the Ninevites, in order to complete their repentance process, are commanded to let go of "the violence that is in their hands"—a violence that included the waging of war and notorious acts of cruelty to victims. Not until the Ninevites abandon their ways of bloodshed does God turn to them in mercy.

What ancient Israel saw and experienced we see and experience: violence in terms of hostile and aggressive activity, individual to individual and community to community, is a part of the human landscape. In terms of a biblical approach to this aspect of our existence, we can confidently say that the God of biblical faith is not in accord with this type of violence, does not approve of it, faces people with their responsibility for it, and envisions for the human community an existence without this dominant reality. In addition, people have a choice in terms of the exercise of violent action. Once violence is born in the imagination, it is still possible to control it (Gen. 4:7). Moreover, the story of Nineveh's repentance of its violence and God's subsequent change of heart furnishes an example of both the possibility and the power of such decision making.

THE PRACTICE OF VIOLENCE

> Hamas is therefore not only an act of aggression by the stronger toward
> the weaker; it is also a betrayal, a betrayal of the other
> but also of one's own reason for being.
>
> Jacques Pons, *L'Oppression dans l'Ancien Testament*

The absence of war does not guarantee the absence of violence. War is simply the most obvious form of communal violence. More often than not, the violence that occurs in the biblical records is that which results from the injustice practiced by neighbor to neighbor.[9] This kind of violence is less glamorous and therefore less obvious than the activity of war, but it is more consistently and severely denounced in the Scriptures. Two common arenas for the practice of violence are the society and the legal system.

Violence in Social Structures

In the ancient Israelite society, violence is extended to the poor, the ones without resources, who are consistently victimized by the rich. The ancient covenant community was to model itself on a God who cared passionately for the plight of the poor. The prophets thus speak sternly to the community against the violence perpetrated on this group in its midst. Amos, well known for holding the society of his day accountable for divisions between rich and poor, accuses the well-to-do of bringing down "a reign of violence" (Amos 6:3, with *"hamas"* in the original Hebrew). Micah denounces dishonest practices of the wealthy and berates them for being "full of violence" (Mic. 6:12, again with *"hamas"*). In fact, the central and great theme of the prophets of ancient Israel everywhere addressed the people at the point of the connection between the welfare of their common life and their relationship to God. The prophets show this relationship to be inextricably intertwined with the common life of the community. The people are at all times called to establish and strengthen and continue their relationship to God by their life together as a community. This theme is never turned around, in the sense that the relationship with the neighbor would automatically arise out of the right relationship to God. In terms of the prophetic theme: wonderful spirit-filled worship does not create well-being in the community.

Poverty is viewed in the Bible as a direct result of unjust structures and practices. Where injustice prevails, oppression of the poor and the needy is the result, and this is depicted as violence. The needy in the Bible are equated with the righteous and the innocent. When these suffer oppression, the prophets denounce in the strongest possible terms the groups that oppress them and the community within which this deprivation occurs (see, for example, Amos 5:10–13). Justice and righteousness are those qualities that uphold the life of the weak and the poor; injustice and unrighteousness are the marks of a society where those qualities are lacking.

To deal justly and uphold the cause of the poor in the Bible is equated with the knowledge of God—that is to say, the intimate familiar relation with God. In this respect, the leaders of the community are to set an example, and they are taken to task when they have failed to do so. In Jeremiah, the heirs of King Josiah are upbraided because of their lack of concern for the poor, living in luxury while laborers work for nothing and the innocent are deprived of life. The biblical writer asks sarcastically:

Are you a king
  because you compete in cedar?
Did not your father eat and drink and do justice and righteousness?
  Then it was well with him.
He judged the cause of the poor and needy;
  then it was well.
Is not this to know me?
  says [God]. (Jer. 22:15–16)

Conversely, the ideal ruler is the one who protects the poor and who defends their cause. Psalm 72 elaborately describes the actions of such a leader, who delivers the needy, has pity on the weak, and saves their lives. "From oppression and violence he redeems their life; / and precious is their blood in his sight" (Ps. 72:14). The same characterization is given to the servant of God in Isaiah 42. The servant, who will be a light to the nations and who will bring them justice, will not "break a bruised reed nor quench a smoldering wick" (Isa. 42:3).

God is so opposed to the violence that victimizes the poor that the worship of a community that perpetrates this injustice is declared unacceptable. In a stark saying of Isaiah, the prophet declares that God has no pleasure in any of the rites of worship and will not pay attention to the people's prayers as long as the same hands that they stretch out to God in prayer are "full of blood" (Isa. 1:15). Isaiah 58 depicts a group of believers that keeps faithfully the religious practice of fasting and, in view of their fervent worship, questions God's seeming absence and lack of attention for their plight. The biblical writer then declares that this is not a "day acceptable to God" (Isa. 58:5). Rather, the acceptable fast consists of liberation of the oppressed, sharing bread with the hungry, and other actions of compassion and mercy. Only such religious practices will bring about the healing of the community (Isa. 58:1–12). It is well to keep this in mind as we consider how to prepare liturgies and preach about sexual and domestic violence.

Violence in the Legal System

In the legal system, it is assumed that there are classes of disadvantaged people who do not have the means to procure justice for themselves. Into this category fall the poor, the aliens, the needy, all those indicated with the phrase "those who have no helper"—in modern terms, people who cannot afford a private lawyer. The laws in the Bible exhort the community on behalf of these folk, in order to guarantee for them a measure of equal rights and privileges in court. The taking of bribes, agreeing with the majority or the powerful, are to be avoided (Exod. 23:1–9). A witness who aids the guilty for any of these reasons is termed a "violent witness" (Exod. 23:1); that is to say, such a witness commits violence toward those who cannot defend themselves. Particularly when caught in the net of the legal system, the poor may become aware of the violence that is the mark of their lives. Thus, the victim may cry out "Violence!" much like the English "Help!" (Jer. 20:8; Hab. 1:2; Job 19:7).

The Psalms especially abound with the pleas of those who feel themselves unjustly accused, against whom violent witnesses testify. Preaching about sexual and domestic violence should be filled with this spirit of complaint and advocacy. In Psalm 27, for example, the believer describes false witnesses as those "breathing out violence" (Ps. 27:12). These latter are compared to hunters that set traps or to beasts of prey (Ps. 35:7–16). They "lurk," complains the psalmist, "in secret like the lion in its covert; / they lurk that they may seize the poor; / they seize the poor and drag them off in their net" (Ps. 10:9; see also Ps. 57:4–6). The "net" and the "pit" are common imagery for the evils that befall the "innocent" who cry to God to defend them (Ps. 31).

Mockery and insult constitute a common affliction of the poor, who cry for help in the Psalms. The believer who speaks in Psalm 42 is throughout beset by the taunting of the enemies who say all the day, "Where is your God?" (Ps. 42:3, 10). Just so do the enemies of the community mock and deride it when it is bowed down and afflicted (Pss. 44 and 74, for example). All the afflicted may call on God and trust in God, for they believe that in God's presence is their liberation.

The notion that the poor and the needy demand special attention and that harsh treatment of them is denounced in the strongest language resides in the conviction that the people of the ancient covenant community were to emulate God. God was seen by them as a lover of freedom, an opponent of shackles and burdens, yokes and prisons. Not only did God set the slaves free from Egypt, it was understood that God extended this same zeal to all who are in need of liberating activity. God is the one who gives "food to the hungry." The Maker of heaven and earth is the "Maker" of justice for the oppressed (Ps. 146:7–9; see also Deut. 10:12–22).

This understanding of God's nature has profound ramifications for the life of the community that understands itself to be in covenant with God. Christians, together with the Jews, are the inheritors of the traditions of ancient Israel. They, too, understand themselves as a community in covenant with their God. The Christian community views itself, as did ancient Israel, as freed from bondage toward the end of living the life of a redeemed people, an alternative community. The special relationship between God and this alternative community is lived out by its emulating the preferences of the God of Israel, by upholding justice for the oppressed in its common life.

THE VICTIMS OF VIOLENCE

> With rare exceptions hamas is the action of a human agent upon another human being. This agent is in a position of power: the king vis à vis the people, the priest vis à vis the law to be interpreted, the husband vis à vis the wife, the warring nations vis à vis Israel, the judges and false witnesses versus the innocent, the rich merchants vis à vis the producers and consumers.
>
> Jacques Pons, *L'Oppression dans l'Ancien Testament*

Who are the ones especially affected by violence? In the Bible, there are certain terms employed for these folk, as "the poor," the needy," "those who have no helper," or "the abused." One way to ascertain the identity of groups who are recipients of violence is to identify the victimizer. In terms of the word "*hamas,*" it is noteworthy that the perpetrators of this type of violence are mostly men. The description "a man of violence" does not find "a woman of violence" as its counterpart in the Bible. "Men of violence," on the other hand, abound (see, for example, Pss. 18:49; 140:12; Prov. 3:31; 16:29; 2 Sam. 22:49). Does this mean that men are more prone to violence than women in the view of the biblical writers? I believe that we should rather understand this prevalence of males in connection with the perpetration of violence as an inevitable feature of the structures of patriarchy. Where males are in charge of the structures of family and society, they have the power also to practice violence. Violence then belongs also and foremost to patriarchal structures, and among the victims of violence in these structures, women take a primary place.

WIDOWS, ORPHANS, AND STRANGERS

A typical list of folk in the Bible who are in need of special protection includes "the widow, the orphan and the stranger." These three—women, children, and those who do not belong—constitute together, throughout the Hebrew Bible, a category of people who exist by definition on the margin of life. They are people who in the social reality of ancient Israel were deprived of a context that provided them with the security that was available to others. Because of their prominence in the laws, the narratives, and the prophetic texts, it is clear that these groups were, in ancient Israel, indeed in need of help. They were automatically victimized by the structures of that ancient society. Again and again, the text stresses that God is on their side and is their protector and helper. Psalm 146, a text I quoted earlier to illustrate God's attention to the poor, specifies the group and God's special protection for them as follows: God "watches over the strangers; / God upholds the orphan and the widow, / but the way of the wicked God brings to ruin" (Ps. 146:9). In Deuteronomy, this watchful support from God's side is made even more specific when God is said to give them food and clothing (Deut. 10:18; see also Deut. 14:29; 24:19–21; 26:13; 27:19). In the laws of Exodus, the direst threats are uttered against those who abuse the stranger, the widow, and the orphan, whose cries are heard by God (Exod. 22:21–24).

Widows were women who had lost their husbands and therefore existed without a male provider. Their situation was extremely precarious. Of the more than fifty times that widows appear in the biblical text, the vast majority of these references points to their marginalized and vulnerable existence. Socially, economically, and psychologically, widows led not only a deprived existence; outside of the family context, lacking a male provider and protector, life for a woman was not viable.

In ancient Israel, the children of a widow were orphans. Orphans basically were children without a father, since essential economic support was lacking without the paternal presence. Yet the existence of children, especially sons, at least provided widows with some hope for the future. The abyss loomed again if fatherless children were taken away from a widow to make good on a debt left by her deceased husband. The children would then serve the creditor until the debt was judged to be paid. These realities point to the vulnerability of both the widowed woman and her children.

Strangers in ancient Israel were persons without the rights and privileges held by the full members of the community. They were outsiders, not necessarily foreigners, although these would be included if they became permanent residents. A "stranger" (in Hebrew, *ger*) may connote someone from outside the family, clan, tribe, or nation. These people lived most vulnerable lives and were in constant need of protection, since they were all potentially marginalized people. Whereas the widow and the orphan were a class of people for whom protection also was required elsewhere in the ancient Near East, the concern for the stranger is unique to the Bible. In addition, the laws protecting the stranger are among the most frequent and most extensive in scope among the law codes. The community is required to love strangers (Deut. 10:19; Lev. 19:34), to provide for them (Deut. 24:17–22; Lev. 19:9), and is prohibited from oppressing them (Exod. 22: 21–23; 23:9). Abuse, exploitation, and oppression of the stranger are actions that the community must repudiate.

Strangers in the Bible may be defined in general as those who were different from the dominant group and did not share in the same rights and privileges. In our society and church, strangers may be identified in a similar way. They include members of ethnic minorities, women, persons of different sexual orientation, people with different abilities, the poor; all these come to mind. Neither the status of the stranger nor the character of violence has changed radically; the existence of the stranger may even be more threatened today than it was in the Israel of the past. More than ever, we in the church communities need to take to heart the biblical directive to seek the knowledge of the heart of the stranger (Exod. 23:9).

Frequently, in the Bible, it is with the stranger or the impoverished woman that liberation is found from a predicament. When there is drought in the land, God sends Elijah to a widow in Sidon where he finds sustenance and an opportunity to show God's life-giving power in spite of her dire situation and deprivation (1 Kings 17:8–24). It is through the foreign widow Ruth that new opportunities for leadership arose in Israel and because of the orphaned Esther that the community in the dispersion is saved from destruction. Jael, who liberated the tribal confederacy from one of its fiercest oppressors, Sisera, was, like Ruth, a stranger, not a member of the covenant community (Judg. 4:17–22). For preachers to hear a liberating word, therefore, it is important to show hospitality to strangers and to include them in our exegetical and homiletic practices.

WOMEN AND THE PRACTICES OF VIOLENCE

> Are they not looting, dividing the spoil?—
> One or two girls for every man. (Judg. 5:30)

Rape and War

Rape is one of the most commonly practiced weapons of intimidation and victimization of women throughout human history.[10] The Bible contains a few well-known examples of this practice and some allusions to its commonality especially in times of war. Sisera, a Canaanite general during the period of the tribal confederacy in ancient Israel, was late in coming home from the battlefield. In pondering possible reasons for his late arrival, his mother and her attendants came up with the answer quoted above. Naturally, raping a few women is an excusable delay for any warrior worth his salt. During the recent war in former Yugoslavia, it was estimated that by 1993, the number of women raped as a part of a systematic policy of terror came to twenty thousand. During the Second World War, approximately two hundred thousand women between the ages of fourteen and thirty were used as so-called comfort-women, by Japan, forced to have sex with an average of thirty to forty Japanese soldiers a day.

Vulnerability Outside the Household

The story of Dinah furnishes an example of a woman's vulnerability once she moved outside of the household. Dinah reportedly "went out" to visit with the neighbors, and it was then that she was raped by Hamor, "a prince of the land."[11] As a consequence of this episode, Dinah's brothers unleashed a violence of stunning proportions, killing the

Shechemite males and taking everything else, including the women, as prey. Unbridled violence, including mass rape, is also the result of the rape and murder of the Levite's concubine (Judg. 19) and of the rape of Tamar, the daughter of David and Maacah (2 Sam. 13; see also Judg. 20–21 and 2 Sam. 14–20). Violence that begets violence surely meets with the divine disapproval aroused by the oppression of all innocent victims. Even if the passages themselves do not spell out an indictment of the behavior depicted in them, we may confidently view these rapes and their aftermath as being opposed to God's intention for the creation.

In addition to falling victim to such overt aggression as rape, women in ancient Israel were more vulnerable than men to victimization by social deprivation. For preachers, it is important to draw the lines that connect women's experience in biblical times with women's experiences today. It is equally important to be clear about disjunctions between the lives of women then and now. What Elisabeth Schüssler Fiorenza terms "kyriarchal oppression" certainly dominated the social, economic, and religious pattern of life for women in biblical times. Violence against women is an integral part of that pattern, woven into the warp and woof of the fabric. Distinctions must be made, however, in the particulars of this pattern.

In terms of the economy, for example, the entire biblical period was marked by a pre-industrial, pre-urban, agricultural lifestyle. This fact needs to be taken into account when delineating the lives of women in this period, in the process of drawing on their experience for comparison with women's lives today. In some ways, the particular economic context provided women with more scope for their talents and authority.[12] Furthermore, the social context for women had radically different features in biblical times. Women's lives took place in the context of the extended family, clan, and tribe. Outside of these communities, their lives were not viable. Such a realization heightens the perception of the precariousness of the situation of certain individuals such as Tamar, the daughter-in-law of Judah (Gen. 38), or Ruth and Naomi (Ruth), or Bathsheba (2 Sam. 11–12). Today, women in Western industrialized societies are able to lead viable lives outside of the household. It is, however, striking that even in the contemporary context, the situation of homeless women may become desperate. According to Carol J. Adams, "At least forty percent of homeless women are women who were abused by their partners, and left. They now face rape on the street rather than battering in the home. They also face sexual harassment from landlords and building superintendents in seeking apartments."[13]

Physical Vulnerability

In physical terms, women were far more vulnerable than they are today, at least in the Western industrialized world. Weakened by constant childbirth, they were more open to contagious diseases, more prone to succumb in times of the regularly occurring famines.[14] These observations should serve to avoid simplistic messages that take for granted improvements in women's experiences today over those of women in biblical times. Rather, delineating distinctions as clearly as possible may help to focus and sharpen questions in terms of contemporary women's lives. For example, in terms of childbirth, given that we live in a world that is threatened by overpopulation, we might explore the extent to which a woman's status is still determined today by her reproductive capacity and her willingness to give birth. Such issues preachers may raise constructively to call into question patriarchal practices and ideologies.

Women in the Bible are among the recipients of overt physical violence, as servants, as daughters, and as wives. Phyllis Trible in her book *Texts of Terror* has explored the narratives of four such biblical women in detail, with compassion and counsel for contemporary interpretation.[15] Hagar (Gen. 16 and 21), Tamar, David's daughter (2 Sam. 13), the Levite's concubine (Judg. 19), and Jephtah's daughter (Judg. 13: 29–40) represent the four tales that have no happy endings. The actions depicted in these stories do not always find the expected response of explicit condemnation either in the narrative itself or elsewhere in scripture. Yet we may consider such actions of violence perpetrated on women as condemnable under general biblical guidelines which demand protection of people who belong to a vulnerable category (such as the orphan, the widow, and the stranger) in the law and the prophets. Hagar was a stranger in the household of Abram and Sarai (Gen. 16). Tamar became a virtual orphan as she continued to live her life after her rape in the household of her brother, rather than that of her father (2 Sam. 3:20). Although the Levite was not literally a foreigner, he and his household, including his concubine, were treated as strangers (that is, outsiders) in the city where they take refuge (Judg. 19:16–26). The young came under special protection of the ancient laws because they belonged to a fragile category, especially if they were deprived of parental protection. The story of Jephtah's daughter exhibits a grotesque reversal of this law of protection, whereby the protector, her father, became the young girl's destroyer (Judg. 13:29–40).

Violence within the Household

Preachers may note with interest that the violence that overcame Hagar, Tamar, David's daughter, the Levite's concubine, and the daughter of Jephtah took place within the household. The household should provide a measure of safety to all contained within it, and the most threatening situations ensue when the walls of the protective household prove to be permeable. Biblical narratives thus verify a reality that dominates many women's lives today.

CONCLUSION

The liberative word from the Bible issues from the biblical indictment of relationships of violence as contrary to God's intent for the creation and the community called into covenant with God. Law and prophets denounce such relationships as destructive of the community's relationship to God. Although the Bible does not offer a paradigm for alternative structures to patriarchy, the text condemns consistently the violence that permeates patriarchal practices and thereby judges them to be violent and abusive. In order to forswear the violence that is a part of patriarchal structures, it is necessary to seek new solidarities. In the Hebrew Bible, the requirement for the covenant community is to be on the side of the widow, the orphan, and the stranger, to show allegiance to them. Nothing Jesus said or did brought any change in these requirements; in fact, Jesus' words and actions rather underscored their importance. In Jesus' violent death, the devisings of the human mind are exposed once more. In breaking the bonds of Jesus' death, God once more demonstrated the incapacity of violence to restrain the force of peace. Preachers need to state clearly the choice that is before the faithful community. It is up to us to choose where we place ourselves: on the side of violence and death or on the side of peace and life. Fatalism and existence doomed to violence are not a part of biblical thinking. As the biblical text exhorts: "Choose then life, that you may live; you and your children after you" (Deut. 30:19).

3

The Wounds of Jesus,
the Wounds of My People

M. Shawn Copeland

> The wounds of . . . my people wound me too. . . . Is there no balm in Gilead?
> Who will turn my head into a fountain and my eyes into a spring of tears
> so that I may weep all day, all night for the wounded out of my people?
>
> Jeremiah 8:21–23 (adapted)

The chief task of the Christian church is to witness concretely, comprehensively, compassionately to the life and ministry, suffering, death, and resurrection of Jesus of Nazareth, the Christ of God. The church always lives and works out its witness and ministry in particular cultural and social matrices, in particular moments in history. Today, the church carries out its mission in the midst of violence.[1]

Violence is not peculiar to the cultural matrix or social arrangements of the United States: it is an irrational and tragic event of the human condition. What is troubling about violence in the United States is that the offenders and victims are becoming younger and younger. What is troubling about violence in the United States is that more and more young children assault adults—especially those who have been made most vulnerable by age, health, income, neighborhood, and gender. What is troubling about violence in the United States is that violence has become the "first, quick, often pre-emptive recourse," not only in conflictual intragroup relations, but in the most casual of interpersonal encounters.[2] What is so very troubling about violence in the United States, especially with regard to the mission and pastoral practice of the church, is that it is no longer shocking. Violence has subjugated our imaginations, and those who primarily and literally bear the brunt of twisted and distorted imaginations are women and children.[3]

The Christian church and Christian theology demonstrate considerable ambivalence toward violence. On one hand, Christianity displays a subtle intelligence in dealing with societal violence. In certain carefully defined situations, Christian tradition has tolerated, even sanctioned, armed conflict between nations or political groups. In certain carefully defined and other situations, the tradition has condemned—albeit sometimes diffidently —armed conflict between nations or political factions, political repression and torture, genocide, chemical and bacteriological assault, hostage-taking, and random bombings.

At the same time, Christian tradition has promoted nonviolence as both a universal principle and a strategy for achieving social justice—often in the face of anarchical state terror. On the other hand, Christian pastoral practice has repudiated acts of violence in the domain of private or domestic or personal relationships and has tended to uphold nonviolence as the ideal response to face-to-face private or domestic or personal violence. What the church thinks and teaches about violence, then, is conditioned primarily by the rules or conventions of large-scale societal confrontation. This has had fatal consequences for women and children. These, the least powerful in every society, all too often have been enjoined to submit silently, patiently, meekly to violence—all too often in the name of the suffering and cross of Jesus Christ.

Theology mediates between Christian communities of witness and worship and the cultures in which they exist. If theology is to assist pastoral practice in dealing with violence, it has to come to terms with violence in the measure that it has been affecting and wounding our culture, wounding the imagination. At the same time, theology has also to come to terms with the biased ways in which women have been and are perceived in church and society. In this chapter, I probe the relationship between violence, culture, and the imagination with the aim of making a contribution to African American preaching against violence, particularly against face-to-face private or domestic or personal violence. First, I map the social (that is, political, economic, technological) setting in which violence has become a practice. In this analysis, I propose that (for African Americans, at least) some of the root causes of violence lie in dislocations and value disorientations in the wider U.S. cultural matrices. While the causes of violence arise from and are maintained by these dislocations and disorientations, the very ubiquity and banality of violence stems, at least in part, from distortions of the imagination. Here the ambiguous cultural practices of rap and hip-hop come under some scrutiny. Finally, within this context, I discuss the role of the sermon in the recovery and healing of distorted imagination, in preaching against sexism, sexual abuse, and domestic violence.

SOCIAL DISLOCATION AND VIOLENCE

Within each and every one of us there is a fear. . . . My worst fear is dying in the street. Every morning I wake up and I kiss my daughter and I thank God we have made it through the night. I live in Spanish Harlem, and I am surrounded by crack heads and drug dealers. This is not the type of environment I want to raise my child up in. But I'm stuck here until I get to a higher level. . . . Sometimes I sit in the dark and I think about when is it all going to end. Or is this the end? I just keep feeling pain in my heart when I look at all the children in the street suffering. It just keeps getting worse and worse. Tears run down my face when I embrace my daughter and I pray she doesn't become another victim of life. . . . Everyone is born an innocent baby that is full of joy. All they want is to be loved and comforted and they want to have playtime and food. I began to wonder what goes through the minds of these teenagers that still receive love and comfort and playtime from their parents. Why do they resort to violence as a baby resorts to crying when hungry? What are they hungry for?[4]

Officials and friends struggled yesterday to understand the desperation of a 23-year-old mother who pushed her three children from the roof of their 14-story apartment building and jumped herself on Sunday (24 November 1996). A makeshift memorial grew at the site where the mother, Chicqua Roveal, died, with one of her 7-year-old twins, Andre. The other twin, Andrea, and her 2-year-old sister Shando, remain unconscious and clinging to life. A neighbor said Ms. Roveal was determined that her children would never be subjected to the abandonment she had experienced as a child, when she lived in a series of foster homes.[5]

We were on the freeway, going home from San Francisco. He was driving. We were arguing. He told me repeatedly to shut up. I kept talking. He took his hand from the steering wheel and threw it back, hitting my mouth—my open mouth, blood gushed, and I felt an intense pain. I was no longer able to say any words, only to make whimpering, sobbing sounds as the blood dripped on my hands, on the handkerchief I held too tightly. He did not stop the car. He drove home. I watched him pack his suitcase. It was a holiday. He was going away to have fun. When he left I washed my mouth. My jaw was swollen and it was difficult for me to open it.[6]

"You feel the rage of people, [of] your group . . . just being *the dogs* of society."[7] What is violence? "Violence" is defined as "rough or injurious physical force, action, or treatment; or as unjust or unwarranted exertion of force or power, as against rights, laws; rough or immoderate vehemence, as of feeling or language; or injury, as from distortion of meaning or fact."[8] Violence is an act of aggression. It may be either an impulsive or a predetermined response to perceived or actual threat, and it may be aggravated by a person's or a group's sense or need of power.

Although violence takes many different and twisted forms, basically it is transmitted either through structures (social institutions or systems) or through face-to-face (personal) confrontation. Structural violence is indirect, faceless. While it is mediated by a society's institutions (for example, educational and religious institutions, language, and art), structural violence is "shaped, maintained, and eventually transformed within margins of plasticity" by the decisions of the members of a society, including its victims. Moreover, "structural violence flows inside social structures and stems out of them into interpersonal relationships."[9] As face-to-face confrontation, personal violence allows for the victim to identify, to name, to know the aggressor, the actor, the perpetrator. This knowledge, even familiarity and familial relationship, causes the victim of personal violence profound and traumatic psychic shock.[10]

Violence entails the direct or indirect exercise of "physical, biological or spiritual pressure" by one person [or group] on another. When that pressure exceeds a "certain threshold [it] reduces or annuls [human] potential for performance, both at an individual and group level."[11] Most basically, then, violence is the coercive attempt to restrict, to limit, to thwart the exercise and realization of the essential and effective freedom of a human person or a social group. Violence aims to obliterate the fundamental liberty or active, dynamic, determination of self by the human person. And as the above accounts imply, violence seeks to destroy not only the body, but the spirit as well. Violence breeds despair, hopelessness, and rage.

As a form of social oppression, violence is a structural or systemic phenomenon, and, as such, it does not depend upon the choices, decisions, and actions of a few men or women. Rather, as political theorist Iris Marion Young argues, the causes of structural violence are embedded in the unquestioned standards, symbols, habits, patterns, and practices of a given society or group. These causes of structural violence are also woven into the epistemological, moral, and religious assumptions that underlie the performance of various social, cultural, and religious roles and tasks. They subtly convey the individual and collective consequences of following (or not) approved social, cultural, and religious codes or rules. So, any individual act of violence against a particular class of persons (such as children and women) or a social group (for example, Asians, Blacks, Latinos, gays and lesbians) is reinforced by the structural or systemic oppression of those persons or that group. Thus structural or systemic oppression sanctions individual acts of violence.[12]

Members of oppressed social groups suffer from systemic or structural violence. They also live with the knowledge that they must fear random, unprovoked attacks on their persons or property. In the United States, Asians, indigenous or first nations peoples, women, gay men and lesbians, Arabs, Jews, Puerto Ricans, Mexican Americans, and African Americans, in various regions of the country, live under such threats of violence. A key dimension of random xenophobic violence is its irrationality and unpredictability. While such violence may be motivated by "fear or hatred of those groups . . . [or] simple will to power, to victimize those marked as vulnerable," Young concludes that "what makes violence a phenomenon of social injustice, and not merely an individual moral wrong, is its systemic character, its existence as a social practice." And as a social practice, "a social given" that everyone has come to expect, violence is "always at the horizon of the social imagination, even for those who do not perpetrate it."[13]

Even the most cursory analysis of the broader U.S. cultural and social matrix reveals that there are at least two Americas. One America is *overdeveloped:* privileged, educated, predominantly white but including members of other races, and possessing the economic, political, and ideological means to sustain and justify a way of life defined almost exclusively by the attainment of wealth and the exercise of social (read "capitalist") power. The other America is *underdeveloped:* marginalized, segregated, miseducated, overwhelmingly black, brown, and red but including members of other races, and deprived of the economic and political means to accrue wealth and social (read "capitalist") power. At the same time, however, this other America exercises creative forms of cultural and social resistance to the hegemony of capitalist power.

This other America is, in large measure, the result of the economic restructuring of U.S. urban centers. Over the past twenty-five years, employment has shifted away from manufacturing toward corporate, public, and nonprofit service. This has split the labor market with high-paid directors, managers, and professionals at the top and low-paid manual and service workers at the bottom. In the postindustrial United States, too many African Americans are locked into the bottom half of this market with dead-end, forced part-time, no-benefit jobs. Such economic dislocation causes psychological anxiety; damages the fabric of family life; impairs neighborhood cohesion; enervates schools; and undermines the presence of strong, positive male and female role models. This environment is the product of violence—corporate greed, planned obsolescence and decay, and iniquitous public policies. Such an environment is ripe for the practice of violence.[14]

Consider that more than 33 percent of black families in the United States live below the poverty line and that of these families, nearly 75 percent are headed by single mothers.[15] Consider that each day 1,118 black teenagers are victims of violent crime, 1,451 black children are arrested, and 907 teenage girls are impregnated.[16] Consider that the poorest fifth of households in the United States collects only 4 percent of the national income, while the richest fifth receives more than half.[17] Consider that black women are significantly more at risk for death by homicide than either white women or white men.[18] Consider that black Americans have a "three times greater chance than whites of dying from a police [officer's] bullet."[19] Consider that the United States has the world's highest rate of incarceration. Between 1980 and 1990, the prison population increased by about 130 percent. The federal prison population is over half black and Hispanic; the state prison population is about 46 percent black. The United States imprisons black males at a rate almost five times higher than South Africa did under apartheid.[20] Consider that more and more black infants are born to younger and younger mothers who are immature and poor and that these infants are twice as likely as the children of white women to have serious health problems including asthma, deafness, and developmental and learning disabilities, and to endure the effects of maternal drug and alcohol abuse.[21] Consider the most recent public assault on poor black women—so-called welfare reform. Here legislation strips black women, their children, and their partners of the most basic public assistance, ties black humanity to the market wage, and attaches black citizenship to participation in the labor force.

Sociologist Henry Louis Taylor observes that this context of social dislocation, constituted by low wages, tenacious unemployment and joblessness, planned neighborhood decay, and miseducation, stands as a "material reflection of American [vicious] cultural values."[22] Taylor writes:

> In this country all human activity is viewed through the lenses of profit and economic costs and benefits. Money, profit, and greed are placed over people. Every need and want is turned into a commodity that is bought and sold, with income level determining the quality of one's life. Money decides the quantity and quality of food, clothing, shelter, health care, and education available to people. Not surprising, within this scenario, wealth and power define and reference success and the "good life." How much you earn, rather than what type of contribution you make to society, determines the degree of personal success. Indeed a high-paying job, big house, luxury car, suave clothes, conspicuous consumption, casual sex, exotic vacations, and fancy entertainment are viewed as characteristic features of the good life and the just rewards that accrue to the successful. These are the ideas, values, and beliefs that are conveyed by American cultural industries: movies, television, music, radio, videos, and popular publications. Everywhere the message is the same: comfort, convenience, machismo, femininity, and sex are the symbols of the good life and material success.[23]

It is in this wider U.S. cultural and social context, driven by base preferences (money over people, expediency over long-term solutions, immediate gratification over fortitude, duplicity over the truth) that African Americans and other members of oppressed groups kill one another, sell drugs to one another, assault and maim and rape one another. It is in this social context of vicious values that violence permeates every sector of a woman's life: from waking to sleeping (and even during sleep), at work and school, in places of leisure and cultural refreshment, in restaurants and public parks, in concert halls and libraries, on the gynecologist's table, on the therapist's couch, in the pastor's office, even in her own home, a women may be subject to physical, psychological, emotional, mental harassment, abuse, and life-threatening danger.

To be sure, it is no longer possible to speak of women as if mere female embodiment erased an individual woman's social class, economic status, culture, ethnicity, race, religion, age, personal development, preferences, and geopolitical positioning; yet violence against women precisely disregards all these lines. Women who are members of oppressed social groups endure the intensifying marginalization of racism, of class exploitation, or of sexual orientation as well as the numbing refracted violence perpetrated against them by oppressed men. Still, given the hegemony (even mimetic) of patriarchal and what Elisabeth Schüssler Fiorenza has aptly termed "kyriarchal" power, women—individually and collectively, medically and spiritually, metaphorically and literally—live daily with the fear of violence: of sexual abuse and rape, of physical assault.[24]

VIOLENCE, CULTURE, AND THE IMAGINATION

There are, of course, a variety of definitions of "culture." Here I wish to consider culture as "the set of meanings and values that informs a way of life."[25] This heuristic proposal allows us to grasp culture, not merely as something extrinsic, material, and static, but as dynamic, spiritual, and in-process. Moreover, this proposal adverts explicitly to human persons whose inquiry, understanding, persistence, and imagination are responsible for creating, sustaining, and transforming culture. For as culture realizes in the concrete the meanings and values that mold personal and interpersonal, religious and moral, economic and political choice, *imagination* has a crucial role.[26]

Imagination is a central activity in culture-making—that is, in realizing what values we esteem and cherish. Because the (dis)values of secularism and materialism have become so decisive in shaping contemporary U.S. culture, there is widespread breakdown in the moral and spiritual, religious and cultural formation of many (black) youth. Any attempt to counter this deformation must begin by grasping just how these (dis)values have been extended by modernity, advanced by cultural attitudes toward direct or personal and indirect or structural violence, and legitimated by language and art, religion and theology.[27]

The advent of modernity has generated a mass society "glutted by sensate gratification, ordered by benevolent governors, [and] populated by creatures who have exchanged spiritual freedom and moral responsibility for economic psychic security."[28] This society promotes the confusion of comfort, convenience, (hyper)masculinity, (hyper)femininity, and sex with the "good life"—that is, with authentic happiness, self-realization, and personal fulfillment in community. Not only has this confusion spawned a crisis in values, it has brought about, for many women (and men), especially members of oppressed social groups, a collective experience of psychic breakdown or deterioration and nihilism. For many, the lived and material result is a kind of "outlaw culture informed by Social Darwinism, [vicious] individualism, violence, conspicuous consumption, hedonism, consumerism . . . hopelessness, alienation, and self-hatred."[29]

For African American youth and young adults, rap music has become the "central cultural vehicle for open social reflection on poverty, fear of adulthood, the desire for absent fathers, frustrations about black male sexism, female sexual desires, daily rituals of life as an unemployed teen hustler, safe sex, raw anger, violence, and childhood memories."[30] Rap music and hip-hop culture provide a dynamic, innovative intellectual, political, and spiritual form of resistance to the "cultural fractures produced by postindustrial oppression."[31]

At the same time, rap music and hip-hop culture have benefited from marketing and commercial packaging on a global scale. Savvy young "rappers 'hijacked' the market for their own purposes, riding the currents . . . not just for wealth but for empowerment, and to assert their own identities." Moreover, rappers are critically aware of the angular contradictions and tensions between commercial exploitation and creativity, between protesting capitalist and white-supremacist forms and having that protest transformed into mass-produced commodities and, then, incorporated or appropriated by the dominant culture itself.

Still, for many black urban youth, rap music and hip-hop provide the primary way of interpreting the world, of "negotiat[ing] the experiences of marginalization, brutally truncated opportunity, and oppression within the cultural imperatives of African-American history, identity, and community."[32] Rap music and hip-hop shape the imagination of these youth.

Rap music and videos have been denounced as thoroughly sexist, but the charge demands some nuance. In gangsta rap, the images and discourse of male rappers construct and sell degraded and debased representations of black women. The cartoon on the cover of Snoop Doggy Dogg's *Doggy Style* is lewd and obscene: a naked black female on all-fours, her head in a doghouse, her naked buttocks with a dog's tail offered to the viewer. The photographs on the covers of 2 Live Crew's *As Nasty As They Wanna Be* and *Shake a Lil' Somethin'* edge toward the pornographic: black women wearing thong bikinis, standing with their legs wide apart, their buttocks displayed to the camera, the rappers lying between their legs. D.R.S. (Dirty Rotten Scoundrels) rap about the torture and dismemberment of women as a sexual act. Such instances disclose an imagination in bondage, diluting and defiling the real mysterious joy of passion and erotic power.

At the same time, rap's rampant sexist lyrics reflect the sexism and misogyny that pervade U.S. culture, that mark the wider male attempt to establish heterosexual masculine identity by abusing and dominating women. Yet, as bell hooks so correctly observes:

> When young black males labor in the plantations of misogyny and sexism to produce gangsta rap, white supremacist capitalist patriarchy approves the violence and materially rewards them. Far from being an expression of their "manhood," it is an expression of their own subjugation and humiliation by more powerful, less visible forces of patriarchal gangsterism. They give voice to the brutal, raw anger and rage against women that it is taboo for "civilized" adult men to speak. . . . The tragedy for young black males is that they are so easily duped by a vision of manhood that can only lead to their destruction.[33]

Certainly, the deaths of Tupac Shakur and Christopher Wallace (The Notorious B.I.G.) have made it so very plain that "gangsta image—for all its force and bluster—is nothing if not tragic, a *myth* of empowerment."[34]

Rap, hip-hop, and violence meet at the "crossroads of lack and desire."[35] In the social matrix on which rap comments, and often so prophetically, human life has lost preeminent value. "In our urban centers," writes theologian J. Deotis Roberts, "life is a useless passion."[36] Life is snuffed out with little or no remorse, treated as a disposable commodity. Such vicious attitudes are related to and sustained by dysfunctional family life, a social setting satiated with poverty, unfulfilled yearnings, and hostility to genuine moral growth and development.[37] Contemporary Christianity—African American

Christianity in particular—must reaffirm the sacredness and transcendent quality of (black) human life, (black) women's human life. Contemporary Christianity—African American Christianity in particular—must retrieve a notion of the human person as a dynamic acting moral agent, rather than a passive consuming being who is the product of randomly advertised and marketed external change.

The media and the film industry bathe violence in surreal and romantic light. Violence is excessive, gratuitous, made strangely compelling, roughly erotic, determining and redetermining "thresholds" of pleasure, pressure, and pain.[38] This was sickeningly obvious in trailers for the film *Crash,* with its unmistakably titillating connection between sex and violence. But the film *The Piano* "seduce[d] and excite[d]" while serving up an "uncritical portrayal" of misogyny, sexism, and white-supremacist capitalist patriarchy.[39] Black films like *She's Gotta Have It, School Daze,* and *Boyz N the Hood* eroticize black women, and do "violence and mayhem to body and soul."[40]

At the same time, we cannot overlook the real collusion of (black) women in these displays. In her study of rap and hip-hop culture, Tricia Rose writes that the women who participate in rap videos, who allow themselves to be photographed for the purpose of marketing hip-hop culture, are called "video ho's" or "skeezers." Their motivation for such cooperation and "participation in this video meat market is closely related to the rock/sports/film star groupie phenomenon, in which fans, especially female, get momentary star aura by associating closely or having sex with rich and famous figures."[41] How great must be the desire, how profound must be the need of these young women for attention, for care, for affirmation. How poignant, how piteous that their complicity in their own debasement is understood or misunderstood as a means toward a career in the entertainment business or a way out of economically fragile circumstances.

Whether intentionally or not, Hollywood "in black and in white" desensitizes, manipulates, and manages our response to violence—to blood and gore, to seduction and rape, to betrayal and violation, to torture and killing. Whether intentionally or not, print and visual media, films, MTV, and video games transmit gross and violent images that penetrate our subconscious. Unnoticed and unreflected upon, these images suffuse our thoughts, speech, bodily reactions to others, judgments, and ordinary practices of everyday interaction.[42]

Thus, violence becomes common, ordinary, expected; in the absence of countervailing instruction, it becomes normative.[43] For even as violence sustains our aggression, violence undermines our efforts to respond and critique that aggression, to engage in and be engaged by nonviolent personal and social transformation. Violence has deformed our imagination. Violence leaves us discouraged, dispirited, and numb; wounded culturally and socially, psychically and physically, morally and religiously.

THE SERMON IN THE HEALING OF DISTORTED IMAGINATION

Thus far, I have mapped the matrix in which violence has become a social and, for many, a personal practice. I have proposed that at least some of the root causes of violence in African American communities lie in our internalization of the dislocations and value disorientations of the wider U.S. cultural and social matrices. And by focusing critically on rap music and hip-hop, I have tried to make thematic how violence stems, at least in part, from distortions in the imagination due to psychic breakdown and nihilism.

But I have only hinted at the role the Christian church—and African American Christian churches in particular—might take in addressing the subjugation of imagination by violence. I hope, in this last section, to suggest how the oratory of the black sermon can make a contribution in excising religious attitudes and theological positions that foster sexist representations of women and that (unintentionally) condone violence, in healing distortions of the imagination, and in creating and nourishing a counterimagination that contests the reign of violence, nihilism, and despair.[44]

The religiocultural world from which the black sermon emerged was forged in the fusion of fragmented elements and beliefs drawn from several West African cosmologies. Although the enslaved peoples fitted Christianity to their own situation, that fusion laid the ground on which that adaptation took place.[45] The most essential characteristics of an African American (Christian) worldview include: (1) creative and tensive holding of both sacred and secular, without separation or dilution; (2) profound respect for all human life and interpersonal relationships; (3) individual identity-formation from and in relation to community, along with regard for the wisdom of elders; (4) empathetic, symbolic, diunital, and associative understanding; (5) unity of being and doing; (6) commitment to freedom and liberation due to centuries of oppression and communal and personal anxiety; (7) ambiguous toleration and transcendence of a notion of limited reward in the context of slavery and stigmatized social history; (8) indirection and discretion in speech and behavior; and (9) affirmation of styling (that is, intentional or unintentional improvisation in language, gestural or symbolic mannerisms to favorably effect the receipt of a message).[46]

As perhaps the *chief* exemplar of an African American (Christian) worldview, the black sermon is also the key to understanding and projecting this worldview. The sermon is a rhetorical space in which the preacher and the people "articulate the self, challenge the dominant culture's ordering of reality, and contest its authoritative discourse." In that space, the preacher recovers the community's voice and binds the present to the past while striving against social dislocation, value disorientation, and psychic breakdown, to imagine and "project a benevolent cosmology and teleology" in which black people apprehend and know themselves as subjects of their own history and destiny, as a people of God's own making.[47] For those who respond to its beauty, truth, and power, the sermon signifies and effects a healing shift in religious, cultural, social, and psychological imagination.

One of the ways that the preacher does this is by *drawing out* the centuries-old history of African Americans and by *drawing on* what literary critic Stephen Henderson terms "mascon" images and symbols. With the word "mascon," Henderson denotes words that mediate a "massive concentration of Black experiential energy which powerfully affects the meaning of Black speech, Black song, and Black poetry."[48] Henderson contends that "certain words and constructions seem to carry an inordinate charge of emotional and psychological weight, so that whenever they are used they set all kinds of bells ringing, all kinds of synapses snapping, on all kinds of levels." These words and images are mined from what Henderson calls "the soul-field," the dense set of "personal, social, institutional, historical, religious, and mythical meanings that affect everything we say or do as Black people sharing a common heritage."[49]

A final illustration should suffice: "Let My People Go." This is perhaps the most powerful mascon in the canon and is drawn from the great spiritual "Go Down Moses." Drawing on associative understanding, in the recording "Go Up Moses," Roberta Flack prophetically turns the mascon on black people's descent into materialism and self-hatred.[50]

Through improvisational word construction, symbols and images, music and song, mascons configure and mediate meaning, constitute and effect community, generate appreciative awe. Deceptively simple while never simplistic, common while never clichéd, mascons possess what black Catholic liturgist Clarence Rivers terms "magnitude."[51]

For generations, African American people have used mascons (1) to remember and to pass on their unspeakable suffering under slavery, their thirst for life, their unyielding spirit, and their relationship with the divine; (2) to bind the people to one another and to themselves (although this may never be fully realized in the here and now); (3) to liberate themselves, if only briefly, from the material power of the capitalist dispensation; and (4) to transcend societal and personal limitations. The use of mascons in the black sermon is all but required.

Womanist ethicist Katie Cannon maintains that while most African American churchgoers are capable of grasping and judging the aesthetic landscape of the black sermon, we find it difficult to identify, analyze, and articulate its patterns of misogyny, androcentricity, and patriarchy.[52] Theologian Garth Baker-Fletcher concurs. "How," he asks, "can Black churches really mount a sustained critique of woman-degrading rhetoric when so many preachers and churches devalue women on a regular basis?"[53] If the sermon is to heal distortion and to nourish imagination, then the preacher is morally obliged to grasp and plumb the experiences of the *whole* congregation, to "satisfy the whole congregation's spiritual hunger." Cannon proposes a womanist critique of homiletics that will "identif[y] the frame of sexist-racist social contradictions housed in sacred rhetoric that gives women a low image of ourselves."[54] This critique involves asking and answering these questions: "how is meaning constructed, whose interests are served, and what kind of worlds are envisioned in Black sacred rhetoric?"[55] This critique, then, calls the preacher and the church to jettison that *aesthetics of submission* through which the central images, symbols, metaphors, narrative interpretations, traditions, and rituals of Christian practice, explicitly and implicitly, coach tame women to surrender to patriarchal and kyriarchal prerogatives and privilege.

If the sermon is to heal and to nourish imagination, then its message must be rooted in exegetical and theological content that project an eschatological reality worthy of African American Christianity. Given the failure of the church to take women seriously, given the culture's and rap music's reduction of (black) women to body parts, and given the sexual and physical violence against women, the preacher's theological attitude toward personhood, toward the humanity of women, is of special concern. For centuries, religion and theology have used women as a "special symbol of evil."[56] The contemporary residue of this usage coupled with cultural disregard for human life has, quite literally, had fatal consequences for (black) women.

The identification of women with nature, with bodiliness, with emotion, and the identification of men with culture, with spirit, with reason advocate the subordination of women to men in nearly all spheres of human activity. Long-standing theological debates about the constitution and origin of female being (body and soul) have left even women suspicious of their authentic humanity. And although we recognize that the soul is without gender, we still doubt women's *full participation* in the imago Dei.

The notion of woman as a self-transcending, autonomous human subject, a moral agent capable of forming and acting in accord with her responsibly formed conscience remains, for not a few men and women, still disquieting. Contemporary Christianity, particularly African American Christianity, must contest the imagination's downward spiral into the lewd and pornographic—wordplay that warps (black) women's bodies, photographs that simulate steamy violent sex, sadomasochism, and addiction.

At the same time, however, Cannon insists that African American Christianity purge itself of "biblically based sermons [as well as representations and messages] that portray female subjects as bleeding, crippled, disempowered, objectified, purified, or mad." These representations trivialize and distort the humanity of women, for young black girls and women inevitably internalize these malformations. These representations undermine the "historical contributions of African American women's leadership and participation in the church" and in society.[57] These representations deface the divine image in the person of women.

SUBVERTING THE REIGN OF VIOLENCE

We are in a position now to suggest how the sermon might recover and heal distortion in communal and personal imagination, how the sermon might begin to subvert the reign of violence. *First,* since the primary "purpose of preaching is to call the worshipping congregation to *an ultimate response to God,*" the preacher stands between God and the people—"with one ear to the ground hearing the cries and longings of the people and the other ear at the mouth of God."[58] The sermon is the vehicle by which the preacher defines, interprets, and instructs the congregation in what it means to live a just and holy life, what it means to be God's own people in history. Thus, they are called to grasp, incarnate, and proclaim the liberating character and deed of God. In the sermon, preacher and congregation dramatically, rhythmically, and existentially reenact the history of the mighty acts of God. Through "a rhetorical methodology of definition, elaboration, exemplification, and justification," the sermon reestablishes "a line of continuity inside the mind."[59] The psychic and aesthetic aspects of the imagination are engaged and energized, cleansed and refreshed, reanimated and redirected.

Second, the sermon structures a symbolic universe in which, in response to the sound of the preacher's voice, an aggregate of isolated individuals emerge as a community. The preacher "encodes the corporate community with a culturally regenerating vision as preacher and community assert their rights to genuine existence."[60] This vision must project a prophetic critique against all that threatens to maim and destroy (black) life, against all that presents itself as misogyny and androcentricity. And it must grapple with social dislocation and cultural disorientation, equipping women and men for dignity in life and creative social praxis aimed at transformation.

The community as community evaluates and judges this vision, even at the affective height of its delivery. "African-American congregations are not driven to uncontrollable frenzy [even] at times of seeming emotional abandon . . . and do not suspend judgment."[61] In the sermon, the preacher charts a series of imaginal constructions and intelligible conceptions that convey the community's ideal meanings and values. If those ideals are transgressed or exploited, disapproval is expressed, and the direction of the sermon will shift.

Third, the sermon heals and frees the congregation and each of its members from dread, from psychic breakdown, from nihilism. Hortense Spillers writes that the passional thrust of the sermon as oral poetry aims for "a complete expression of a gamut of emotions whose central form is the narrative and whose end is cathartic release . . . binding once again the isolated members of a community."[62] The sermon gives back to the community its own history, its cultural memory, its creative potential, its "soul." The sermon pours out a healing balm and binds up psychic and spiritual wounds of a community oppressed and violated by structural violence, of women (and men) abused and assaulted by direct acts of violence. As the community becomes its "authentic self," each member finds her or his own "self" and discovers personal history and potential nourished, alienated and disordered affective patterns remade. Each member experiences a sense of release, of being at home, of being at one with the other members of the community. The sermon reestablishes the principles of truth, trust, justice, and integrity as the norms by which the community and its members evaluate and reorient themselves. The sermon clears a path for the intervention, the irruption of the Spirit in lives of disorder and disgrace.

Fourth, the sermon is a challenge to the members of the community to question, to analyze, and to transform their social and historical situation, and, to do so *as* and *in* community. It proposes practical solutions to the social dislocations of joblessness, homelessness, hunger, and poverty and thus "invites the congregation to make a decision for or against emancipatory praxis."[63] The community and its members in response act out their self-determination and self-actuation in responsibly life-valuing ways. The day-care centers, job-training programs, housing plans, and social ministries of African American churches represent efforts to realize the symbolic vision of a human, whole, and holy life in the concrete. To the cultural, social, moral, and psychic alienations that give impetus to irrationality, chaos, and evil, the sermon evokes an *aesthetic of redemption* that orders a vision of another kind of city. Insofar as the sermon enacts an *aesthetic of liberation,* it intentionally, attentively, intelligently, rationally, responsibly, and lovingly recovers appropriate mascons, brings forth and tests fresh images, symbols, metaphors, and narratives; it engenders a nondominative, antiviolent, nonsexist, truly human and Christian future.

And, *fifth,* sexual abuse of (black) women and children, battering, and psychological assault are deeply disturbing; they are sins as well as crimes. Inasmuch as preacher and people believe and act and move as if the authority of the sermon comes directly from God, then the sermon must be a self-critical practice. It must continually measure the vision it projects and the message it proclaims against "God's Agapic love."[64] Indeed, the blood of raped, battered, abused, and murdered (black) women (and children) summons the church to its own *kenosis.* If the church, is to be a credible, purified, authentic witness and servant of the message of that love, then it must effect in its own life and structures what it preaches.

CONCLUSION

The black sermon can be a crucial instrument in the recovery and healing of distorted and wounded imagination. At the same time, the context from which the sermon emerges—African American culture and religion, exegesis and theology, language and art—all too easily can be implicated in the legitimation of violence. The sermon achieves its aesthetico-medico function only insofar as preacher and congregation participate in the retrieval of those meanings and values that constitute African American culture as a good, choiceworthy, just, and beautiful way to live.[65] The sermon's ability to shape and to project realizations of aesthetic consciousness demonstrates just how imagination constitutes the ground not only of our cultural, social, and historical transformation but of our eschatological hope.

Part 2

Pastoral Resources for Telling the Truth

4

Preaching Forgiveness?

Marie M. Fortune

The single most common pastoral concern that I hear expressed by victims and survivors of sexual or domestic violence is their anxiety about forgiveness. Painful stories abound.

"Do I have to forgive my grandfather who molested me for five years?"

"Baby, I'm sorry. I didn't mean to hurt you. Please forgive me and come back home."

"He raped me and beat me—in my own home. And you expect me to forgive him? I hope he rots in jail."

"But the Bible says I must forgive seven times seven. I don't know if I can do that."

"Preacher, do I have to forgive a man who murdered my four sons?"[1]

When we consider the meaning of forgiveness and the pastoral needs of our people in the midst of these circumstances, these assumptions apply:

1. We are dealing with real and immediate experiences of violence and abuse in the lives of our congregants (and in our own lives).
2. There are always three groups of people present when we gather: victims/survivors of sexual and domestic violence, perpetrators of sexual and domestic violence, and bystanders (those who knowingly or unknowingly have stood by before, during, and after acts of harm done by one person to another).
3. Whenever we preach or teach, we must remember that all three groups are present, and we must speak to each group in its particular experience. We must attempt to meet our pastoral and ethical responsibility to all three groups—which is no easy task.

MISUNDERSTANDING FORGIVENESS

In contemporary Christian teaching and practice, the burden to forgive seems always to be placed solely on the shoulders of those who have suffered physically and emotionally. The same is true in New Age ideology. In speaking about family violence, Alan

Reid, a Canadian lawyer, comments: "In my opinion, forgiveness, not confrontation, is the 'systemic remedy' that can bring about the needed attitudinal change. Forgiveness takes us beyond the belief in our victim-victimizer roles to the realization of our inherent equality. Those who are willing to forgive receive instant healing. Those who are not willing to forgive continue to experience conflict, and to see themselves as victims and victimizers caught up in the violence syndrome."[2]

This is the most common response that victims or survivors hear from family, friends, and the church. The first thing that those who are trying to be helpful want to discuss is forgiveness, meaning that the one victimized should simply forgive and then be rewarded magically with healing.

In Judaism, the burden rests with the one who causes harm. Maimonides explains that the Day of Atonement, Yom Kippur, provides corporate atonement for sins against God. But sins against one's neighbor (or intimate partner) are not pardoned unless the offender compensates the victim and apologizes. This means confession, taking responsibility, repentance and restitution to the one harmed (2:9). Then repentance is real when there is an opportunity to repeat the offense and the offender refrains from it because of his/her repentance (not because of fear) (2:1).[3]

In fact, the teachings of Jesus in the Gospels are congruent with the teachings of Judaism on this issue (which should be no surprise to any of us). In Luke 17:3–4, Jesus says that if another disciple sins, you must rebuke the offender, and if there is repentance, you must forgive. And then the seven times comes in: if that one sins seven times and repents seven times, you must forgive.

As we shall see later on, the Christian scriptural teachings are more complex than might appear at first. But fundamentally, both Judaism and Christianity link the expectation of forgiveness on the part of one harmed to genuine confession and repentance on the part of the offender. This is the context of justice, which we shall examine as necessary for real forgiveness and healing to occur.

The problem for Christians is that somehow the notion and practice of forgiveness has been romanticized and placed in a vacuum due in large part to the canonization of "forgive and forget" theology. If we ask most Christians today where to find "forgive and forget" in the Bible, none of them will know where it is, but they will swear that it is in there somewhere. It is not. It appears in Shakespeare's *King Lear* (act 4, scene 7). But it has struck a resonant chord in the public psyche I believe precisely because it is simplistic and allows us to ignore the power dynamics of the situation in which harm has been done by one to another.

When the expectation of agency in response to harm done by one to another is passed to the one harmed and away from the one causing harm, then three things happen:

1. No one (including us as bystanders) ever has to deal with accountability for the offender. This is particularly advantageous for the nonrepentant offender.
2. The victims, whose priority is their own individual healing, can decide that they have the power to bring about this healing by their own agency in the "act" of forgiving. This is a cruel hoax for the victim.
3. The bystanders (often you and I and many members of our churches) can stand by and do nothing, self-righteously reassured that we have no lines in this play.

As a result, the victim is shamed or cajoled into saying the magic words "I forgive him," convinced by us that now she will feel better; now God will love her; and now she can remain in good standing within her church. In the following hypothetical situation, these dynamics are painfully played out.

I am the pastor of a local church. A congregant whom we will call Lisa comes to me and shares that she was raped several weeks earlier. She reported to the police; they have apprehended the suspect; he will be prosecuted. Lisa is now getting in touch with her anger, and she wants to discuss it with her pastor. She is hesitant because she learned in Sunday school that anger is un-Christian and not ladylike. But she presses ahead with my support, for I believe that anger is healthy and important for victims of violence. She returns a week later still venting her anger. This continues for four to five weeks. Finally, because I am concerned about what this anger may be doing to her, I decide to encourage her to move beyond it. But if I am honest with myself, I have a second agenda: I am tired of hearing about her anger every week and would like her to move beyond it. So I suggest the following: "Don't you think it's time you forgave him?" Lisa is a thoughtful and committed Christian, and she thinks that I know what I am doing; she trusts me. So she goes home and thinks about it and prays about it; she returns once more and says, "Well, I've forgiven him," but her clenched teeth and tight body suggest otherwise. This is the moment of truth for my pastoral sensitivity.

My temptation here is to say a prayer of thanksgiving and send her home. If I do this, I will communicate that the topic is closed to further discussion and that I am not available to her any further in this situation. She has followed my direction, gone through the motions, and doesn't feel any better. In fact, now she feels worse: she doesn't feel forgiving; she has disappointed her pastor, and so she must not be a very good Christian; plus she can't bring her concerns here in the future. This is not a helpful scenario for Lisa. What is missing in this picture is any experience of justice for Lisa and the time and space that she needs to deal with the possibility of forgiveness.

LEARNING FROM OTHER CONTEXTS

If we place the issue of forgiveness in a larger context, we can begin to see its limits and possibilities. In the Holocaust, humanity is faced with the unspeakable horror of genocide, a reality being repeated today in places like Bosnia and Rwanda. But individual persons were and are faced with personal suffering and a longing for healing in these situations. Simon Wiesenthal, a Jewish survivor of the camps who has spent his life bringing Nazi war criminals to trial, tells a story of his experience in a camp in Lemberg, Poland. He was in a work detail assigned to move boxes at a hospital. A nurse called him out and told him to follow her to a hospital room, where she left him standing before a bandaged figure in the bed. A weak voice from a man named Hans told him that he was an SS man and that he was dying. He had asked the nurse to bring him one of the Jewish laborers to speak with. He confessed to an atrocity in which he participated, where they had herded Jews into a house, locked the doors, and then blown up the house. He asked Wiesenthal to forgive him. Wiesenthal listened to Hans, reflected briefly, then turned and left the room without a word.

Wiesenthal questioned his decision immediately, and it has continued to haunt him ever since. In his book *The Sunflower,* he tells this story and also shares his own and others' reflections on his decision. He is very clear that his silence in response to Hans was not an act of revenge or anger; and he believed that Hans's confession was genuine. His reason was this: "How could he forgive someone for harm that person had done to someone else? Isn't it only the injured person who may decide to grant or to withhold forgiveness?"[4]

Wiesenthal argues against himself when he questions whether the fact that a person who has caused harm fully acknowledges responsibility and attempts to amend the harm he has done should not suffice. And if so, then can someone other than the victim(s) be the agent of the community to offer pardon and forgiveness? This would reflect the common practice of the church. On Sunday mornings, pastors in many congregations pronounce that "Your sins are forgiven."

The questions are legitimate: How can anyone presume to forgive on behalf of someone else? Is it necessary to confess and be accountable in order to be forgiven? And what does it mean to forgive anyway?

If we allow the context to guide us further, let us consider the aftermath of apartheid in South Africa. Here we see a whole society struggling to find a way to heal the wounds caused by the violence of apartheid which was visited on so many individuals and families. It is a moral laboratory in which the success of the experiment is necessary to the survival of the nation; the stakes could not be higher. The Truth and Reconciliation Commission was established by law and is chaired by Archbishop Desmond Tutu. Anyone who fully discloses a politically motivated crime committed between 1 March 1960 (Sharpeville massacre) and 5 December 1993 (the last day of apartheid) may receive indemnity from civil or criminal action. But there is no guarantee of amnesty. Some crimes will be viewed as too horrendous or not politically motivated, and prosecution will follow for these.

Archbishop Tutu's leadership of the Truth and Reconciliation Commission is key. And his commitment to it as a Christian leader is at the core of his ministry. But the process is complex and difficult. Many criticize it: the family of Griffiths Mxenge, for example. He was a lawyer for the African National Congress who was assassinated in 1981 by the South African police. One of the officers involved has come forward and named names. Mxenge's family questions whether this is sufficient and criticizes Tutu's efforts: "Tutu is a man of the cloth, a man who believes in miracles. But I cannot see him being able overnight to cause people who are hurt and bleeding simply to forget about their wounds and forget about justice. It is President Mandela's wish, too. But that is not normal. That doesn't happen. Unless justice is done it's difficult for any person to think of forgiving."[5]

But what is the nature of this justice? Tutu responds:

"There are different kinds of justice. Retributive justice is largely Western. The African understanding is far more restorative—not so much to punish as to redress or restore a balance that has been knocked askew. The justice we hope for is restorative of the dignity of the people." This is an expression of the African notion of *ubuntu*—interconnectedness, the idea that no one can be healthy when the community is sick. "It's a deeply Christian concept," Tutu said. You are not saved as an individual, but through incorporation into a body. Ubuntu really is a good deal more Biblical and Christian than Western individualism is."[6]

This is all well and good. But what about the family of Griffiths Mxenge? And thousands of others who carry the excruciating memories of violence done to them and their loved ones?

RETHINKING FORGIVENESS

Forgiveness is not always possible. Berel Lang asserts: "Some acts are irretrievable by the human will alone: forgiveness cannot always intervene between or among human beings. For some acts, the agents continue to have responsibility for what they do beyond anything else they can do or wish."[7] Lang tries to imagine a world without forgiveness, explaining that it would be a world in which human perfection means that no wrongs are committed or a world in which vengeance would be the norm.[8] And the result of this would be no possibility of healing or reconciliation for victims of harm. Forgiveness is God's gift for victims and survivors. Any benefit that it brings to offenders is a bonus. Likewise, any benefit it brings to the bystander is a bonus. Forgiveness brings, first and foremost, the possibility of healing to those harmed.

But what then is forgiveness?

1. It is not condoning or pardoning, making every thing okay as if no harm had been done by the perpetrator (It is our temptation to "heal the wound lightly, saying 'peace, peace,' where there is no peace" [Jer. 6:14]).
2. It is not the sole responsibility of the victim/survivor: "Don't you think it's time you forgave him?"
3. It cannot happen in a vacuum.
4. It is very difficult absent the accountability of the offender.
5. It is about letting it go and getting on with one's life.

FORGIVENESS REQUIRES JUSTICE

An adult survivor of incestuous abuse came to talk with me about her recent memories of sexual abuse by her uncle. She was getting in touch with her anger, which she was also hesitant to share. She quickly moved to the point of wanting to confront her uncle, only to be stymied because her uncle was deceased. So she decided instead to write to her father (her uncle's brother) and tell him what had happened. She wrote the letter; we discussed whether she wanted to send it. We explored the possible responses her father might make. She decided that she didn't care how he responded; she just needed to break the silence.

Her father received her twelve-page letter and immediately got on a plane and came to her. He said how sorry he was that all this had happened. He said he didn't know that his brother was abusing her, but he knew she was having a hard time and he didn't check that out with her. He said that he should have protected her, because that was his job as her father. He asked how much her therapy had cost, and said that he would send a check for the expense as soon as he got home. When I saw her a week later, she was a different woman. She still had work to do; she stayed in her survivor support group. But her burden had been lifted; she had forgiven—that is, let go of the immediacy of her pain because she experienced justice in her father's response.

Justice is necessary. This is what I have learned from my pastoral work with victims, survivors, and perpetrators of sexual and domestic violence. I didn't learn this in seminary. I learned it when I slowed down long enough to listen to survivors. I learned to ask them the question "What do you need to find some healing and resolution from the abuse that you suffered?" If, as helpers, we bother to ask this question, victims and survivors usually will have fairly straightforward answers, such as the following. I need:

- My abuser to acknowledge what he did to me.
- A chance to tell the bishop what the priest did to me.
- An apology from my uncle.
- To be sure that he won't do this to anyone else.
- Compensation for my expenses as a result of all this.

If we think categorically about these concrete requests, we begin to see what justice looks like.

Truth-telling: Telling the story of what happened in order to break silence.

Acknowledgment: Being heard and acknowledged by someone significant to the victim/survivor; hearing "I believe you and it was not your fault."

Compassion: The bystander's willingness to suffer with the survivor and not try to "fix" the situation.

Protection of the vulnerable: Whatever steps are necessary to protect others from this person who caused harm.

Accountability for the offender: Being called to account in whatever ways are possible. This is where the community communicates that this harmful behavior must stop.

Restitution to the survivor: The offender offers or is required to make material restitution to the survivor in order to attend to the material cost of the harm done.

Vindication for the survivor: To be vindicated is "to be set free." Justice enables a survivor to be freed from the burden of memory, self-blame, and pain in order to get on with her or his life.

OFFENDERS MUST BE HELD ACCOUNTABLE

"But what about the offender in all of this? This seems much more retributive than restorative." This assertion is based on the assumption that anything that makes the offender uncomfortable or requires him or her to give anything up is punitive and unfair. This assumption reveals a fundamental lack of understanding of what accountability is all about.

I was asked to meet with a group of incest offenders in a court-mandated treatment group a number of years ago. In a group of twenty-seven men, twenty-five were active Christians. The Christians were presenting a real challenge to the therapists because they kept wanting to talk about theology and scripture; the therapists were not trained for these issues. So we met and discussed a number of questions. But at the end of the meeting, as they summarized, almost to a man they said, "Whenever you talk with church leaders, tell them for us: don't forgive us so quickly." Each one of them, when he was arrested, had gone first to his minister, who had prayed over him and sent him home "forgiven." The offenders said this was the worst thing anyone could have done for them, because it meant that they could continue to avoid taking responsibility for the harm they had done to their children.

Their witness is important for pastors and the church to hear. The incest offenders were reminding us that premature forgiveness without repentance, without accountability to those harmed, is cheap grace and is very unhelpful to them—not to mention to those they have harmed.

To be held accountable is to be called to repent, which is basic to both Judaism and Christianity. And this is not some abstract notion about eternal salvation; it is a very concrete expectation that one change his or her behavior here and now. So it is necessary to discuss accountability as part of justice-making if we are ever to get to forgiveness and reconciliation—whether in the family or in South Africa.

Consider these two contrasting methods of the community requiring accountability. A judge cleared a man convicted of beating his wife after defense attorneys argued that the conviction was preventing the man from joining a local country club. The man was convicted of battery, paid a fine, received domestic violence counseling, and has served three years of a five-year probation he must sucessfully complete. The judge acknowledged that the beating was a bad thing, but ruled that keeping the conviction on record served no purpose. The judge wanted to remove the stigma that this conviction carried with it. The prosecutor argued against removing the conviction and the man's domestic violence counselor described him as extremely resistant to counseling. His estranged wife was upset by the decision.[9]

In contrast, members of the indigenous Tlingit tribe in southeast Alaska describe their memory of a time one hundred years ago when wife-abuse was not tolerated in the tribe. Wives were valued members of the community, and husbands knew they were not to use violence in their homes. If a husband did violate this custom, then the consequences were clear: his family clan would make a material payment to his wife's family clan in a public potlatch gathering of the whole tribe. Wife-abuse was very unusual in early twentieth-century southeast Alaska, because it was shameful and expensive. Since the arrival of white settlers and alcohol, the incidence of wife-abuse among the Tlingits equals that of the dominant community. The advantage that the Tlingits have over those of us from European cultural backgrounds is that they at least have a memory of a time when wife-abuse was not an accepted part of family life. They can go back to that memory and that value today and build upon it to reestablish a community norm that says there is no excuse for domestic violence.

The community and church have the potential to help make justice, which invariably then helps call the abuser to account and frees the survivor to forgive. It is our job in preaching to bring the entire community into this picture.

THE BIBLE AND THE MEANING OF FORGIVENESS

So what about the biblical take on all of this? In "Structures of Forgiveness in the New Testament," Fred Keene does the biblical homework that corresponds to the ethical and pastoral framework presented here.[10] He asks the important questions about power, which remind us again that we are always dealing with three groups of people in this discussion: the victim/survivor, the perpetrator, and the bystander. Keene wants us to consider the power relationships among these three groups as we interpret the Gospels' teaching about forgiveness.

His point is that if we look at the way Jesus taught about forgiveness, we can see that he never expected anyone who had less power in a relationship to "forgive" a more powerful person who had exploited him or her. The only way that the more powerful person could expect to be forgiven was by giving up power and thus leveling the playing field. Then the offender's repentance might have some integrity, and forgiveness might become an option. And finally, Keene reminds us that from the cross, Jesus did not forgive his murderers but asked God to attend to this. In his powerlessness and vulnerability, Jesus could not forgive, and so he does not ask us to, either. But he calls upon us to forgive those who truly repent, which means those who are willing to give up the power they may have had over a victim. Only then do healing and reconciliation become real possibilities.

GUIDELINES FOR FORGIVENESS

What Forgiveness Is Not

1. Forgiveness is not condoning or pardoning harmful behavior, which is a sin.
2. Forgiveness is not healing the wound lightly, saying "peace, peace" when there is no peace.
3. Forgiveness is not always possible.
4. Forgiveness is not an expectation of any degree of future relationship with the person who caused the harm.

What Forgiveness Is

1. Forgiveness is letting go so that the immediacy of the painful memories can be put into perspective.
2. Forgiveness is possible in a context of justice-making and the healing presence of the Holy Spirit.
3. Forgiveness is God's gift, for the purpose of healing, to those who have been harmed.
4. Accountability is God's gift to those who have harmed another for the purpose of repentance (read "fundamental change").

THE CHALLENGE TO PREACHERS

If a preacher is to preach effectively about sexual and domestic violence, he or she must address the Word to all three groups present on any given occasion: victims/survivors, offenders, and bystanders. While each group needs to hear a particular portion of the message directed to its situation, each needs to hear the other's portion as well. The victim/survivor needs to hear accountability preached to the offender; the offender needs to hear support offered to the victim/survivor; the bystander needs to hear both, so as to learn how to participate in providing both and thus making justice.

The preacher often feels overwhelmed by this task. It is important to remember that the preached word that addresses sexual or domestic violence is a seed that may not bear fruit for months or years to come. The preacher may not see the pastoral impact of this word. But it is a critical word, nonetheless. It can set in motion the possibility of individual and collective healing where brokenness has been the norm. So the writer of Hebrews encourages the preacher: "Therefore lift your drooping hands and strengthen your weak knees, and make straight paths for your feet, so that what is lame may not be put out of joint, but rather be healed" (Heb. 12:12).

Our people do not need platitudes, sentimentality, and offers of cheap grace. They do not need to be urged "to forgive"; in fact, in many cases, they need to be urged "not to forgive so quickly." They need guidance and support to help them face head-on the painful realities and memories of violence and abuse in their lives. They need to hear about a God who stands with the exploited and abused; who calls the powerful to account; who offers justice and forgiveness as the tools of healing; who expects bystanders to support victims and call abusers to account. This is the good news that they deserve.

5

Preaching to Survivors
of Child Sexual Abuse

Nancy J. Ramsay

I have chosen a startling phrase to convey the central themes of this chapter—God's fierce tenderness. It is crucial for survivors of sexual abuse in the faith community to recover or construct images of God's power and love that unequivocally disclose God's righteous anger in response to their abuse, fierce commitment to their healing and empowerment, and tender compassion for their wounded bodies and spirits. The image I have in mind is described often in the Hebrew Bible. A good example is found in the anger of the good shepherd (Ezek. 34) who condemns those who have failed to protect the vulnerable entrusted to their care. The shepherd provides tenderly for the imperiled and assures justice for them.

There are, of course, a variety of images for God and God's power in scripture. The more monarchical ones, still predominant in contemporary North American religious culture, suggest a hierarchical, unilateral exercise of power that encourages dependency or a fated passivity. Such images may seem painfully familiar to one who has experienced betrayal, violation, and domination at the hand of a trusted adult or sibling whose love and protective care they had relied upon. I want to discuss here the importance of preaching that helps survivors recover two things: (1) theological worldviews in which God's power is on behalf of love and justice—reliably redemptive and empowering, and (2) empowered and tender images of their embodied selves.

As Calvin has helped us realize, to reflect on the nature of God also points us to our own experience. It is important to help survivors reimagine their embodiment in God's image so that their bodies—once the locus of betrayal, violation, and domination—may open for them opportunities for trustworthy, mutually respectful, and joyful relationships of love and care. A theological worldview in which embodiment is a gift for deepening our communion with God and one another is crucial for survivors' full recovery. It is also important to help survivors overcome the bondage of fear which is the legacy of betrayal, violation, and domination. Fearful self-protection undermines a survivor's ability to embrace his or her gifts and share them on behalf of the freedom for love that is the vocation of all believers.

At the heart of effective preaching for survivors lie these two themes of God's empowering love and tender power, and our embodiment as creatures called to love in mutually empowering and tender ways. Preachers need to have an informed understanding of the reality and consequences of abuse in order to use well the power accompanying the privilege of preaching and ritual practice. Preachers exercise powerful knowledge as they interpret and name reality. Whether and how they name the reality of violence and abuse makes a world of difference.

THE SITUATION

The grim statistics of the incidence of child sexual abuse are painfully familiar, so I will refer to them only briefly.

> One in three girls and at least one in seven boys are sexually molested before the age of eighteen. Between 75 and 90 percent of the time, the abuser is an adult the child and those who would protect her or him know and trust, thus lowering the likelihood that she or he would reveal the identity of the perpetrator or that she or he would be believed. Estimates are that half of the incidents of sexual abuse occur in the immediate or extended family as incest. Sexual abuse in the family is likely to begin when the child is as young as three to six years of age and, if unreported, continues into adolescence. In this country a girl is molested every ten minutes, and a daughter is molested by her father every thirty minutes.[1]

These are sobering reminders of the level of brokenness, often beneath the surface, but surely present in every congregation. For pastors, such statistics are peopled by those who seek their care or perhaps seem unable to receive it. There's Sam, a young pediatrician who recently shared that he has entered therapy and is taking an antidepressant to help him keep going after his recovery of memories of abuse by older boys at the private school he attended. His memories were triggered by an abused child in the emergency room. He says he struggles with how to speak of God's love. Joyce and Jim have come in to talk about the difficulties in their marriage and especially their sexual relationship, because Joyce has been working through memories of abuse by her father. Joyce reports that her father has told the family she is crazy and that her accusations are threatening her mother's heart condition. Joyce says the quality of her work has suffered, and she has been warned that her job is in danger. She fears she may lose her husband, too. "Where is God's justice?" she asks through tears.

As we seek to offer hope and encourage healing for persons such as Joyce and Sam, it is important to understand how it is that abuse can be so damaging. These predicaments I have described point toward the tragic structure of human existence at intrapsychic, relational, and social levels. Intrapsychically, human beings are quite vulnerable to distortions in our emotional and cognitive development because that development continues for years before we reach maturity. Who we are is not the result of instincts that are programmed to unfold or an identity that develops in isolation from other factors. Rather, our identities emerge in dynamic interaction through a continuous relational pathway.[2] Who we are and the way we live are significantly shaped by the relationships that shape our worlds. This is especially so in the early and most-formative years of our lives. The betrayal, violation, and domination of abuse significantly alters our otherwise relatively unselfconscious oscillation between those formative relationships and our individuality.

Shame ruptures the trust on which that relational bridge relies. Our intrapsychic structures are not compartmentalized so that shame could be neatly localized around memories of the abuse. Rather, shame is able to metastasize to other emerging aspects of identity and relational development. The abuse that Joyce experienced as a preschool child and into her elementary-school years and that of Sam as an early adolescent came at crucial developmental junctures. This is so both with regard to their particular identities and with the relationships in which such identities are formed. Precritical ingredients necessary for an adequate sense of trust, competence, self-esteem, agency, and hope, for example, have been undermined by their experiences of betrayal, violation, and domination. For Joyce, this came from a parent whom she trusted for an adequate sense of safekeeping and a reliably loving world. For Sam, just beginning to shift his relational world to his peers, abuse by older boys in an environment that taught him to "take it like a man" was similarly devastating for his sense of trust and well-being. As a child and as a young adolescent, their experiences of abuse remind us that our cognitive abilities to make sense of experience are also unfolding. Children are not little adults. Joyce, for example, needed a safe and ordered universe more than the truth of her father's culpability. To keep her world safely ordered, she presumed she was the one at fault.

What both Sam and Joyce as children demonstrated is an accurate estimation that they were powerless in relation to the older and larger persons who abused them. They knew "their place" in the hierarchy of power that shaped the social structure of their lives. The likelihood is great that they would have been placed in more danger by telling the truth about what was happening to them. In the lives of these two children, we see illustrated the vulnerability of human identity development, familial and larger relational networks, and social norms that privilege the credibility of adults. I describe these vulnerabilities as tragically structured because they are inherently present alongside possibilities for enhanced well-being.

Effective preaching needs to acknowledge that we are born not into Eden's paradise but into a milieu of suffering. Most of us emerge through the various stages of development with a good enough balance of such strengths as self-esteem, agency, trust, and hope to function responsibly most of the time. The evil of sexual abuse, however, takes a more serious toll. The stories of Sam and Joyce illustrate the way in which the victimization of child sexual abuse continues into adult life. Its effects are cumulative because of the deficits it creates in personality structure and relational skills as well as the affective toll it exacts as survivors come to terms with what was done to them and seek to heal their losses.

This attention to our tragically structured environment is crucial because, unless the context of suffering and violence is named, it is easy to respond to survivors with categories of guilt and sacrificial love separated from justice. This is the theological origin of injunctions from clergy to battered women to return to husbands as more attentive wives, or the injunction to forgive a perpetrator of sexual abuse regardless of his or her repentance. The church's complicity in the abuse of power and the invisibilization of those who are abused are the consequences. Clergy, especially preachers, have the opportunity and obligation to exercise their powerful knowledge and name violence and the abuse of power as the problems, not the survivor's guilt and hard-heartedness. To name reality this way is to include a helpful systemic and contextual analysis which may encourage the congregation to engage in structural and systemic dimensions of ministry.

THE LOSSES

As preachers, we intend to offer survivors hopeful healing and empowerment for new life. We need to be mindful of what losses are likely. Of course, the consequences of abuse vary because of such issues as the age of onset, identity of the perpetrator, nature of the abuse, particular personality of the child affected, and other factors. Although these losses are profound and often debilitating, preachers need to remember that while human development is characterized by a certain fragility, it is a resilient fragility. Neither Sam nor Joyce is huddled in a corner unable to function. The consequences of abuse are real in their lives, but they have not exhausted their resources for both recovery and contributing to the lives of others. They need our compassion, not pity that would keep them in a powerless victim role.

Fear

Fear is one of the prominent consequences of child sexual abuse. It is difficult for us adults to reenter the profound vulnerability we experience as children utterly dependent as we are as children on the trustworthy care of those on whom we rely for everything— food, shelter, nurture, love, protection. The innocence we associate with childhood derives in part from a child's naive trust that his or her world is safe. As Alex Kotlowitz and others have alerted us,[3] the length of time many children in this society can enjoy such naiveté is far too brief, but our hope for children is this sense of security so that they can focus on being the children they are. A poster at the pastoral counseling center where I work pictures a doll in pieces. It reads, "Childhood ends when sexual abuse begins." What ends is trust in one's safekeeping. What begins is a fearful posture of self-protection, being "on guard" even as one knows one is vulnerable in every sphere of life. Of course, such fear is not confined to the particular context of violation—wanting a night light, checking the closet, and the like. It becomes a habit of being. Those who define the child's world either have harmed them or have failed to protect them—where can they turn?

When we think of fear, hiding is an image that comes to mind. Adults don't hide like children do. Perhaps they grow silent, refusing to risk their own ideas or even imagining they have them. Perhaps they refuse to risk extending themselves in relationships, since intimacy involves risk. Perhaps they live through the accomplishments of others rather than risking the possibility of failure. Fear is one of the forms of bondage that abuse creates. Its spiritual implications are also serious because fear undercuts our ability to risk responding to the opportunities for love and relationships with God and others.

Shame

Shame has devastating consequences in the experience of survivors. It organizes their psychological reality. Gershen Kaufman describes shame this way: "To live with shame is to feel alienated and defeated, never quite good enough to belong. And secretly we feel we are to blame. The deficiency lies within ourselves alone. Shame is without parallel a sickness of the soul . . . an inner sense of being completely diminished or insufficient as a person. It is the self judging the self."[4] Shame is more primitive than guilt. It condemns the self rather than an action of the self. It is a wound we cannot correct ourselves, for we are the problem.

All of us have some acquaintance with shame simply through the predictable defeats and failures inherent in growing up. But the shame that arises through severe or chronic trauma within significant relationships is internalized as alienating self-contempt.[5] It may well set in motion repression and denial.

Shame occurs as unmet needs are exposed and brings to mind efforts to cover up or hide. The survivor hides because of an internalized sense of unworthiness rather than their fear of what another will do again. Shame is debilitating for healthy relationships and vital spirituality. Survivors closely guard against others' discovery of their presumed inner inadequacy. Because shame arises from the experience of betrayal, anger or rage may well emerge as a protective mechanism and response to the betrayal of trust and experience of violation. Unfortunately, such anger may only assure distance from those who wish to offer care.

Preachers need to be aware that the shame associated with child sexual abuse is intimately related to a survivor's experience of embodiment in general and sexuality in particular. Spirituality is also depleted because it relies on our connectedness with God, one another, creation, and ourselves. That sense of connectedness begins in our embodied selves. The violation of sexual abuse is located precisely in that dimension of human being that is intended to deepen the experience of intimate communion, mystery, and joy. This means that the alienation of shame is even more devastating in its consequences, as Joyce and Jim's marital struggle attests. Shame has an alienating effect within persons as well as between persons. Joyce's difficulty with embodiment is not confined to the sexual dimension of her marriage. In order to survive her abuse, Joyce learned to separate herself from her emotional and physical feelings. Like many survivors, she grew keenly aware of the emotional needs of others but rather numb to her own. It was hard for her to take enjoyment in or even accept her own body as attractive and strong. She struggles to live as an embodied person aware of and valuing her feelings and appreciative of her sensuality.

In her book *Women's Sexuality after Childhood Incest*, Elaine Westerlund describes some of the predictable consequences of sexual abuse for embodiment. These consequences seem proportional to the level of self-blame the survivors carry regarding their abuse. Psychic numbing and some forms of estrangement from the body predominate. These defenses arise in the context of abuse as a survival mechanism. But they continue in a debilitating way. Many learn to feel their bodies are "dirty," "nasty," "evil," "out of control." Westerlund recorded one survivor as saying, "My body isn't mine. I have no rights over it. I have no boundaries." Another survivor described her experience of estrangement saying, "I can't be in my body fully because I'm afraid to physically feel." Regarding her experience of her gender, one survivor wrote, "I don't want to have breasts, I don't want to have a uterus, I want not to be female"; another wrote, "If I were a male, I would not be disgusting to others and to myself."[6]

Emotional anemia and the experience of alienation from one's own physical body are cause for serious concern because compassion and empathy as well as emotional intimacy rely on our differentiated awareness of the feelings of another and our selves. Emotional needs do not go away if we are unaware of them, but they are more likely to be met in distorted and covert ways if they are outside of our awareness. Similarly, ethical action relies on an imaginative empathic connection with those we seek to assist. To the extent we truncate our affective awareness from intellectual reflection, we have distorted, if not diminished, our capacity for ethical responsiveness with our neighbors.

When understanding oneself as culpable and dirty or stained, self-love is difficult to imagine. Likewise, if persons cannot imagine themselves as lovable, it is difficult to receive God's love or that of others as trustworthy. Predictably, we find victims living a rather graceless life. They have narrowed the love commandment to exclude love of self. The diminished capacity to give and receive love is one of the most serious deprivations of abuse. This difficulty emerges in the vortex of betrayal, violation, and domination. We learn to imagine ourselves as lovable through the physical and emotional nurture we receive, especially in the early years of our lives. Victims of abuse predictably internalize the shame of their experience, blaming themselves rather than soliciting the aid and comfort of others.

Betrayal and violation, often precisely by those whose safekeeping we need to presume for a sense of order in our world, have sobering consequences for the quality and resiliency of trust in relationship to God and others. As Erikson reminded us, trust is born of care.[7] Undermining the capacity to trust and the willingness to risk it has many levels of significance. Trust, of course, is the bedrock of physical and emotional intimacy. Spiritually, it is foundational for faith. Abuse represents radical evil that confronts victims with questions about the very presence (reality) and care of God.

Hopelessness

Abuse seriously affects the capacity to live with hope, an essential dimension of being human. We all imagine a certain trajectory for our lives. But fear and shame together create a sense of bondage that constricts or distorts a victim's experience of agency or power. He or she may wonder, is it possible that what I think or feel could matter or make a difference? Do I have a right to feel angry? A kind of passivity or living through or behind others may take shape. Expressing what one thinks or feels is an expression of power that involves some tolerance for the risk that these ideas or plans won't be effective or that one's needs won't be met. Sometimes victims respond to the experience of betrayal, violation, and domination with remarkable needs for control which obviously are risk-avoidant. This might take the form of rigidity in their personal, intellectual, and spiritual lives. Whether through passivity or constricted control, one's sense of agency in the world is limited. If one's sense of agency is depleted or constricted, then it is difficult to imagine a future that is life-giving and empowering.

Hopelessness may take the form of despair or depression. Despair is related particularly to a loss of meaning that arises as a survivor tries to make sense out of senseless, arbitrary, and undeserved suffering. This is especially likely to occur if the survivor only has access to a theological worldview that links suffering and guilt. Depression often is related to unarticulated or unfinished grief work for the emotional and relational losses that accompany child sexual abuse. Innocence, unself-conscious enjoyment of one's body, self-esteem, a sense of safety, and trust in oneself and others, for example, are not easily recovered—especially when such losses occur in childhood.

Fear, shame, and hopelessness each pose significant and problematic barriers to the freedom for love which God intends for humankind. They also interact to further deplete the spiritual, emotional, and relational resources of survivors.

PRESENT ECCLESIAL AND THEOLOGICAL CONTEXT

Awareness of what adult survivors of child sexual abuse are experiencing is important but not sufficient. There are contemporary cultural and theological issues that color any discussion of effective preaching that addresses child sexual abuse. Culturally, we have witnessed the tremendous backlash evidenced by the "false-memory syndrome" movement and news accounts of overzealous social workers who disregard parents' rights on the basis of a child's remark or an unnamed accuser's suspicion. Expert-witness testimony in Kentucky supporting the reliability of a child's report of abuse, for example, has been seriously eroded by these reactionary times. Denial of the reported scope of the problem is back on the rise.

Theologically, I suggest there are five complicating issues. The first is the focus Wendy Farley has addressed—that is, limited understandings about the nature of God's power and love. In part, that reflects a narrow understanding of power itself as some form of unilateral or dominating force. But professed mystification about the presence of radical suffering in the midst of the creation of a good God has served to stifle resistance to evil. We have spent precious time and energy debating the limits on God's freedom and will to act rather than joining God in resisting evil and acting compassionately.

Ours is a culture quite ambivalent about love for self. For a long time, our sermons and liturgies have reflected a long-standing interpretation of the love commandment as really a twofold command, because supposedly our love for self can be presumed and is invariably problematic. Sin is singularly understood as pride by the vast majority of Christians in this culture. Prayers of confession prescribe selflessness, only rarely acknowledging the struggle of many to be the self they are called to be.

This ambivalence about love also contributes to the confusion among us regarding forgiveness, which Marie Fortune has so helpfully addressed. Her discussion of forgiveness rejoins love and justice in a way that presumes mutuality rather than selflessness as the norm for love. For many Christians, sacrificial love is the ideal for Christian life rather than a means toward mutual regard and care.

We also are confused about freedom and accountability. Is freedom autonomy defined by the goal of one's fulfillment? If it is more of a responsibility, how do we discern accountability from the limitations that arise from experiences like abuse? How free are we to act? This question is especially pertinent in responses to perpetrators who also have a history of abuse and in survivors' self-doubt about their complicity in their abuse.

Finally, many Christians in this culture have not been invited to consider the church's complicity in the level of violence perpetrated against women and children. There is little mobilization at congregational levels to consider how it is that child sexual abuse is epidemic in a country where many persons describe themselves as Christians. Denial is a major factor in congregations and perhaps among many ministers who preach.

The cultural and political reactivity of our time and the theological ambivalence and confusion I described shape the context for victims of abuse who participate in communities of faith, as well as the context for many of those who preach.

RESOURCES FOR HEALING, EMPOWERMENT, AND HOPE

Keeping in mind that contemporary context for ministry with survivors and the losses survivors experience, I turn now to resources available for preachers who want to facilitate healing, empowerment, and hope for adult survivors of child sexual abuse.

By all accounts, child sexual abuse represents radical suffering. As Wendy Farley reminds us, such suffering is undeserved and "assaults and degrades that about a person which makes her or him most human."[8] Toinette Eugene suggests, "Sexual abuse is a sacrilege of God's Spirit in each of us."[9] Distinguishing radical suffering from guilt is important so that we remain clear we are not concerned with atonement for sin but with an experience that calls into question the character of God's power and the nature of God's love.

In my judgment, the first priority in our work as preachers is to preach in ways that express what Wendy Farley describes as "active resistance and compassion." To do so is to reframe and redefine God's power in the context of God's love. In *The Vulnerable God*, Bill Placher reminds us that as we preach such themes, we must repeatedly clarify that we are describing God's power as quite different from what has long been assumed.[10] God's power is not coercive or controlling; it arises through the witness of vulnerable, active, tender, empowering, faithful love. As the resurrection attests, such power is sufficient to triumph over death, but it does not operate in a dominating way most familiar to us.

Radical suffering that results from the evil of child sexual abuse includes a horrific list of losses: the betrayal of trust and love, the bondage of fear and shame, powerlessness, distortions in a capacity to love self and others, estrangement from one's body and shame about embodiment, and depleted possibilities for hope. Clearly, survivors of abuse will not find naive or substitutionary theodicies very compelling. Rather, sermons that locate divine power in the context of God's fierce and tender love faithfully describe God's presence as safe, empowering, and hopeful. Such sermons are lenses for interpreting God's Word that will help survivors reweave the narrative of their lives into the larger and hopeful story of God's redemptive love.

Let me illustrate what I mean by using this hermeneutic of resistance and compassion as the lens through which to reflect on Psalms 22 and 23 and the themes they pose for Christology—especially the passion narratives. I am particularly indebted for these reflections to Patrick Miller's book *Interpreting the Psalms*.[11] Psalm 22 is painfully familiar to survivors of child sexual abuse because its themes have to do with abandonment, betrayal, powerlessness, despair, hopelessness, self-loathing, and being scapegoated by others.

[1] My God, my God, why have you forsaken me?
Why are you so far from helping me,
from the words of my groaning?
[2] O my God, I cry by day, but you do not answer;
And by night, but find no rest.
[3] Yet you are holy,
enthroned on the praises of Israel.
[4] In you our ancestors trusted;
They trusted, and you delivered them.

5 To you they cried, and were saved;
in you they trusted, and were not put to shame.
6 But I am a worm, and not human;
scorned by others, and despised by the people.
7 All who see me mock at me;
they make mouths at me, they shake their heads;
8 "Commit your cause to God; let God deliver—
let God rescue the one in whom God delights!"
9 Yet it was you who took me from the womb;
you kept me safe on my mother's breast.
10 On you I was cast from my birth,
and since my mother bore me you have been my God.
11 Do not be far from me, for trouble is near
and there is no one to help.
12 Many bulls encircle me,
strong bulls of Bashan surround me;
13 they open wide their mouths at me,
like a ravening and roaring lion.
14 I am poured out like water,
and all my bones are out of joint;
my heart is like wax; it is melted within my breast,
15 my mouth is dried up like a potsherd,
and my tongue sticks to my jaws;
you lay me in the dust of death.
16 For dogs are all around me;
a company of evildoers encircles me.
17 My hands and feet have shriveled;
I count all my bones.
They stare and gloat over me,
18 they divide my clothes among themselves,
and for my clothing they cast lots.
19 But you, O God, do not be far away.
O my help, come quickly to my aid!
20 Deliver my soul from the sword,
my life from the power of the dog!
21 Save me from the mouth of the lion!
From the horns of the wild oxen you have rescued me,
22 I will tell of your name to my brothers and sisters;
in the midst of the congregation I will praise you. (Ps. 22:1–22)

It is appropriate to turn to a psalm of lament, because, of course, laments presume the value of giving voice to the experience of injustice, loss, and suffering. Survivors know the form of lament by heart, but perhaps not in their own voices. As Brueggemann has reminded us, empowerment only comes after this process of giving voice to one's complaint.[12] Laments presume the right to complain because of one's covenantal relationship with God, through which expectations of faithfulness arise. Notice, for example, the interplay of "trust" and "cry" in verses 4 and 5 of Psalm 22. Laments embody active resistance to evil and suffering. They are clear that suffering is not deserved or instructive. Out of a context of the larger narrative of faith, psalms of lament call God to account on the basis of a relationship. This psalm's alternation between complaint and memory of faithfulness also reminds us of the empowering quality of memories of God's compassionate love and saving power. These memories challenge any assumption of God's absence or indifference.

In verse 21b, we find the assertion that God's active resistance to evil and compassionate love is present precisely in the midst of evil. Moreover, God does not turn from our suffering or affliction—for example, in horror of children's violated bodies. Rather, God joins us in that suffering and transforms it. This is good news for those who feel shame, self-loathing, and abandonment. Psalm 22 is also helpful because it describes God's tender power as stretching far beyond this one person in need. Rather, God is able to set right relationships throughout the world and to save those who have died as well as those yet unborn. Psalm 22 offers a ringing affirmation of God's tender and empowering love, which knows no geographical or temporal bounds.

The passion narratives link this psalm of lament to Jesus' death and resurrection rather than to Paul's focus on guilt and justification. The Gospels choose to attend to God's active and compassionate resistance to evil and suffering. Many contributors to this volume, such as Wendy Farley and Barbara Patterson, remind us that God's response to evil and suffering is incarnation.[13] Incarnation occurs not so that Jesus might suffer abuse but so that we might see the power of love to actively resist forces that destroy and deform human life. Here, the cross becomes a symbol of God's active, determined resistance to evil and triumph over it. Obviously evil is not utterly defeated, but the larger power of compassionate love is demonstrated convincingly. These images of the cross and resurrection, when rescued from a singular focus on guilt and atonement, offer a healing and empowering hope to one who has felt abandoned in her or his suffering. It is also helpful to recognize that a hermeneutics of compassionate resistance doesn't valorize suffering.

> God is my shepherd, I shall not want.
> God makes me lie down in green pastures,
> leads me beside still waters,
> restores my soul,
> leads me in right paths as befits God's name.
> Even when I walk in the valley of the shadow of death,
> I fear no evil;
> for you are with me;
> with rod and staff you comfort me.
> You set a table before me
> in the presence of my enemies;
> you anoint my head with oil,
> my cup overflows.
> Surely goodness and mercy shall pursue me
> all the days of my life,
> and I shall dwell in the house of God forever.

Psalm 23 seems to extend the trust restored in Psalm 22. Through a lens of resistance and compassion, this psalm helps us to recover a linkage in the prophetic and pastoral dimensions of the shepherd's care. One can overhear the fiercely protective love of the good shepherd in Ezekiel 34. God's provision and saving presence in the exodus and the wilderness are recalled in the image of one who does not "want" (Neh. 9) or a "table" (Ps. 78) in the presence of enemies. It is precisely in the midst of enemies that God's presence can be relied upon. In the context of one who has known betrayal, violation, and domination (the valley of the shadow of death), we are reminded that there is no need to fear, so that we overhear the annunciation of the angel at the empty tomb beginning with the words "Do not be afraid." Instead of enemies pursuing, we learn from translators that God's goodness and mercy don't simply follow us, they actively pursue us. This psalm reminds us that Jesus, as the shepherd, is the host for us in the presence of our enemies and the host for all the world.

Preaching these psalms through the lens of active resistance and compassion provides a powerful resource for survivors of child sexual abuse. They provide preachers with an opportunity to clarify that compassion is real power, not just sympathy. It is power that offers both healing and love's transformation individually and on a worldwide scale. Psalm 22 validates the anguish and the anger of a survivor. It also opens a way in the wilderness experience of victimization to recover the hope of God's tender and empowering love. God's love is vulnerable to others' abuse of freedom. God could not prevent their abuse, but God can help them resist and overcome the power of evil to keep them in bondage. Together, these two psalms imagine a life-giving future story for survivors that invites them to claim the empowerment of God's fierce and tender love.

This hermeneutic of God's resistance and compassion also informs our ritual practice. In *Ritual and Pastoral Care*, Elaine Ramshaw was right to remind us of the transformative and ethical power of ritual practice.[14] Imagine the possibilities for survivors at Holy Communion to hear us referencing the Twenty-third Psalm's words about a table in the presence of our enemies or a God who will not let us want for what we need even as we wander in the wilderness. Imagine an Ash Wednesday service through this lens of compassionate resistance so that Psalm 22 describes a God who joins with us to resist evil and whose power is sufficient to empower us to overcome it. What a difference this hermeneutic would make for a service of healing and wholeness.

Through the lens of resistance and compassion, we find in scripture compelling images of God's tender and empowering love. These allow our proclamation and ritual practice to mediate life-giving hope, courage, and power that is not naive about the reality of evil and suffering.

The second thematic lens I suggest for our preaching about abuse shifts the focus from God's love as the context of God's power to love as the context of power in human experience and relationships. My goal is that our preaching helps survivors reconstruct empowered and tender images of their embodied selves as created in the image of God. With these self-images, their bodies—once the locus of betrayal, violation, and domination—may open for them opportunities for trustworthy, mutually respectful, and joyful relationships of love and care.

Rather than beginning with Jesus' death, preachers will find it helpful to make our creation in the image of God the foundation for our reflection about love and power. With this shift, mutually respectful and empowering love and care become the normative criteria for our relationships. Sacrificial love voluntarily chosen for a period of time is put in its proper place as a means toward restoring mutual love and care. As Gene Outka reminds us, "We are called to love whom God loves."[15] To be created in the image of God is to be created for life in a relational web of interdependence. Justice and love are reunited in such a context.

With this groundwork, it is possible to preach a clear understanding of the love of God experienced in the death of Jesus. The norm of mutuality makes the forfeiture of power in the service of empowering love more apparent. Marie McCarthy, a pastoral theologian, suggests that when neighbor love is reduced to self-sacrifice, we have "no basis for distinguishing between attention to others' needs and submission to their exploitation. Nor . . . [is there] any warrant for resisting the latter."[16] McCarthy has put her finger on the problem in popular Christian interpretation of the relation of love and power. When self-sacrifice defines love and power, survivors are left with the category of guilt to define their experience and trying to forgive what has often never been repented.

When we name violence and abuse of power rather than pride or guilt as the problem, it is easier to focus on resisting the evil of violence and its disempowering consequences. Daniel Day Williams reminds us that "love is that expression of spirit that has communion in freedom as its goal."[17] He is right to identify empowerment as the norm of power in authentic love. While the criterion of mutuality in relationship supports broadening definitions of sin beyond pride, it is less common to hear discussions about sin as the refusal to be a self.[18] It is important for preachers to help survivors avoid the temptation to remain victims who do not risk exercising the freedom and responsibilities of love. Our encouragement to survivors to value themselves and recover a sense of power is not equivalent to popular definitions of self-gratification. The freedom for love moves us to speak of discipleship, vocation, and solidarity with those whom God also loves.

What I have shared also has implications for ritual practice. Rare indeed is the occasion when I read prayers of confession and assurances of pardon that are appropriate for survivors of abuse in the congregation. I am not saying that sin as pride is irrelevant to survivors of abuse. Rather, I am suggesting that more often their struggle is to risk embracing the freedom to be in mutual relationships of care and love. When this is the case, prescriptions of selflessness are toxic.

Forgiveness is complicated in this culture because of the confusion that surrounds the relation of love and power. However, recognizing the radical mutuality that neighbor love envisions helps us recover the Bible's linkage of justice and forgiveness. Forgiveness is at the end of a process that begins with truth-telling and repentance.[19] It is intended to restore mutuality. In the context of radical suffering, forgiveness of the perpetrator cannot be coerced, and it certainly must not be cheapened by demanding that it precede evidence of changed behavior. The perpetrator of abuse must give up the pretense of power over the victim and request forgiveness. Paradoxically, the perpetrator's presumption of the power to dominate must yield to an acknowledgment of her or his sin and include a request for forgiveness. It is the victim's forgiveness that restores the perpetrator to mutuality.[20] Even then, forgiveness remains an act that the survivor offers as she or he is able. It may well be that a survivor is able only to entrust forgiveness of their perpetrator to God—the strategy Jesus employed from the cross.[21]

Finally, I want to take one other slant on the problems posed by preaching from the pulpit out of a singular focus on sacrificial love. Such a focus can express complicity in distorting survivors' experiences of embodiment and sexuality. Typically, this focus on sacrificial love not only arises from Paul's interpretation of the atonement. It also reflects a long-standing dualism of body and spirit in Western intellectual thought.

In his commentary on Romans, Luther suggested that while one could interpret the command to love as threefold, it was better to read it as a twofold command, because love of self was presumed as inevitably dominating any relationship.[22] He stated that no one was such a nonentity that he or she did not love him/herself. Luther presumed a dualistic notion of the self in which all of us are engaged in a battle to subdue our self-absorbed carnal selves. The call to humility that agape includes would help discipline unruly desires of the flesh. It is very important to name such dualism as a distortion in a tradition that relies so heavily on God's incarnation. God's response to evil and suffering is embodied love. Christian tradition rightly understood values embodiment more generally and sexuality in particular. How often do we hear about that in sermons?

Ethicist Jim Nelson got it right when he said, "We either experience God's presence in our bodies or not at all."[23] Our perception of reality and our conceptualization about it is inevitably through the experience of our embodiment. Our capacity for love, accurate empathy, and ethical connection with others and the creation all arise from our affections. These are important avenues for deepening connection with God and one another.

Colluding with this dualism is not just mistaken; it is dangerous. It obscures the relation of love and justice, the reality of power in relationships, the possibility of exploitation, the privatization of love and freedom, and it denigrates the gift of embodiment that is a primary source of our experience of love and joy as God's gifts for us.

These dangers are particularly striking for survivors of abuse whose bodies were the locus of betrayal, domination, and violation. When our sermons say nothing to contradict this dualism, the silence is deafening to those who are already predisposed to reject or fear or distance themselves from their embodied experience. It is not hard for them to imagine that such silence means their bodies are a source of shame and dangerous desires.

There are many persons in the pews on Sunday morning who have experienced radical evil in the form of child sexual abuse. They experience evil that we must resist not with silence but with sermons that name this evil for what it is: a terrible betrayal of the love God intends for human life and relationships; an abuse of the power that God intended for our mutual empowerment; and a sacrilege of the embodiment that God intended as a gift for deepened communion in freedom, mutual love, and care. The word that can respond to this evil is one in which God's power is always on behalf of love and justice, and in which survivors are able to reconstruct empowered and tender images of their embodied selves.

6

Preaching to Perpetrators of Violence

James Newton Poling

When George was arrested for sexually abusing his teenage daughter, he was remorseful and wanted to be forgiven by God and by his church. When I asked him what he thought this meant, he didn't know. As a faithful church member all his adult life, he had heard sermons about sin and forgiveness, and he had engaged in confession before the eucharist. But he had never heard a sermon that named sexual and domestic violence in the family as a sin that could be brought to God for redemption. After he was arrested, he was shunned by friends and members of his church. He felt rejected and alone, and he didn't know whether there were spiritual resources to help him through this crisis in his life. On the one hand, he wanted to avoid any consequences by being restored to the [community] of the church. On the other hand, he needed to hear genuine words of judgment and grace that pointed the way toward spiritual renewal.

Encountering people such as George points to a problem—preachers of the gospel have not been preaching sermons as if there are perpetrators of violence in the congregation. So perpetrators have not been getting the sermons they need. On one hand, perpetrators are not hearing clear ethical guidelines against family violence—as a problem that includes church members. In order to correct this problem, we need to realize that every congregation includes perpetrators of family violence, who need to hear that God hates violence so that vulnerable persons are protected. On the other hand, perpetrators are not hearing about the redemptive value of confession, repentance, and the possibilities for new life after they cease their violence and turn their lives in a new direction. So they hide their problems and hope everyone else will ignore them also. Perpetrators need to know what it takes to repent of their sins and how to find their way back into the honest and full community of the church.

WHO ARE THE PERPETRATORS OF VIOLENCE?

The credible research on violence indicates that 25 to 50 percent of women and children will be victims of physical or sexual violence, either as children facing physical, sexual, and emotional abuse and/or as adults facing assault, battering, rape, and psychological control. As a result, victims and survivors of violence face substantial physical and psychological injuries that last a long time. These statistics do not diminish with social class, race, religion, or faithful church attendance. This means that more than 25 percent of the members of the typical congregation have experienced violence. The most frequent perpetrators of family violence are other members of the immediate and extended family and trusted friends and community leaders. The public fear of the stranger who mugs or molests prevents us from facing the fact that the most familiar persons in our families and communities are not safe.[1] If these studies are true, then victims, survivors, and perpetrators of interpersonal violence are present in every congregation whenever a sermon is preached. It is urgent that preachers of the gospel begin to address domestic and sexual violence from the pulpit, including the needs of perpetrators.

PRINCIPLES FOR SERMONS FOR PERPETRATORS OF VIOLENCE

The principles for developing sermons on sexual and domestic violence are the same for perpetrators as for victims and survivors. These principles have been emphasized in other chapters in this volume and are summarized clearly in educational materials from the Center for the Prevention of Sexual and Domestic Violence and many other victim advocate groups.[2]

These principles are:

1. Protect the vulnerable from further abuse (hospitality).
2. Call the abuser to accountability (confrontation, confession, repentance).
3. Restore the relationship (between victim and abuser), *if possible*. Often this restoration is not possible. The harm is too great, the damage too deep, the resistance of the abuser to change too formidable. *If not possible*, then mourn the loss of that relationship and work to restore the individual (comfort to the grieving).[3]

The practice of preaching to perpetrators of violence is complicated because of the church's long history of silence and complicity on these issues. In the balance of this chapter, I will review some of the challenges facing preachers who want to preach the whole gospel to the whole people of God, including perpetrators of violence. First, I will share the witness of a survivor. Then I will discuss some of the historical issues that have created this problem. Finally, I will review several hermeneutical principles and look at some New Testament texts that need reinterpretation in our increasing awareness of the presence of perpetrators in our congregations.

WITNESS FROM ONE SURVIVOR

Linda is a survivor of family violence by her mother. When she heard that I was planning to write an article on preaching to perpetrators, she sent me the following witness.

> The only way I can even begin to think about perpetrators deserving God's love is if I let myself imagine (and this is painful) that one of my sons raped a woman. I do not believe this would ever happen; but trying to fathom my response if it did brings me the closest I can get to what you will be lecturing on in March.

Each of my sons feels like a gift to me, and I love them both deeply. But if one would ever commit the crime of rape, my empathy would be with the victim. I could forgive murder before rape; because I know too well the kind of living death that rape can mean for those who survive it. If my son was the perpetrator, I would be outraged and grief-stricken— but I would not stop loving him. I would want to see justice for the victim—but not the "justice" of our current system which in reality does nothing for the victim or the violator. I would want my son to understand the horror of what he had inflicted on another human being, and be given the opportunity to make whatever restitution is possible.

In a humane system, the victim would be protected and a primary goal would be giving her (or him) whatever resources are needed to heal . . . unlike our current structure where the victim is often doubted, disbelieved, and ridiculed in court and the only compensation she might receive is the dubious satisfaction of sending the person who raped her to prison . . . where he will most likely suffer what he inflicted on her, thus continuing the cycle of violence. In a human system, a perpetrator might be consistently confronted with the painful stories of rape victims until he or she finally began to glimpse the tragic consequences of rape on a human being. Instead of spending years in the brutal system of a prison, s/he might do supervised work with the majority of the money earned going into a fund to meet the needs of victims.

This has been hard for me to think about—even for a little while. I think that God is outraged at rapes, beatings, mutilations, incest . . . and I think God holds those who abuse their power accountable. But I also believe God weeps for both victims and violators, given that we live in such a broken society where cycles of violence are passed down from generation to generation.

I do not weep for my mother. I do not forgive her. This is beyond me, and is an unfair thing to ever ask of survivors of violence. Still, I stop short of saying that because she tortured me God does not love her. God knew her before whatever awful circumstances she was born into twisted her mind and spirit toward evil, and made her who she finally became. God knows who she could have been. I do not. Linda.[4]

In this witness, Linda reveals several of the challenges facing anyone who would preach the gospel with awareness of the presence of perpetrators of violence in the congregation. First, although with the example of her own sons, she feels emotionally bonded with the potential perpetrator, she does not allow that attachment to cloud her ethical commitment to solidarity with victims and survivors. Having a relationship with a perpetrator does not set aside the moral commitment to oppose violence in all its forms and support the need for safety and healing for those who are most vulnerable to such violence. Second, Linda expects accountability for the perpetrator of violence. He or she should not be allowed to continue life as if nothing happened. The church cannot count on the individual conscience of the perpetrator of violence to be adequate for safety. The whole community must become involved in holding the perpetrator accountable for his or her behavior. Third, after safety for victims and accountability for perpetrators are assured, then attention can be turned to issues of transformation. God's grace is sufficient to help victims and perpetrators alike engage in healing with the resources of the larger community. However, Linda is clear that the victim should not be given any responsibility for forgiveness, reconciliation, or healing for the perpetrator. Whether the perpetrator of violence benefits from the healing resources of the community should never be the responsibility of the victim, but must remain between the perpetrator, his or her counselors, his or her faith community, and God.

A HISTORY OF PREACHING DOMINATION

In order to preach to perpetrators we must ask *why* some people perpetrate violence against others—especially the violence against women and children that occurs in families and other intimate relationships. My work with perpetrators and my research have led me to conclude that the answer is complex. According to Victor Lewis, in the video *Broken Vows*,[5] men feel entitled to own and control women and are willing to use violence to enforce their power. This sense of entitlement has very old roots. Scholars such as Patricia Hill Collins have convinced me that, especially in the United States, the ownership of other people and enforcement of that right by violence is rooted in three hundred years of slavery and oppression of women.[6] I have been especially interested in the role of religion in helping to construct arguments for the legitimacy of owning other persons along with whatever violence was necessary to enforce that ownership.[7] We know that U.S. slavery not only included physical violence but also sexual violence against women and children who were slaves. We live in a country that for three hundred years officially promoted the ownership and abuse of people, and religious leaders and theologians supported these policies and practices.

Kelly Brown Douglas, in *The Black Christ,* asks how ownership of persons was justified religiously. Her answer: by spiritualizing the meaning of Jesus. "Evangelists were able to spiritualize the themes of Christian freedom and equality. . . . Jesus' salvation had nothing to do with historical freedom."[8] For example, many slaves, at the time of baptism, were required to "declare in the presence of God and this congregation that you do not ask for Holy Baptism out of any design to free yourselves from the Duty and Obedience you owe to your Master while you live, but merely for the good of your Soul and to partake of the Graces and Blessings promised to the members of the Church of Jesus Christ."[9] By imposing this vow as a requirement for baptism into Jesus Christ, pastors justified the physical and sexual violence necessary to enforce enslavement and ownership of other Christians. They said that Christian freedom was a state of grace that would take effect only in the next life and had nothing to do with freedom from violence in this life. This spiritualization of the gospel helped perpetuate three hundred years of violence in support of slavery in the United States.

According to Riggins Earl, the miracle of God's action in history is that Jesus' spirit of compassion for all people has lived on in spite of the evil of those who justified slavery. How could the slave community in resistance confess Jesus in the midst of profound evil? Through trusting their own religious experience of Jesus' presence and rejecting the lies that created their captivity, converted slaves resisted evil and confessed the love and power of God in Jesus Christ. In the process, they found a precious interior spiritual space of freedom from domination, a sanctuary from evil.[10]

Jacquelyn Grant, Delores Williams, and other womanist and feminist theologians articulate the long history of African American resistance to slavery, racism, and violence. Jacquelyn Grant says we have to rethink our use of servanthood language because of the history of slavery and the domestic servitude of black women.[11] Delores Williams says we have to rethink our theories of atonement based on surrogacy because of the enforced surrogacy of black women in the United States.[12]

There is a parallel story about the oppression of European American women. The "cult of true womanhood" emphasized the importance of piety, purity, submissiveness, and domesticity—all of which justified the property rights of men.[13] Christian theologians were in the forefront of this debate in the nineteenth century to justify the subordination of women to men and the violence required to enforce this oppression. The Women's Rights Act of 1848 protested the fact that women could not vote, own property, have custody of their children, or protect themselves from drunken husbands. Rita Nakashima Brock questions our doctrines of innocence, such as the cult of true womanhood, which we project on Jesus to protect ourselves from the disclosure of actual evil.[14]

These brief references remind us of the longer history of theological justification for the idea that certain people can be owned as property and that ownership of persons can be enforced by violence. As Gerda Lerner says, we are trying to overturn a very long tradition.[15] I think it is fair to say that the liberal view of individual human rights has not changed the underlying ideologies of white supremacy and male dominance in the United States. As the writers of this volume have emphasized, the struggle has to go much deeper.

From my work with perpetrators—that is, men who have been convicted of sexually abusing children and/or battering their partners—I know that we theologians have much work to do. In the immediate future, we must support the justice work of shelters and the legal system to protect women and children by stringent consequences. In the long run, our work to reconstruct Christian theology and thus change our preaching is crucial.[16]

A HERMENEUTICS OF SUSPICION AND CONFESSION

In terms of hermeneutical method, I start with the premise that human beings do not have access to a pure gospel undistorted by history and social location.[17] While attempts to recover "the historical Jesus" can be helpful by showing that descriptions of the first-century peasant are not identical to the debates about Christ throughout history,[18] the results of this research do not resolve the conflicts between contemporary religious groups. Even conservative religious creeds teach that the Scriptures must be "rightly explained" (1 Tim. 2:15) and interpreted by the Holy Spirit.[19] Historical research is crucial because it forces the church to uncover the layers of distortion starting in the oral traditions and continuing through every version of the Bible and its interpretations.[20] Searching for the truth is a crucial aspect of deconstructing any lies about Jesus. Therefore, we must have a *hermeneutics of suspicion* of attempts by Christian groups to misuse the gospel for their own privilege and power.

My method is also based on a *hermeneutics of confession,* that Jesus is a spirit that continues to empower those who are faithful to God. The love and power of Jesus lives in the people's struggles for survival and freedom in the face of massive evil and injustice. Church leaders are called to become attuned to Jesus' spirit in the scriptures and to bring voice to the gospel. Jesus lived and died and was resurrected in the past, and Jesus lives, dies, and is resurrected every day when violence against the vulnerable is resisted. Learning to see Jesus in the present is a way of remaining faithful to the Jesus the Bible proclaims as cosufferer.

In practice, the hermeneutics of suspicion and confession work together to define the method for interpreting the scriptures. We must be suspicious of every individual and group who calls on the name of Jesus in such a way that their claims to power create systems of domination and evil. We are reminded in Matthew 7:21 that not everyone who calls on God will enter the realm of heaven, but only those who do God's will. We must also hear the confessions of those for whom Jesus has been a liberating and empowering figure of religious piety. Finding a healthy balance between suspicion and confession is a challenging task.

Clarice Martin, a womanist New Testament scholar, describes this tension when she distinguishes between a hermeneutics of truth and a hermeneutics of effects.

> "Hermeneutics" is not simply a cognitive process wherein one seeks to determine the "correct meaning" of a passage or text. Neither are questions of penultimate truth and universality solely determinative of meaning. Also of essential importance in the interpretive task are such matters as the nature of the interpreter's goals, the effects of a given interpretation on a community of people who have an interest in the text being interpreted, and questions of cultural value, social relevance, and ethics.[21]

Martin continues by quoting from *The Responsibility of Hermeneutics*: "What is at stake in hermeneutics is not only the 'truth' of one's interpretation, but also the effects interpretation and interpretive strategies have on the ways in which human beings shape their goals and their actions."[22] This form of hermeneutics involves a rhythm or dynamic interplay between biblical texts from the canon and the lived faith and experience of communities of resistance. An interpreter cannot understand Jesus by studying the Bible in isolation, but must also be immersed in a community of resistance which lives out faith in Jesus today. Without participation in resistance today, one cannot comprehend the spirit of Jesus' resistance in the past. The truth of Jesus in Scripture is revealed in the ongoing resistance in the name of Jesus.

Another version of the hermeneutical circle can be described as a dialectic of preaching and pastoral care. The preacher preaches the gospel as the truth of the Bible; the people speak back to the preacher through the problems they bring in pastoral care. This relationship could be visualized as a circle, in which the practice of Christian life results in problems of pastoral care, which in turn yield questions for preaching; these questions call for Bible study, which influences preaching, which in turn influences the practice of Christian life. The questions the people bring to the pastor in pastoral care represent the problems and questions that arise as the people try to live the gospel that the preacher preaches within a particular historical and social context.

Some of these problems are a critique of the culture in which Christians live—for example, individualism, hedonism, materialism. When members of Christian community try to live according to love, justice, and the Holy Spirit, they come into conflict with the culture, and the people need pastoral care to sort out their confusion and strengthen their resolve to live according to the gospel. Some of these pastoral-care problems are a critique of the gospel that is preached. That is, every preached gospel is only a partial description of the triune God who created the universe. Whatever accommodations the church and its preachers make to the world will create problems when the people try to live out the gospel. For example, when preachers urge people to forgive perpetrators too quickly and endanger children and other family members, they create problems for the survivors. In this case, preaching distorts the real gospel in favor of the ways of the world.

Therefore, a preacher/pastor must be able to hear both critiques—of culture and of the preached gospel (as distinguished from the whole gospel).

Sexual and domestic violence, including child abuse, is a new pastoral-care issue (though not a new behavior) because of the denial and silence of church leaders. In what way is domestic violence a critique of the culture of the United States? In what way is domestic violence a critique of the preached (not the whole) gospel? In this volume, we see many examples of the way in which domestic violence is a critique of the culture— sexism, racism, distorted sexuality, idealized marriage and family. I believe sexual and domestic violence is also a critique of the gospel that has been preached for many years. If we listen to the information we are getting from pastoral care, we hear distorted theological messages about male headship, nuclear families, parental authority, obedience to authority, suffering and forgiveness, and the nature of salvation.

In our preaching, we have to pay attention to both the hermeneutics of truth (the relationship of preaching to Bible) and the hermeneutics of practice (the lived experience of the body of Christ). In terms of the hermeneutical principles, we must ask whether a sermon is true in relation to the Bible and also whether it is true when practiced in a particular historical and social context.

THE PRACTICE OF PREACHING THE BIBLE TO PERPETRATORS OF VIOLENCE

In this section, I make some practical suggestions about preaching the Bible when there are perpetrators of violence in the congregation.

Pastoral Care as Worship

As preachers and pastors, we should mention victims and survivors in our pastoral prayers and in sermon illustrations: abused children, teenagers facing dating violence, battered women, adult survivors of child abuse, abused elders. In addition, we should pray that the perpetrators of violence will see the sin in their lives and come to the church for accountability and repentance for their destructive behaviors. This is the extension of the loving care of God for all persons in all circumstances. When we bring such prayers and examples, religious leaders must be prepared with referral resources when members disclose their experiences of violence. All congregations must know the names and phone numbers of shelters for battered women, child-abuse hotlines, elder-abuse services, rape counseling centers, so they will be ready to respond to the pastoral-care needs of their members.[23]

Ethical Sermons on Family Violence

As preachers and pastors, we need to take clear ethical positions about family violence and its root causes. The following are ethical positions recommended by the Center for the Prevention of Sexual and Domestic Violence.

a) Violence and abuse have no place in the family. There is no legitimate justification for striking or otherwise abusing a family member. "People are not for hitting under any circumstances" is one way to express this value. Hitting or abusing another person is a violation of that person's very self. Violence sets up and enforces an imbalance of power based on physical strength. It minimizes the potential for trust, openness, and intimacy in the family.

b) A strong, vocal public stance against violence in the family is needed. Traditionally, violence committed against persons by strangers has been righteously condemned as a social evil that threatens our community. All too often, however, violence in the family has been silently condoned and seen as no one else's business. Rarely has anyone publicly asserted that family life should not be violent and abusive.

c) Families are [an] important social unit in our communities. Families, which come in many different forms, are the groupings from which we receive nurture and caring, through which we learn to share intimacy and trust. Many families do not fulfill these expectations. These families are in trouble. Many are literally being destroyed by violence and abuse.

d) The problem of violence in the family is a social problem, not an isolated, individual problem. Personal incidents of violence in the family take place in a larger societal context.

e) Preventing violence in the family means addressing the root causes of the problem.

f) Education is a primary means of changing the destructive patterns of violence in the family.

g) Sexuality is a very important dimension of every person's life.

h) Intervention from the outside into families where abuse occurs is often needed to stop the abuse.

i) Religious resources can be indispensable for family members who come from a religious background.

j) Ultimately, violence in the family is about power and control.

k) The sum of all efforts to address violence in the family in religious communities must be justice making.[24]

Reevaluation of Certain Doctrines

We need to listen to our own sermons, prayers, hymns, litanies, and all worship materials to determine how they will be heard by persons who are experiencing violence in their families, by persons who are in crisis right now because of violence, by adult survivors who are recovering from the effects of violence in their past, and by perpetrators of violence. "The least of these" principle of solidarity with the most vulnerable is crucial when preaching to perpetrators of violence.

Subordination of Women, Dominance of Men. Certain scriptures have a long history of being used to promote the subordination of women, and these texts are among the most frequent rationalizations by male abusers to promote violent domination of their partners. For example, "Wives, submit yourselves to your husbands as to [God]. For a husband has authority over his wife just as Christ has authority over the church; and Christ is . . . the Savior of the church, [Christ's] body. And so wives must submit themselves to their husbands just as the church submits itself to Christ" (Eph. 5:22–24). Thousands of sermons on this text have made the idea of male domination a part of the general religious piety of U.S. society. Male children have been socialized into this dominance throughout their lives in many ways. When men become husbands, they feel entitled to dominance and control; and when they feel threatened, they often feel justified to use violence to maintain their control. Fortunately, there is a spirited feminist discussion about the "household codes," which seem to contradict other scriptures that call for equality and freedom between women and men.[25] Other scriptures, for example, promote a view of gender equality between women and men.

> It is through faith that all of you are God's children in union with Christ Jesus. You were baptized into union with Christ, and now you are clothed, so to speak, with the life of Christ himself. So there is no difference between Jews and Gentiles, between slave and free, between men and women; you are all one in union with Christ Jesus. If you belong to Jesus Christ, then you are the descendants of Abraham and will receive what God has promised. (Gal. 3:26–29)

Preaching equality and freedom in Jesus Christ for women and men will make a big difference for some couples, and eventually will begin to change the traditional themes of male dominance that have caused so much violence.

Subordination of Children in the Family. Certain scriptures have been used to promote absolute parental authority over children, so that children have no ethical claim on adults for safety and protection. In *The Abuse of Power*, Karen gives witness to the effect of hearing the commandment to honor her parents which kept her silent about the incest she experienced from her father.[26] Scriptures like the following need to be carefully interpreted so that parents realize there are ethical limits to their authority. Parents cannot use violence to injure or sexually assault their children with permission of the Decalogue and the New Testament.

> Children, it is your Christian duty to obey your parents, for this is the right thing to do. Respect your father and mother is the first commandment that has a promise added: so that all may go well with you, and you may live a long time in the land. Parents, do not treat your children in such a way as to make them angry. Instead raise them with Christian discipline and instruction. (Eph. 6:1–4)

The end of this scripture provides a soft guideline for parents, but it is not sufficient to counter the authority given to parents in the first lines. Perhaps such scriptures need to be set in contrast to Jesus' words about protecting the children because they are messengers from God.

> At that time the disciples came to Jesus, asking, Who is the greatest in . . . heaven? So Jesus called a child, had him stand in front of them and said, I assure you that unless you change and become like children, you will never enter the [realm] of heaven. The greatest in . . . heaven is the one who humbles him[/her]self and becomes like this child. And whoever welcomes in my name one such child as this, welcomes me. If anyone should cause one of these little ones to lose his faith in me, it would be better for that person to have a large millstone tied around his [or her] neck and be drowned in the deep sea. How terrible for the world that there are things that make people lose their faith! Such things will always happen—but how terrible for the one who causes them! (Matt. 18:1–5)

Doctrines of Forgiveness and Reconciliation. Scriptures about forgiveness and reconciliation frequently are used by perpetrators to avoid the consequences of their violence and to coerce others to remain under their authority. Not infrequently, a perpetrator of violence goes to his or her pastor immediately after being arrested and asks for forgiveness. Because the petitioner appears remorseful and seems to be following the prescribed formula to activate God's grace, many pastors utter the words of assurance: "You are forgiven." Then the perpetrator pleads with the pastor to mediate reconciliation in order to "preserve the family." Counselors who work in shelters often say that the only time they see a pastor is when he or she follows the perpetrator to the shelter and asks the vulnerable woman and her children to return home for the sake of reconciliation. I have been in the presence of a perpetrator when he pressured his wife and child to forgive him as the Bible said they must. Scriptures like the following, when interpreted outside of a doctrine of sin and redemption, endanger vulnerable family members and support the denial and continued control of the perpetrator. "If you forgive others the wrong they have done to you, [God] will also forgive you. But if you do not forgive others, then [God] will not forgive the wrongs you have done" (Matt. 6:14–15).

Preaching on Matthew 18:15–20 and Luke 17:3–4 has also encouraged perpetrators to believe they can demand forgiveness. Fortunately, there is significant work being done on forgiveness and reconciliation which provides much needed reinterpretation of the history and intent of these Scriptures. Perpetrators need help from good interpretations of the Bible to stop their sinful acts. In the video *Broken Vows,* a pastor says to a perpetrator: "My job is not to tell your wife to come back to you to preserve the family, but to tell you that you have destroyed your marriage through violence. You have committed sin in the eyes of God and you must repent to be saved. My responsibility is to tell her to seek life, not death." Perpetrators of violence need to be confronted and instructed that forgiveness for violence is a process of repentance and sanctification that will take many years within a disciplined fellowship of Christians.[27]

Doctrines of Obedience, Servanthood, and Suffering. Other scriptures that cause problems for perpetrators of violence are the texts that seem to identify being Christian with obedience, servanthood, and suffering. Unfortunately, perpetrators do not apply these scriptures to themselves, but they do try to enforce such behavior from those over whom they have power. Parents often expect children to obey them without question, to run errands and do chores for the parents' benefit, and to accept the suffering that comes with punishment. Men often expect to be head of the marriage and the house, to make decisions that their partners have to obey; they see nothing wrong with requiring service from women, and they often minimize any suffering that is caused by their violent behavior.

> It is to this that God called you, for Christ himself suffered for you and left you an example, so that you would follow in his steps. He committed no sin, and no one ever heard a lie come from his lips. When he was insulted, he did not answer back with an insult; when he suffered, he did not threaten, but placed his hopes with God, the righteous Judge. Christ himself carried our sins in his body to the cross, so that we might die to sin and live for righteousness. It is by his wounds that you have been healed. You were like sheep that had lost their way, but now you have been brought back to follow the Shepherd and Keeper of your souls. (1 Peter 2:21; see also John 13:12–17, John 14:15, 21, Matt. 20:24–28, 2 Cor. 1:5–7, Romans 5:15, 1 Cor. 12:26, James 2:15–17)

A perpetrator who thinks of himself as the "shepherd and keeper of your souls" could use this scripture to justify his power and control. He would also have support from a history of interpretation of such passages. The nineteenth-century cult of true womanhood specifically connected the suffering and obedience of Jesus to the preservation of Christian values by women who stayed home during the early years of industrialization. Women who remained undefiled, who loved and obeyed their husbands, and who endured suffering for the sake of the family were the repositories of Christian civilization. While this language has been challenged by women's-rights movements, the rhetoric is alive and well in many Christian homes and is explicitly supported by some evangelical preaching. Preachers need to be careful when preaching about Jesus' obedience and suffering that it does not support the violence and domination of parents over children and husbands over wives and children. Fortunately, much good work on resistance to violence is being developed by liberation theologians as an extension of the stories about Jesus.[28]

Doctrines of Surrogacy and Crucifixion

But God has shown us how much [God] loves us—it was while we were still sinners that Christ died for us! By his sacrificial death we are now put right with God; how much more, then, will we be saved by [Christ] from God's anger. We were God's enemies, but [we became God's] friends through the death of [Christ]. Now that we are God's friends, how much more will we be saved by Christ's life! But that is not all; we rejoice because of what God has done through . . . Jesus Christ, who has now made us God's friends. (Rom. 5:8; see also 1 Tim. 2:5, Matt. 4:17)

Not infrequently, sexual and domestic violence results in permanent physical injury and sometimes death. Over 30 percent of the women who were murdered in the United States in 1995 were murdered by their intimate partners: husbands, ex-husbands, boyfriends, ex-boyfriends. Two thousand children every year are murdered by their parents or other caregivers.[29] With so much violence in families, preachers must be careful how we talk about the crucifixion and about images of surrogacy—that is, the necessity of someone dying for someone else. The idea that persons in authority have the right of life and death over subordinates unfortunately appeals to the sadistic impulses of some perpetrators. Batterers who murder are often heard to say: "If I can't have her, no one else will." Abusive parents sometimes say to their children, "I will kill you if that is what it takes to make you listen."

This leads us to a difficult theological discussion of the purpose of Jesus' death, the theories of atonement. Did Jesus die as a sacrifice to accomplish the victory over evil, to satisfy the wrath of God, to demonstrate the cost of sacrificial love? In our theories of the crucifixion, are we encouraging victims and survivors to identify with Jesus, who died as a sacrifice for the sins of others? These are hard theological questions, but they must be addressed when we realize that perpetrators are listening in order to justify their abuse of power.[30]

CONCLUSION

Are perpetrators of family violence getting the sermons they need? In many cases, I think not. In this chapter, we have reviewed some of the issues that arise when preachers are confronted with the presence of perpetrators of violence in their congregations. As preachers, we must assume that men and women in our congregations have engaged in violence within marriage, against children, and against elders and other family members. Our research suggests that 25 to 50 percent of the members of any congregation have experienced significant interpersonal violence in their lives and are struggling to survive this trauma. As we preach a God of love and power who cares for all people in all circumstances, we need to address this violence. The silence of the church is not an expression of the whole gospel of Jesus Christ.

We need to understand our history within the United States of ownership of persons which developed to justify slavery of African Americans and was applied to women and children within families. We have abolished slavery and have voted for gender equality, but we have not yet purged our theologies of the ideas of domination and submission. This is a crucial theological and historical task as we try to reduce the violence in our families and in our society.

We need hermeneutical principles for interpreting certain biblical texts that mislead perpetrators into feeling justified in their violence. They rationalize their violent acts through submission of women and children in the family; through demands for forgiveness and reconciliation; through appeals to doctrines of obedience, servanthood, and suffering; and through misinterpretation of biblical emphases on surrogacy and crucifixion. Fortunately, significant theological work is being done on these biblical texts and doctrines in light of what we are discovering about violence in our society.

The most important principle for preaching to perpetrators of violence is to listen to the witness of victims and survivors of violence. They have the authority of their experience as victims of violence, and they have the witness of their own religious experience. As preachers listen carefully in their pastoral care, we can begin a new dialogue about the meaning of the gospel for our time. And through such pastoral work, the saving stories of Jesus' life, death, and resurrection become real for another generation. In this work, God is glorified and the church becomes the body of Christ.

7

Preaching in a Violent Situation

David Emmanuel Goatley

I once played baseball on a Little League team, and the most exciting part of the game for me was being on offense. I particularly enjoyed batting. I was exhilarated every time I got a base hit. Further, getting a base hit advanced the collective efforts of my team. Although I was never a "heavy hitter" with frequent doubles, triples, and home runs, I became a pretty good batter.

Before I became a good batter, however, I had to learn to step up to the plate. "Stepping up to the plate" meant standing in the batter's box close enough to home plate so that I could hit the ball whenever it was in the strike zone. Being able to stand close enough to the plate to have the chance of hitting the ball was not something that came instinctively to me. I was innately afraid of being too close to the plate, because I did not want to risk being hit by a wildly pitched ball.

I knew enough about Little League pitchers to perceive danger of two kinds. First, these child pitchers were sometimes out of control, and they would occasionally unintentionally pitch a ball that would nearly or actually hit the batter. Second, some pitchers would deliberately throw the ball at the batter. This was intended to intimidate, rendering the batter ineffective: a batter who was afraid to step up to the plate had little possibility of hitting the ball.

Learning to step up to the plate meant that one could not be intimidated by fast-moving pitches that might come extremely close to, or indeed even strike, the batter. The only way to be a good batter was to overcome the fear of being hit. One could not be paralyzed by the possibility of random or intentional wild pitches. One had to risk injury to succeed. All good hitters must step up to the plate.

RELEVANT PREACHING IS LIBERATING PREACHING

Stepping up to the plate may be a useful metaphor for contemporary preaching that seeks to be relevant. When a preacher steps up to the plate, he or she practices effective preaching that advances the liberative thrust of communities of faith who are committed to living and declaring the good news of Jesus Christ. Effective preaching is relevant preaching, and preaching of this sort is never done without risk. Effective and relevant preaching moves against the flow of the ordinary currents of contemporary life. It challenges the assumptions of the lying voices that excuse violence and explain away destructive aggressive behavior. Consequently, the relevant preacher will discover him/herself often facing wild and potentially dangerous accusations and responses (like wild baseball pitches) from many places.

The relevant preacher may be accused of not preaching the Bible but of offering commentary on current events. The accusation of not preaching is a devastating one for anyone who claims to be called to preaching ministry. He or she may face cold, piercing, and venomous responses from people who feel convicted of their wrongs and claim that the preacher is meddling. During the U.S. civil rights movement, some European American pastors who dared to preach the gospel authentically faced censorship and termination. Because they challenged the racist systems and individuals who benefited from the structures of oppression, they found themselves terminated by church leadership. These courageous preachers were fired because they proclaimed the liberating good news of Jesus Christ and moved against the contemporary flow of popular opinion and ideology. Just as a few preachers of that era risked their physical and economic well-being, today's pervasive violence signals an urgent need for preachers who are prepared to step up to the plate. Stepping up to the plate as a preacher means that the preacher will sometimes be hit by the injurious rhetoric and actions of perpetrators and enablers of violence. The church and our world, however, desperately need relevant preachers and relevant preaching.

Some people—in and out of the church—believe that "preaching" and "relevance" are ill-fitted for the same sentence. In other words, they are said to be contradictory terms. These critics interpret their experiences to teach them that churches and the proclamation within churches are essentially irrelevant for contemporary life. Whatever the cause, it is clear that relevant preachers must enter into the worlds of people. Relevant preaching engages the realities of people—their progress and struggles, joys and sorrows, victories and defeats, successes and failures, hopes and fears. Henry Mitchell agrees inasmuch as effective preaching is carried out within the cultural milieu of a particular community; language, imagery, and other aspects of the sermon must relate to the cultural context of a given people. Otherwise, communication is hampered or prevented.

Two principles related to hermeneutics in black preaching are: (1) the gospel must be preached in the vernacular of the people; and (2) preaching must relate to the hearers' contemporary needs.[1] As Paul Brown argues, liturgy as the context for relevant preaching must also reflect the church's living in the world rather than providing a shelter that allows people to hide from the world.[2] Consequently, the language of liturgy, which certainly includes preaching, must speak with and to the historic and contemporary experiences of people.

Good preaching is preaching that is delivered well, but good preaching needs more than eloquent oratory and dramatic flair. Good preaching is more than panache. Good preaching is good theology, and good theology seeks to speak responsibly, coherently, and with integrity something of faith in who God is, what God does, and what God desires for creation. When preachers preach like this, they are stepping up to the plate.

Relevant preaching today must confront directly the pervasive violence that infects our world. Relevant preaching for African American life must unapologetically challenge violence that is experienced within and inflicted from without their communities.

LIVING IN VIOLENCE

Violence is a dominant theme in the portrait of African American life in the United States. For nearly four centuries, African Americans have lived in a culture with prominent strands of violence woven throughout the fabric of life. Violence takes many shapes and has a myriad of nuance, but its core identity is that of aggressive, combative, and destructive behavior.

African American experiences of violence in the United States are rooted in the oppressiveness of chattel slavery. Chattel slavery did violence to enslaved people both physically and psychologically. Men, women, and children were subjected to vicious beatings and physical mutilations inflicted upon their own bodies, or they were forced to witness the imposition of violence on the bodies of others. Additionally, the abusive patriarchy of the antebellum period meant that women and girls faced the added brutality of sexual exploitation. This abuse is normally, and perhaps normatively, identified with the atrocious aggression of enslavers and overseers. One must acknowledge, however, that females in nonenslaved environments were also vulnerable to sexual assault. Likewise, African American females additionally faced expressions of sexual exploitation at the hands of some African American males who were socialized to view females as objects of violent sexual aggression.

The abolition of slavery did not eradicate barbarous exploitation. Postbellum life yielded its own expressions of hostility. Examples flourish in Jim Crow America, where African Americans were assaulted, attacked, and lynched by racist European Americans who fashioned themselves as judges, juries, and executioners. Individuals, families, and communities could be victimized by the brutalities that reigned in many parts of the country. A horrid chapter of this kind of malevolence has been unburied in recent years through the recollections of the Rosewood massacres. In the 1920s, impoverished white citizens of a community neighboring Rosewood, Florida, set out to destroy the relatively prosperous black town when a white woman alleged that she had been beaten by a black man. By the time the story had taken on a life of its own, the alleged victim had been raped as well as beaten, and the white men of the area did not intend to tolerate the violation of one of the women of their community. The allegation was false: she in fact had been beaten by her white lover and was afraid of her husband's reaction. Consequently, an entire African American community was obliterated. While such massacres may not have been frequent events, that the Rosewood massacres could occur, be buried in history, and receive mostly muffled outrage is indicative of the callousness that characterized much of the European American attitude toward African Americans.

In spite of the alleged progress of contemporary life in the United States, violence is still a substantial ingredient in African American life. Many African Americans are subjected to violence exclusively because of their culture and color. Among the manifestations of violence are economic, educational, and environmental assaults. African Americans consistently are paid less than their European American counterparts for both comparable and identical work. Further, racial discrimination is consistently practiced by financial institutions which refuse loans to African Americans who are equally, and sometimes more highly, qualified in terms of income, credit history, and such. Public schools with high percentages of African American students often receive lower degrees of investment in their facilities and educational programs. It is commonplace to see industrial sites that spew pollutants in the air and water located in African American urban communities as well as in poor European American and African American rural communities.

Living in environments that are at least substantially—and perhaps dominantly—shaped by the encroachment of violence and its injurious impacts has contributed to a contemporary experience of oppressed peoples internalizing the behavior of oppressors. While empirical data may yet need production, it is reasonable to propose that those who are victims often victimize others. Schoolchildren experience this when the high-school bully intimidates the middle-school child, who in turn terrorizes the grade-school child, who in turn horrifies the preschool child. And on it goes. The victim becomes the victimizer. The assaulted becomes the assaulter. Some African Americans have become inundated by the violence to which they have been culturally, emotionally, psychologically, and physically subjected. This results, in part for example, in the growing crisis of gangs among African American young people. African American gangs are in part, in the words of Malcolm X, "made-in-America Negroes."

I assert that African American gangs are "made-in-America Negroes" because they have espoused some of the same principles in much of contemporary corporate America. To say that gangs are related to for-profit capitalist corporations is to say that gangs use the tools available to them to achieve the perceived profits which benefit the gangs. Gangs do not have tools of stock options, buyouts, downsizing, and the like. They use the tools they have at hand—physical intimidation, illegal business activities, and various forms of coercion. The exploitation of the weak by the strong is characteristic of gang violence and the violence of many. This is also akin, in principle, to U.S. corporate practices of maximizing profits in the interest of stockholders. Corporate profits are often maximized by considering employees and the environment as expendable commodities. This expendability of the powerless means that a corporation can behave assertively, combatively, and destructively toward workers and natural resources because of the unequal distribution of power. Employees and the environment become tools for "profitability"—in sometimes perverted understandings of the term. Consequently, the strong often advance their agendas at the expense of the weak. For example, numerous cases may be made for the mutuality of corporate profit when companies downsize to save the jobs of a few vis-à-vis the loss of jobs for an entire organization. However, one is hard-pressed to justify the aggression of corporations toward vulnerable employees and environments while simultaneously rewarding corporate officers with obscenely large compensation packages. Is this not what gangs often do? They exploit relative weakness or vulnerability in the name of what is in the best interest of the gang. Hence, gangs have internalized the self-serving interest strategies of those who function in the economic system that arguably makes the United States the economic superpower in today's world. It follows then, that the United States, through its principles of economic power and progress, may have created the very cancer that will lead to its own demise.

A particular problem of gang behavior is the overt control gangs seek to exercise over their own members. Two cases stand to illustrate this point. A church with a vibrant youth ministry has been reaching many youth in its evangelistic thrust. Two teenagers—one female and the other male—responded to the inspiration of the Holy Spirit to become disciples of Jesus. They both approached the gang to which they belonged to explain their new commitment of faith and their need to leave the gang. The gang leaders responded that these two new Christians should not bring that kind of request. Continuing their relationship with the gang was nonnegotiable. The counsel they received from their new church was to make themselves less accessible to the gang: remain home more, and eventually, the gang would turn to others to fill the minor roles these two young people played. This kind of intimidation and control is common in gang life.

Sherry (a pseudonym) was a member of a gang. She joined a branch of the armed services to escape the hopelessness of her impoverished neighborhood and the emptiness of the life ahead. Having experienced progress in her new life many states away from her home, she was surprised to be contacted by a member of her old gang, who informed her that she had not left the gang. Joining the armed services and moving to another state did not sever her relationship. She reasoned, pleaded, and appealed to be left alone by the gang. Eventually, her leaving the gang was agreed on, subject to one condition: the only way out of the gang was to have sexual intercourse with twelve male gang members; otherwise, she still owed loyalty to the gang. After weighing her options, she was subjected to the violence of sexual exploitation as her rite of expulsion from the gang.

Gang violence, however, is only one expression of sexual violence. Most expressions of abuse and violence are not imposed upon people through ganglike behavior. Most expressions of sexual violence are imposed on victims by acquaintances. Violence is a real and pervasive experience in the lives of women, and contemporary research indicates that "both the threat and reality of sexual abuse prevail in the majority of the lives of African-American females."[3] This threat and reality are not new phenomena. The case has been convincingly made that the violence of exploitation by coerced and pseudo-voluntary surrogacy is a dominant presence in the lives of African American women. Antebellum surrogacy was imposed on black women in the forms of: (1) mammies, who were household managers and raised the children of their enslavers; (2) masculinization of slave women, with the women being forced to do field labor identical to that by male slaves; and (3) surrogate sexual partners, who were subjected to the sexual exploitation of white males. Postbellum economics forced African American women into somewhat refurbished, nonetheless surrogate, roles. While African American women obtained legal standing that allowed them to reject mandated sexual submission, economics still caused these surrogate roles to continue in various forms.[4]

One can argue convincingly that being subject to violence is prominent in the portrait of African American life in the United States. From the earliest periods of physical servitude, enslavement, and savagery to contemporary sophisticated and subtle expressions of hostility and despisement, Africans and their descendants in "the land of the free and the home of the brave" have embodied Langston Hughes's sentiment, "Life for me ain't been no crystal stair." Indeed, life for far too many has been like that of Richard Wright's Bigger Thomas in the classic novel *Native Son*—"a hot and whirling vortex of undisciplined and unchannelized emotions."

It is false to say that African Americans experience violence in any homogeneous or monolithic way. It is true, however, to assert that life for virtually all African Americans is lived against a backdrop of, in close proximity to, or with actual engagement with a disproportionate probability of knowing violence. Further, these imposing experiences of violence are all too frequently related to being black and in America. Preaching that is relevant for African American life must be prepared to speak coherently, responsibly, and with integrity in the harsh and hostile realities of violent situations.

PREACHING WITH RELEVANCE

African American preaching can be characterized as art, craft, and gift. As an art, it is an expression of human creativity. Preachers are attempting to build messages with strength and beauty or to weave messages with durability and grace—messages that make a difference in the lives of those who hear. As craft, it is a skill well refined. The preacher is continually striving to chip away at the rough edges and knead a sermon into a smooth and consistent texture. As gift, it is freely offered by God through the divine call to the preaching ministry. To acknowledge this gift is to accept it and seek to be a faithful steward of the gift, despite one's frailties.

In addition to the above characterization, preaching is a dynamic event. Something truly happens. There is an experiential quality in black preaching on the part of the preacher and the listener. It is an event approached with anticipation of something about to happen. To speak of this event-oriented nature of black preaching is akin to Molefi Kete Asante's articulation of *nommo*, "the generative and productive power of the spoken word."[5] Asante's discussion of oratory in his Afrocentric perspective moves toward the understanding of the spoken word as functional art. Rather than art existing for the sake of art, art in this perspective is purposeful and fits into the world and experiences of the people. As a result, the spoken word as art serves to produce something in and among the community. This idea contributes to perceiving the spoken word as alive. It follows that black preaching, which stands in the African-centered tradition of functional oratory, is dynamic. To say that black preaching is dynamic is to say that it has a living quality, movement, contours, and textures. It is always evolving and rarely duplicated. It intends to make something happen.

Dynamism in African American preaching has sometimes been interpreted as the manifestation of style with limited substance. This dynamic kind of preaching has often been mislabeled as anti-intellectual preaching. Preachers who voice empty rhetoric do so irrespective of cultural heritage. There are poor preachers in all cultures who may or may not be energetic and dramatic. To accuse emotive African American preaching as stylistic but lacking substance is an ill-placed criticism. The charge of "anti-intellectualism" sometimes leveled against African American preaching is assumed in part because the degree of extroversion, emotional intensity, and demonstrative response to the sermon from the preacher and the hearer in some settings is assumed to lack intellectual rigor. What leads to this conclusion is the idea that the expression of passion in certain African American contexts occurs devoid of reflection. Warren A. Stewart offers an insightful response to this charge as part of his structure of hermeneutics for preaching. Defining intellect as the power of understanding, Stewart claims:

> The survival tactics and intuitive hermeneutics of black people living in America under the oppression, discriminatory practices, and racism of white Anglo-Saxon Protestants have proven that black people are *highly intellectual* in the *weightier* issues of human existence, namely, survival and religion. The ability to know God as a liberator *is* in part an *intellectual* experience. And it does not take a diploma or a scholastic degree to exercise the mind or to show its intelligence and understanding (emphasis in original).[6]

For our purposes, then, relevant preaching in African American contexts *must* have the quality of *nommo*. It must be a creative constructive force that functions for the transformation, production, or promotion of the good of a community. This observation is critical for an appreciation of the point I am trying to make. For it is this idea of *nommo* that distinguishes my understanding of relevance from that of some other people.

What does it mean to be relevant, and how can preaching be relevant? First, relevant preaching is not therapeutic commentary that enables people to cope with issues more ingeniously. Relevant preaching does not have as its primary goal (and probably not as a secondary or tertiary goal) soothing the anxious consciences of those who are socio-economically upwardly mobile. Relevant preaching does not seek to comfort the socially comfortable. Second, relevant preaching does not aspire to confirm one's place of relative privilege. Some people want a gospel (small "g" intended) not to which they must say "Amen," but which says "Amen" to their relative comfort. Relevant preaching does not lend itself to complacency. Third, relevant preaching is not eloquent observation upon contemporary events. Simply to mention or even to talk at length about what may be occurring during a particular time is not to be relevant. Preaching that is needed does not talk *around* subjects. To the contrary, it tackles complex, contradictory, and confounding issues squarely.

Relevant preaching is not content to talk about where one *is*; instead, it is concerned about what one *does*. Relevant preaching is productive preaching. It challenges us in ways that are often discomforting. It does so not simply for the purpose of discomfort, but it proceeds along this way because of our need to be continually re-created. Relevant preaching seeks to birth something new, fresh, alive, and meaningful—something that makes substantive contributions to the world in which we live. Relevant preaching intends to move us from where we are toward where God desires us to be. It seeks to call us to the purpose of liberation for all who are oppressed, victimized, and marginalized in various ways.

Samuel Proctor asserts that there are four pressing issues with which all preachers who seek to be relevant must contend: "(1) Is God alive, aware, and active, and is God willing and able to intervene on our behalf? Is the universe a friendly place? (2) Can this carnal package of drives and urges be controlled, restrained, and reconciled to the will of God? (3) Is a blessed, genuine community possible? (4) Is our space–time frame of reference the only one, or is eternity moving through time?"[7] These are critical questions.

Proctor answers the above questions by affirming that God is present and active in the lives of humanity. Consequently, God enables people to resist evil and pour out compassion upon the victims or survivors of violence. This present God can renew and transform lives, leading to meaningful and moral living. Genuine community that overcomes the pervasive experiences of "noncommunity" with its barriers that separate people is possible. And people can know the eternal quality of life amid the artificiality of our commercialized and consumer-constructed world.

Proctor recalls an experience of hearing the late Clarence Jordan of Georgia's Koinonia community speak. As Jordan characteristically challenged the assembly to live in a manner consistent with Jesus' teaching in Matthew 5–7, he was asked how one could realistically be a successful, modern, urban pastor and follow Jesus' Sermon on the Mount of Olives. Quoting Jordan, Proctor recalls the response: "Jesus did not give this sermon to successful, modern, urban pastors. He gave it to his *disciples*, and if there is a conflict, you have to choose whether you are going to be a disciple or a successful, modern, urban pastor."[8] This direct, confrontational, challenging tone is necessary to preach coherently, responsibly, and with integrity in violent situations.

Gardner Taylor, to whom *Christian Century* refers as the dean of black preachers and the "poet laureate of American Protestantism," uses the analogy of the sentinel from Ezekiel 33 to talk about the preacher's role. First, the sentinel/preacher is to watch carefully the hills and valleys that surround the community to determine whether danger approaches. The sentinel/preacher is to see clearly and accurately and not sleep or be distracted. Second, the sentinel/preacher is to sound the warning upon sighting an approaching enemy. This is not ranting, but the urgent cry concerning danger to the well-being of the community.[9] According to Taylor, "Whatever a sermon does, it must bring humanity in touch with its Creator."[10] Additional qualities of preaching, according to Taylor, relate to Naomi's comment in the book of Ruth where she speaks of having gone out full and come back empty. Preachers, say Taylor, "must keep ourselves full so we can empty ourselves in the pulpit."[11]

Taylor's descriptions of the preacher's task speak substantively to preaching in a violent situation. The watchful preacher sees the trouble of violence not only in distant plains, but also as having invaded the gates of our communities. Being alert, the preacher sounds an urgent cry about the approach and arrival of violence and the peril it brings. Further, because of confidence in God and God's will for well-being in creation—*shalom*—the preacher empties her/himself with the proclamation of challenge toward violence and the hope of deliverance. Over and over again, the preacher must fill up with this conviction for continuous proclamation.

Relevant preaching must attend to the ways in which women and men will interpret the preaching as well as carefully avoid potentially oppressive implications for the community. Hermeneutics for preaching cannot lean exclusively into an interpretation of what the Scriptures said. This is an impossible task because of the inherent contextualization with which everyone does theology. Hermeneutics for preaching requires one to speak both out of and into the real-life situations in which people live and lose, flourish and flounder.

Katie Canon lends a womanist perspective to the preaching event which must be heeded if preaching is to be relevant for African American contexts. Far too often, she believes, African American preaching has been guilty of "phallocentric" concepts, even in the name of "text-led" biblical preaching.[12] Women cannot be considered at the fringes and men at the center of the community. The centralization of men and the peripheralization of women cannot be tolerated. This means that preaching must be bold and combative, yet attentive and sensitive. This is not a new suggestion. Karen Baker-Fletcher shows us how Anna Julia Cooper (b. 1858) called for preaching that addressed Christ's concern for the poor and oppressed from America's pulpits. Born out of the sexual exploitation of her enslaved mother by her enslaver, Cooper is a prototypical liberationist who challenged the oppressiveness of sexism, racism, classism, and imperialism. Although her ministry was teaching, she called for preaching that spoke unapologetically to the oppressions that characterized her context, and she advocated giving voice to those who suffer and whose very beings are threatened. The gospel message has something to say to those who are victims and to those who chose to victimize.[13]

I contend that African Americans live in a violent situation, and that preachers have something constructive to proclaim. Relevant preaching for African Americans and relevant preaching informed by African American insight cannot shrink from the honest engagement with the reality of violence. Relevant preachers must speak something of challenge and hope in this context .

HOW SHALL THEY PREACH?

Sexual violence is real and far too rampant. Preachers cannot hide from this fact. We must reverse the failure of preachers and Christian communities to maintain the proper perspective on the taboo related to violence, which has produced devastating results. Frances E. Wood contends that the African American church has failed to address adequately the horrendous nature of sexual abuse. This is also true of churches in general. "Abusive behavior, which we call taboo, is not the real taboo, speaking the truth about the abuse is."[14] What then are appropriate responses to the devastating problem of sexual violence?

We must believe and proclaim unapologetically that human sexuality is good when expressed and experienced with integrity, mutuality, intimacy, commitment, and love. This is part of God's creation. Any negativity associated with sexuality is not grounded in the ontology of human sexuality, but is due to a wrong-headed axiology—the assigning of value in human thought and practice which distorts and disfigures what God has made good. Further, humans are sexual beings. That we are such is good. To ascribe some intrinsic evil to the sexuality of human beings is indicative of an erroneous anthropology that associates the physicality of humanity with an inherent sinfulness of the body. While this perspective may be embraced by certain individuals as appropriate for their belief about their own humanity, it should in no way be proposed as universally normative for humanity. Since humans are sexual beings and integral to the reality of the church, the church is necessarily a sexual community. To say that one is sexual simply describes a biological fact. The exercise of sexual intimacy may or may not be part of the life of sexual beings—of humanity. The church as a sexual community is obligated to behave with integrity. To have sexual integrity is to practice and promote appropriate discourse and demeanor that seeks to oppose, prevent, seek appropriate punishment, and work for suitable reconciliation for those who commit exploitation, abuse, and violence.[15]

Perhaps the following positions are among the essentials for relevant preaching concerning the threats and actualizations of sexual violence. First, we must oppose the belief that sexually violent and aggressive behavior is ever acceptable or even tolerable. People are not receptacles to be used as others please. Further, the risk of rape and battery cannot be assumed to be a liability of being female. No one has the license to victimize another.

Second, we must oppose excusing men who batter women because of the stress in men's lives or in response to "nagging" women. One does not relieve stress through hurting another. The need to "blow off steam" must be directed in ways that do not threaten or injure the well-being of others. Additionally, hitting a woman to "shut her up" is unacceptable. Some men who physically batter women claim to do so in response to the women's verbal and intellectual battery of them. The logic here is that if a woman is intellectually more astute than her mate and if she assaults him with her oratory, he may only be able to fight back physically. People use the weapons available to them. We must challenge the idea that assault is acceptable on anyone's part. If a man claims he is responding to his intellectual victimization with physical assault, we must confront him, but we must call both "abusers" into accountability and seek healthier ways of interaction. I emphasize again here my commitment that physical violence cannot be opposed while intellectual or emotional violence is somehow considered less offensive. All aggressive, combative, and destructive behavior must be opposed.

Third, we must oppose the silence that surrounds much domestic violence and enables the violence to continue and intensify. Those of us who keep the "dirty little secrets" assist and encourage the continuation of violence. We cannot stand by and claim that what happens in another's home or relationship is not our business. We are in relationship to all of God's creation, and we are obliged to care for one another and oppose anything that threatens the life and living of one created in God's image.

Fourth, we must affirm the intrinsic value of all people, irrespective of what others have done to them. No amount of battery or abuse can diminish the innate value of a person. Victims of violence are often further victimized by judicial and social systems that somehow blame the victim for her or his victimization. Victims are often shunned or treated with shame, as if *they* had committed an offense. Preaching must not further victimize victims by blaming them or excusing the perpetrators. We must be discerning of what and how we speak to the issues involved in sexual violence. But we must speak! We must affirm that people who are victims of abuse or battery are good; they have creative possibilities. And with God's help and the support of those of us committed to the eradication of sexual abuse and domestic violence, people who have been victims of violence can build lives full of hope and a flourishing future.

Fifth, we must attack the problem of abuse that occurs among and between teenagers. Conversations about sexual abuse and domestic violence often focus on people who live in the same homes or are in familial relationships. There is a massive problem, however, of sexual violence and physical battering among and between teenagers. Perhaps the most acknowledged problem—although too often underemphasized—is date rape. In addition to date rape, however, is the growing occurrence of physical battery between teenagers who believe themselves to be in dating relationships. Some claim that 30 percent of teenage girls will be involved in a physically abusive relationship by the time they are nineteen years old. This does not count the number of boys who also are subject to violent assaults by persons with whom they are in dating relationships. These young people have no political capital; therefore, their experiences with the horrors of sexual and physical violence go unnoticed, unopposed, and unattacked. Preachers must directly confront this issue for the sake of young people today and their future lives. Young people are in the process of learning about themselves and about how to relate to others. They need help now!

Sixth, we must attack the myth that only women are victims of domestic violence and sexual abuse. Men are battered. Boys are sexually violated by males, females, adults, youth, and other children. Beyond the personal problems associated with being victimized, male victims face the social stigma of being labeled as a "wimps" who are unable to care for themselves. Consequently, both their personhood and their idea of "manhood" are at stake. Attending to the victimization of males is not a threat to the overwhelming realities of the victimization of females. Neither should our understanding of the less-frequent occurrences of male victimization diminish the demand for a firm stance on the issue.

Sexual and domestic violence impact individuals and families in devastating ways. Relevant preaching must address these issues forthrightly and unapologetically. Those who perpetrate violence must be called to accountability and responsibility. Those who are victims of violence must be affirmed, supported, and comforted. This occurs when preachers step up to the plate. While there is no definitive series of sermons that would address effectively the problems associated with sexual violence and domestic abuse, perhaps the following might offer some possibilities for development and refinement.

SERMON POSSIBILITIES

The Dignity of Defiance (Esther 1:1–22)

Some people in power erroneously believe that they can use people for expediency or entertainment. This is an effort to devalue and dehumanize. Many men have the mistaken idea that women exist exclusively or primarily for the pleasure of men. Women are toys for boys. This misguided mindset is often excused when exhibited by so-called professionals and people of influence—executives, attorneys, physicians, educators, ministers, and others.

Vashti is a strong woman. Her strength is exhibited in her defiance at the exploitative intentions of her husband and his compatriots. When sent for to parade her beauty, she refuses. She declares that "You won't use me!" She is banned from the king's presence and loses her personal place of privilege because the king's associates recognize the possibilities for liberation for other women who hear of her audacity. There is dignity in her defiance. Other women will be encouraged to oppose oppression and exploitation. No controlling, patriarchal, abusive, exploitative man will be secure. No more unchallenged violence. No more passivity in the face of assertive, destructive, combative behavior. Vashti is onto something. She threatens the established disorder. This defiance just might set the captives free!

When a Man Stands Up (1 Kings 18:1–39)

It seems that many people have little to which they are committed. Our culture in this country is such that we have little "staying power." Nearly everything is temporary. We operate in sound bites and with disposability as a normative paradigm. Since we drive and fly, we have no tolerance for those who walk. Consequently, we often suffer from the lack of commitment to high principles and values. We should remember, however, that it is said that a person who stands for nothing will fall for anything.

Elijah confronts Ahab and the prophets of Baal. First, he stands up to false accusations by the king and against intimidating odds. Second, he speaks up to confront the instability of his own people and to challenge the prophets of Baal to demonstrate whether their god is God. Third, God shows up and demonstrates who is God. Fourth, the people wake up and recognize the identity of God. This can begin a cycle: for those who awaken can now stand for justice, liberty, truth, and the like—and the beat goes on!

True Greatness (Phil. 2:5 – 11)

Many of us want to live in ways that make a difference. Of course, what it means to make a difference has various connotations for various people. Too often, we believe that making a difference does not mean being a blessing to someone or enhancing the lives of people in modest ways. We think we need to make a splash! Being *good* is not enough for many; being *great* is our desire. This is especially true of people of relative wealth, might, or influence. Many in our own country are preoccupied with the designation of being a superpower (whatever that means).

Being great, however, does not mean successful manipulation of opportunities for personal achievement or acquisition. Being great does not mean exploiting the weaknesses and vulnerabilities of others who are not as shrewd. Being great does not mean domination of others by political, economic, or military force. Greatness comes through the commitment of life to the edification of the lives of others. Greatness comes through humble exercise of power to enable the powerless to stand on their own feet. Countries, corporations, communities, and individuals who impose their wills on others are not great. They are simply ones who impose their wills on others.

Greatness comes when one does not have to grasp power. Greatness comes when one expends one's life in the service of God. Greatness comes not by aggression; it is conferred upon those who do not seek it. A great country is one that does not seek to dictate the policies and practices of more-dependent countries. A great country is not one that inflicts economic, political, and cultural violence for the alleged benefit of its corporate citizens. A great country abhors violence in any way and seeks to empower and live in solidarity with the oppressed and suffering and struggling masses of the world. People do not voluntarily relinquish power; it is snatched or wrested from them. But great people relinquish their privilege and share their power, that all may be empowered for life and living.

CONCLUSION

I remember an encounter with a child in an after-school program in the church I served as pastor. Carla was a "challenging" girl who regularly attended the program. She normally had a negative attitude and kept an unpleasant disposition. One day she simply walked up to another one of the children and hit the child in the face with her fist. In our discussion that followed, she told me that she did not know why she struck the other child and that she was wrong to have done so. In spite of Carla's less than ideal home setting (which undoubtedly fueled her problematic behavior), Carla knew, by instinct if not by instruction, what was right.

Because we are made in the image of God, there is a "cognition of righteousness" to which we can, and indeed must, appeal. While my affirmation of the cognition of righteousness may sound hopeful and applicable in the setting mentioned above, one may question the suitability of such an assertion in the context of vicious violent offenders. What of those who terrorize and violate the very humanity of others? What of rapists, murderers, abusers, predators of various sorts? Can we claim to believe in a shred of goodness in those who commit such barbarous acts? One must concede that there are people in whom it is extremely difficult—perhaps impossible—for us to find an element of righteousness. Some who work with sexual abusers and child molesters, for example, will argue that one cannot assume the possibility of reaching any seed of goodness in some nauseating offenders. I concede these points made by professionals who try to work with perpetrators of violence. I also want to cling to the hope, however, that while evil may overpower good for any number of reasons, evil does not have the power in itself to obliterate the potential for good. I believe that God's power can reach and redeem even those who seem to be most disgusting and beyond redemption. I believe in the possibility of redemption. This does not imply, however, that redemption comes cheap or magically. Punishment, therapy, recompense, and more may be part of the cost of redemption. But redemption is possible. It has to be. Evil cannot obliterate the possibility of good.

We must not be discouraged by the prevailing attitudes which hold that one is justified in mirroring violence with violence. I am not suggesting passivity in the face of raw aggressive, combative, and destructive behavior. One's context of oppression may demand aggressive response. But if this response is called for, it should be measured and calculated with an intent to a positive resolution. This places the response in a different context than the initiated behavior. No one can design a universally applicable system of responses to the complex and barbarous expressions of violence in our world. But we must seek to respond in ways that move toward constructing environments that are conducive to growth, harmony, and community. If measured aggressive responses serve that end, so be it. I am convinced, however, that our humanity is not obliterated by original sin. Evil cannot destroy absolutely that which God made good. Preaching in a violent situation demands that we "step up to the plate" and straightforwardly address the problems of violence, strongly challenge the perpetrators of violence, encourage and support the victims of violence, and do so with the intent to produce a world more like the harmonious community for which God is calling.

Part 3

Transforming Homiletic Practice

8

Preaching as Nonviolent Resistance

Barbara Patterson

Preaching can be an activist and transformative response by the church to violence against women. In order for this to happen, we, as preachers, must learn to approach preaching as part of a daily Christian practice of resisting violence. This practice encourages us to ask difficult questions about ourselves, abuse, the good news, and God. What difference will our sermons make for these women, our parishes, ourselves, and God? Will our homilies engender understanding, compassion, and active justice? Can they speak of Christ's incarnate good news in the midst of very painful, complicated, and messy lives?

As baptized believers, all of us are called each day to remember and enact the good news: "Christ has died; Christ is risen; Christ will come again." Our baptismal vows remind us to renounce daily the destruction and evil of violence against women while proclaiming healing power for resistance and transformation. These vows are our incarnational prescription for "being saved." Athanasius wrote of this process as taking on the qualities of Christ.[1] We are participating in the renewal of the whole creation, the living body of Christ. We are becoming sharers of Christ's incarnate qualities—however imperfectly and ambiguously—by Christ's mercy. As preachers resisting violence against women, we are putting our bodies, minds, and souls on the line with women abused, raped, and beaten. These women also, in various states and ways, participate in Christ's body. We are bound to one another, and so we preach about their reality and what we know and experience. But how do we do that in an incarnational sense?

I propose two responses. First, we learn to preach about the cessation of violence against women in connection with our witness about Christ's active presence in our own day. We preach sermons that make clear the connection between the suffering of abused women and the continuing suffering of Christ. Clarifying the linkages between their suffering as unjust and the unjust suffering of Christ, we tell of Christ's incarnate power to touch human suffering, not only in the past but also in the present. Christ's body and blood are not only remembered sacrament, text, liturgy, song, preaching, discipleship, and so forth. They also are profoundly present in contemporary human experiences, including suffering and responses to suffering. These connections with Christ's incarnation provide tested or proved bridges of hope from human suffering to transformative compassion and power. Learning to preach about this incarnate reality engages us in forms of gospel activism and solidarity with violated women.

Second, I propose we learn to preach about violence by approaching this kind of preaching as one among our other spiritual practices or disciplines. Like prayer or scripture study, preaching teaches us to take on the qualities of Christ—in this case, in the arena of violence against women. Preaching about violence in this way roots us in the daily life of Christ, not solely by thinking but also by seeing, hearing, speaking, and being present to violated women and their families. In this way, preaching becomes a spiritual discipline, a practice of formation designed to re-form our hearts, minds, and bodies in the image of Christ facing violence. To tell the good news to these women cannot mean an idealization of Christ's incarnate power in them. Some violated women also abuse others—for example, their children. It requires that we train and develop the skills of discernment that will help us to recognize issues of sin and repentance as well as incarnate hope and transformation. In learning as preachers to take on the qualities of Christ, we recognize that Christ both suffers and redeems now. How can we develop this spiritual practice of preaching against violence toward women?

PREACHING: CONTINUITIES OF INCARNATE LIFE WITH CHRIST

In a mysterious way, Christ's incarnation continues to be actively present in our own lives. As we preach about Christ's suffering and ours, Christ's redemption and ours, Christ's relations with abusers and ours, we are making explicit this *continuing and active incarnation*. We learn to recognize this thread partly in human experience including actual bodies. We recognize it in the body of Christ, the church, but in other institutions, groups, and individuals as well. We look for experiences of redemption, responsibility, and love, and practice discerning the presence of Christ in order to tell the good news.

Participation in the Lives of Victims and Survivors

We begin by discerning the incarnate Christ in the lives of violated women. This occurs as we participate, with permission, in their lives. Their experiences, past and present, are some of the junctures that disclose the life of Christ. There are concrete points where we can learn to recognize human choices to take or not take on the qualities of Christ's divine action in the world. When we put our whole selves in relation with violated women, we are intending to knit our bodies and blood with that of Christ, who already is knitted to their pain and suffering. Our flesh also shares in the body and blood of Christ, redeeming over time these women's pain and/or compassionately inviting them to take responsibility for their own destructive choices and encouraging their actions to restore the beauty of their lives. Learning to preach this way calls attention to points of continuity and discontinuity between us and Christ and asks us to learn to make a Christian embodied witness as best we can.

To preach this incarnating word may be a struggle when the juncture is the body of a beaten and raped woman. Suddenly, texts, creeds, doctrines, even homilies about the continuing sufferings of Christ become radicalized as literal broken limbs, wounds, and agonies. Searching to say an incarnate word in this context is to discover the commitment of divinity to humanity. Now we see, hear, and experience the flesh and blood of a woman whose life is embraced by the incarnate Christ. "Forgive us our sins" becomes "forgive us our literal despisings and murderings of women—this woman." "Test and know our hearts" becomes "expose our too-usual patriarchal language and oppressive assumptions about women." At the juncture of incarnate living and preaching words, the preached Word becomes literal flesh.

For many of us who preach, this tactile, incarnating encounter with Christ is disorienting. On one level, we are shocked by the destruction caused by our having been numbed by cultural camouflages and our own denial. On another level, we are not practiced enough in speaking a word of good news in the face of the suffering Christ knows so well. We try platitudes, but they sound empty even to us. We cannot speak that way with Christ present, and we recognize now that Christ *is* present. To consider preaching out of this experience would put us in a burning rage and/or terrorizing despair, perhaps even struggling to discover the justice and compassion of Christ. But we must learn. We must practice the spiritual exercises that will place us in the incarnate presence of the suffering of Christ and help us respond in Christ's name. We can learn to ask in our homilies why Christ's suffering continues in the flesh and blood of these women. Why are we, the church, Christ's body, so slow to respond? How do we deny the blaze of Christ's compassion resisting violence? Are we dead to the Spirit? too complacent? too afraid? unskilled in spiritual practices? How can we too deny Christ in violated women, saying, "We never knew her"?

Taking these questions seriously, we cannot accept homilies about violence against women that have no literal flesh, no experience with abused women. Those homilies deny Christ's continued suffering in and with these women. We question placating and destructive rhetoric about the "sadness of beaten women's plight"; or even worse, their "complicity in it." When we preach such things, we are claiming tacitly that Jesus taunted his human accusers until they could bear it no more and, caving in, crucified him. Stated this plainly, this view is obviously absurd. Those beaten and abused do not deserve further punishment simply because they confront us with our own capacities for violence. Homilies of transforming resistance and compassion recognize, name, and re-member Christ's incarnating presence with these violated women before, during, and after their abuse. Our word and bodies, too, must wait with Christ on behalf of the women, ourselves, and our communities. We must be there to see the transfiguration.

Feminist theologians such as Rebecca Chopp, Carter Heyward, and Dorothee Soelle have offered reconstructions of Christian justice and compassion rooted in the realities of human lives.[2] Preaching as a practice of discerning Christ's incarnation keeps us anchored in those realities by requiring that we spend time with violated women and begin to know them and their stories. We stand in Christian solidarity with those suffering as witnesses and advocates. An effective preaching practice cannot be developed through one or two nights at a shelter. Such visits might alert us to the realities of women's suffering, but they do not offer the continuity and depth required for a spiritually formative practice that can transform our preaching about violence. We, like the beloved disciple, must be committed to a lifelong process of waiting, listening, and staying at the foot of the cross. We must come to know these women, as they give us permission, over time. Otherwise, we cannot begin to connect the suffering of their real bodies with the wounds of knowledge about Christ's suffering, justice, and healing compassion.[3] But this is the hard work of following Christ and learning to preach against violence. Often, we flee from realities of violence; and even if we stay, it is hard to stay long enough to be transformed in our minds, bodies, and hearts. Remaining in our practice is how we learn to preach Christ's suffering and hope. Remaining, listening, and learning, we can begin offering homilies in solidarity with the violated.

I mean by "solidarity" the kind of preaching that makes appropriate connections between the reality of a particular, violated woman and the reality of Christ's woundedness. The word "appropriate" is important because the correlations of human experience and Christ's experiences among us are not directly equivalent. Though we are taking on the qualities of Christ, our imaging of God is incomplete, messy, and complex. So our preaching needs to point to the life-giving connections that reveal the power of suffering and violence as Christ knew it and as we can see it in other human beings. Our preaching must point to those healing convergences between violated women's experiences of discovered self-love and compassion which reflect the embrace of Christ.

Learning to preach from this participatory perspective, we press ourselves and our congregations literally against the body of the Word, now linked with a violated woman. But our preaching will sound hollow, like an endless abstract waiting, if we do not model actual work with violated women. We must *practice* solidarity in our flesh, because their flesh is not theoretical. To learn to preach incarnationally is to think about suffering, forgiveness, responsibility, and pain, as theology and practice. We put our bodies on the line, when invited, in order to learn how to tell others about the living, incarnate dynamic of Christ's presence, comfort, support, and resistance in her and our lives.

Literally being there and pressed makes it much harder for us to sermonize about women's suffering as a way of being "one with Christ." The practices of participation and solidarity help us see clearly with Thomas that the wounds are real, the damage was unjust, and that we, with Christ, must resist all such violence. Like Thomas, our homilies must cry as we come to know these women and their stories, "My Savior and my God."

Discerning the Broader Dimensions of Violence

The suffering and healing of a woman is unique and specific, as was Jesus'. But her suffering and redemption in certain senses are shared, reflecting the whole creation connected with us, the body of Christ. Her literal flesh and blood are both particular and inclusive in Christ. If our preaching is a discernment of Christ's incarnation, it must be both particular and broad. We learn to preach attentive to both individual and systemic violence. Our preaching is enhanced when we are intellectually and experientially informed about the cultural, gender, and economic issues which shape, deny, and/or dismiss violence. Becoming attentive to the single and systemic dimensions of violence also helps us better recognize violence among people different from us. Christ's renewal of the whole creation is for all of us.

This might mean, for example, that we are willing no longer to quickly forgive abusers, even abusers within the Christian community. We now bring to such situations the whole knowledge of our preaching practice of discerning Christ's incarnation, including the discernment of Christ's compassion, confrontation, justice, resistance, and transformation. With Christ, we want to build real bridges of solidarity by naming, remembering, and responding from our practice that it is not the victim's body only which is torn and bleeding: it is the mysterious body of us all now named, remembered, and responding in Christ. The abuser is part of the body. I am part of the body. We all are involved, all implicated. We all have been given the responsibility to respond as members of the body of Christ, seeking justice and compassion for violated women.

Coming to Terms with Our Own Violence

As we discern the presence of Christ in the lives of the abused, we are confronted with the violence in our own lives. Part of our work as preachers is to come to terms with the violence within us, the gap between our own lives and the incarnation of Christ. We recognize our own capacities for sending Christ to Golgotha. As a result, we can publicly preach more about our own truth—that we are able to kill women, to destroy children by beating their mothers, to deny women dignity and self-expression. As our practice deepens, we also come to realize the grace of Christ present to our violence and our abilities to choose abundant life. We can tell the good news that violence can be resisted, that compassion and healing are possible, that responsibility and forgiveness are real because Christ invites us to participate, flesh and bones, in the ongoing incarnation.

PREACHING AS A NONVIOLENT PRACTICE

Preaching that discerns continuities of incarnate life with Christ increases our capacities to communicate how Christ's woundedness touches the wounds of violated women and our own wounds—all of which are different and yet share in the mystery of the incarnation. What we are engaged in is a nonviolent preaching practice. This practice cannot be learned only from books. We must go out and do it, and the great teachers and preachers of the Christian tradition have always known that. As Abba John, a beloved and respected teacher-monk of the Egyptian desert said, "I never taught anyone to do anything [any of the practices] which I did not first do myself."[4] Abba John reminds us that our credibility as teacher/preachers is nil unless we have experienced the truth of Christ's suffering and healing ourselves. We must intentionally develop a nonviolent preaching practice, in this case in the context of the lives of violated women. How do we do that, and what are the transformative effects when we approach preaching as one among other spiritual practices?

Why Spiritual Practices Are Important for Preaching

The Christian tradition is rooted in practices. There were particular rituals, actions, and attitudes through which believers could practice taking on the qualities of Christ. The early monastic communities placed a great deal of emphasis on practices. They found them to be the most effective, holistic, and enriching path for learning how to participate in the ongoing incarnation of Christ. They provided structures and routines for imitating or exercising the daily actions of Jesus' life, practices of prayer, healing, study, worship, proclamation, community life, fasting and feasting, and so forth. By placing one's body, mind, and soul in their rhythm, one was formed in and by Christ's bridging of human and divine suffering and love.[5] These were the training exercises of Christian incarnation, molding believers' passions toward the passions of Christ. They were not about preparing for rarefied lives of spiritual ecstasy. Practices were about the daily, incarnate work of living and loving in a world torn by violence and destruction and open to the grace of transformation.

The assumption was that spiritual practices such as prayer, healing, study, worship, and proclamation involved a lifelong commitment. Re-forming the human heart, body, soul, and mind is strenuous and takes time. Though these disciplines remain part of our tradition, many Christians are not familiar with them. They no longer shape our daily routines. Fundamentally, this means that much of our Christian witness lacks maturity. We are called to a bold and vital life, but we lack the stamina, the strength, and the wisdom that can only be gained through regular exercise or practice. It is not, therefore, unexpected that our preaching is also lackluster and vacuous with regard to the violence faced by too many women, children, and men.

Too often, we find ourselves, like the disciples, unable to respond to Jesus' call to "stay here and keep watch with me . . . watch and pray not to give way to temptation. The spirit is eager, but the flesh is weak. My heart is nearly broken with sorrow. Remain here with me, stay awake and pray."[6] We clamor for a false peace, afraid of the suffering that Christ knew. There is a human and understandable quality in this response, but as Christ's own, we are about living with Christ in the incarnating hope that violence can be confronted and healed. This is the only path for learning true peace. First, we must have the discipline and practiced strength to face violence even when our hearts and minds are overwhelmed, which they will be when we comfort and wait with a sobbing and beaten woman.

But if we have practiced resisting violence toward women, we have at our disposal the presence of Christ and a fuller range of incarnational responses. We are not preoccupied by a false peace. Rather, facing the realities of violence and suffering, we go to visit the wounded, and through that action, we can preach a living word about God's reformation of violence. Abba Theodore of Pherme had a young novice who struggled to learn the real practices of confronting violence and speaking an active gospel word. His advice was the following: "Believe me, I have been a monk for seventy years, and I have not been able to get a single day's peace. And do you want to have peace after eight years?"[7] Facing violence, preaching about violence is not going to bring a quick peace. Nor can we quickly learn and engage the spiritual insight and strength required for genuine peace-making and healing. What then is a nonviolent preaching practice? It is a spiritual discipline that engages our whole selves, our whole lives in exercises of prayer, study, ministry, and preaching against violence, and for compassionate and just peace.

Nonviolent Preaching Practice

If we commit ourselves to a nonviolent preaching practice, we will be re-formed incarnationally with Christ and Christ's body. We will have opportunities to confront evil, despair, greed, envy, and violence, and we will be better able to preach a gospel word about what we have known and seen of Christ in our own experience. Placing ourselves squarely in the center of our human destructiveness and our God-created compassion and justice, we learn to respond with the qualities of Christ. We may find ourselves preaching about the powerful ambiguities of violence, who is violated, and why, while still proclaiming genuine hope amid the gaps between our human selves and the divine.

Having practiced confronting and reflecting on the deep ambiguities of our own lives and the lives of violated women, we have resources for publicly acknowledging that we as humans—even Christians—can both love women and repeatedly beat and demean them or tolerate their being beaten. We can talk from the pulpit about women's self-named beauty while exposing the cultural pressures on women to conform their bodies to impossible expectations of youth and thinness. We will have genuine resources for preaching about the rhetoric espousing women's rights to name their own arenas of success and self-empowerment—rights that are daily denied as women confront "glass ceilings" and put make-up over their bruised faces and blackened eyes.[8]

Because nonviolent preaching practices put us in the midst of the destructive contradictions in ourselves and our communities, for that is where Christ is, we better realize our need for a deeper relationship with Christ. We will learn from Christ how to negotiate our human ambiguity and destruction with our potential for justice and love. We meet, learn about, and become advocates for violated women because Christ is there, and we want and need to be with Christ. So our work for justice with violated women is also part of our practice of developing more intimacy with Christ. In the same way, our practice of solidarity with violated women is part of our reforming our preaching in the presence and image of Christ. To preach the false peace of a fleeting word about violence against women would be to deny Christ and our responsibilities to Christ.

Additionally, as we pursue our preaching practice of resisting violence, we strengthen our skills for recognizing abusers and how to resist them. We know better what it means to stand with and in support of violated women. We can preach calling for the compassion and forgiveness of Christ or stating that forgiveness is premature. We develop capacities with Christ for pursuing the truth of our lives, and so we cannot proclaim just any "good news" but only the "good news" as rooted in real encounters with violence. Our homilies about violence against women are not predictable in detail, but they are consistently witnessing to real experiences of Christ's incarnate justice and compassion in the face of violence in our own day. How many sermons have we heard that have no shared experience with real women who have suffered violence? Unrooted and unpracticed, these sermons have little to do with the living Christ, but are expositions of lifeless texts and stereotypes. These are the homilies of mouths like "open coffins," acts of a certain kind of violence in themselves. Certainly, violated women do not deserve them, and neither do our parishes or communities.

Separated from Christ and violated women, these homilies blame, patronize, and dismiss violated women and the power of Christ for just transformation. They proffer cheap grace via simplistic forms of obedience or cheap condemnation through distorted labels such as "temptress" or "seductress." They leave women who have suffered violence with two fundamental options. They can choose to deny the destructiveness they know and agree to be enslaved to a patriarchal power that isolates them from Christ and their own created participation in the divine. Or they can search for a faith community in which Christ's gospel, resistant to violence against women, is preached and practiced. By God's mercy and our commitment to a nonviolent preaching practice, they will be able to find one.

Clearly, developing preaching as a spiritual practice of nonviolence is crucial for speaking an authentically incarnating word from our pulpits in the face of violence against women. We and members of our parishes must pursue this practice with our full strength through studying scripture and the writings of the mothers and fathers of the church, and placing ourselves in the flesh-and-blood contexts lived by violated women. We must worship and pray mindful of our solidarity with them. If we make this commitment, our sermons will provide significant teaching about Christian responses to violence and experiences of the power of Christ's healing. As Abba Theodore remarked to a young brother, "If you make some attempt at a thing you are discussing, you will discuss [or in our case, preach] it as it truly is."[9]

Learning Preaching as a Practice of Spiritual Formation

Let me now be more specific about the dynamics of preaching as a practice of spiritual formation. What shape does this practice take?

Action. As I have already suggested, to establish our own specific practice, we need to pursue appropriate opportunities for developing mutual relations with violated women. We need to listen to, wait with, and respond to them mindful of the continuing incarnation of Christ.

Reflection. With and in the context of these women's experiences, we must ask questions relevant to preaching: Where is Christ's passion and suffering? Where is God's justice? Who will wash the wounds? What does forgiveness or compassion or responsibility mean now? How do I/How do we as the body of Christ respond to violated women?

Certainly, reading texts about violence against women as well as relevant theological and scriptural texts will help answer these questions. Taking seminars, participating in discussion groups, and journaling can offer us further insight. But in the context of a spiritual practice, some of our answers require being in relationship with beaten, raped, and healing women. Having received their permission, we reflect with them and those from service organizations committed to supporting them. Of course, as with any spiritual practice, we also are always working with our own responses, quandaries, and biases. We focus on how we can integrate our growing relationships with these women, ourselves, and Christ in order to offer clearer and more-faithful preaching about violence against women.

Facing the Gaps. Practicing Christlike solidarity with violated women, we experience personally and in some sense corporately through our parish relationship how we claim one set of responses as Christians while feeling, saying, and doing others. We practice touching the gaps between our reason, emotions, visceral responses, faith, fears, justice, and compassion. Moreover, we discover that these gaps are not only about our relation to these women, but also about the gaps within ourselves. We are faced with the ambivalences, fears, confusions, and evils which trigger violence in our own lives. Experiencing many levels of inadequacy, resistance, and denial within ourselves through our relationships with violated women, we know on a deeper, practiced level the gaps between our rhetoric of taking on the image of Christ and what we actually do. Of course, these realizations also mean that we can learn to bridge those gaps with Christ's help and more-mature practice.

Although such realizations are painful, frightening, and confusing, we must pay attention to them. They are the crucial paths for maturing into the full stature of Christ, who resists all violence against women and proclaims that resistance. Our process also provides some resources to violated women who are struggling to make sense of God after their experiences. Furthermore, the practice of discerning and facing the gaps between where we are and where Christ is offers communities explicit alternatives for rebuilding relationships appropriately when violence has torn them apart. We are developing the tools by which we as a community can recognize the weekly congregant sitting in the front row who is a regular spouse-abuser. As we begin to tell the truth from our pulpits by power of our practice, our parishioners can begin to tell the truth about who in their very midst suffers from violence. Then, our mutual goal as the healing body of Christ is to actively respond in Christlike ways to the abused and the abuser.

Let's look more closely at an example of learning to preach from this practice of action, reflection, and facing the gaps. For many in our parishes, the assumption is that women "ask for" violence. Our practice will have helped us see the destructiveness of that assumption more clearly in others and in ourselves. We discover that this assumption shapes very damaging sermons which can be more dangerous when associated with distorted interpretations of Christian texts. Add all the traditional patriarchal Christian theology about women and we find ourselves facing a daunting challenge to preach authentic good news. Unless we speak from the pulpit directly about the deep assumptions that women are suspect, seductive, and manipulative—if not evil[10]—we will not significantly change violent behaviors. But we can find the courage and wisdom we need from the experiences of our practice. We know women now as Christ knows them, as cherished friends, trusted comrades, and wise sisters.

Through our *action* of solidarity with the abused, we have heard the stories of women who have bled from the power of our culture's and parts of our tradition's stereotypes and abuse. We have gained insight through shared stories about the fallaciousness of the "asking-for-it" assumption. Through our *reflection* on the theological wisdom contained in those stories, we can offer from our pulpits new insights about misinterpreted texts and reconstructed theologies about women which are affirming and just. As we *face the gaps,* we can share with our parishes that we are learning to face our own fears about violence and women through relationships with these women and the grace of Christ. We can offer different paths for living with women in the image of Christ—paths not shaped by controlling, violence, and demeaning behaviors, but by acts of mutuality, solidarity, and compassion.

The Journey

Having a nonviolent preaching practice, we encounter the living and incarnate Christ in the flesh she assumes before us. We cannot pick and choose the lessons, insights, and/or outcomes. We simply pay attention to our commitments to learn to respond in as Christlike a way as our practice enables us. We practice bridging our gaps, encountering the emptiness of the crucifixion by waiting with a raped woman in a rape crisis center. In the presence of Christ, we learn to acknowledge our feelings of resistance and fear even as we participate in liturgies of healing designed and led by violated women. We may even have to practice learning how to give an appropriate homily in such a service—should we be asked.

But all these lessons will strengthen our preaching as an incarnate witness to the just and transformative power of Christ. And this witness is not solely about struggle. It also includes learning to praise and dance with violated and surviving women, preaching homilies about restoration and new life. We can proclaim and embrace the beauty and power of all women defined in their own voices and on their own terms. Our preaching practice keeps us in close, incarnate proximity to the new things God is doing in the midst of seeming devastation for these women and ourselves. We can learn that violated women are teachers of homiletics. Abusers also can be teachers, showing us how strongly and clearly we need to preach against denial, premature forgiveness, and injustice. We reject the noxiously pat and obligatory homilies on "Anti–Violence against Women Sunday" as disembodied and unpracticed preaching. Such sermons have nothing to do with the living flesh and blood of Christ and violated women to whom we have dedicated this portion of our preaching practice.

Our homilies will reflect the whole body of Christ—centers and margins valued equally and attended to responsibly and compassionately. We speak from our pulpits with those who have power and status, and with those whose power and status have been denied or demeaned or who have been killed. We have seen the damage to the margins of the body of Christ and found the center implicated. But we also have seen and therefore can witness to the grace-filled inclusivity of God's reign and its transformative recreation even in the face of our sin. Our parishes can become alive and responsive to rather than dead and lying about violence against women when we tell the good and often difficult news that we have learned.

Of course, preaching and teaching this homiletics of risk and inclusion assumes the kind of long-term commitment expected in any spiritual practice. We are choosing as Christian preachers to be attentive to violence against women by placing our bodies with them in order to learn of them, of Christ, and of ourselves. As a response to violence against women, our preaching practice commits us to an ongoing process of "being saved" and "preaching saved." To renege on this commitment will mean the loss of real bodies and the loss of our walk with Christ in our own day. To hold to it will mean increased spiritual growth with newfound strength and clarity for resisting violence against women. It may mean that we will have to deal with our parish's resistances, even face the threats of job loss. But our practice has taught us the skills for engaging destructiveness while keeping our own egos in balance. Are we ready to take this risk and make our commitment?

SOME PRACTICAL THOUGHTS ABOUT A *PRACTICE*

I have a few pragmatic suggestions for our preaching practice.

Mentors

Recognize that the staff people, volunteers, and supervisors working every day with raped, battered, and silenced women are excellent mentors and guides for our learning. Observe them carefully and learn how they have learned to be present and in solidarity with violated and surviving women. Develop strong relationships with these "beyond-parish" abbas and ammas, the monastic terms for father and mother spiritual directors. Invite them to be mutual designers with you of your spiritual and practical learning. Usually, they have helpful insights about the format of your work, intentions and expectations, and ways of evaluating how you are doing.

Other Disciplines

Use the resources of other spiritual practices, study of scripture, prayer, worship, discussion and reflection, meditation, and the like, for additional clarity. Use journaling or critical incident reports[11] as concrete ways to develop the skills for bridging your own gaps of fear, denial, reawakened memories, and so forth. Engage in this learning together with others and expect that others will have a good deal of expertise about violence against women. Be prepared for their responses and reactions as you work your own spiritual practice, and encourage them. Periodically, reflect on the sites in which you work. Are they still transformative? Do women still find them healing and empowering? Do they remain attentive to and activist on behalf of violated women? Finally, spend as much time reflecting on your preaching practice as on learning homiletic techniques.

Study

Many other specific techniques have been developed that could be very helpful for developing your practice. Read the monastic mothers and fathers. Study how those working with violence design, implement, and evaluate their work.[12] Consult with Christian educators and pastoral care faculty asking them to help you shape your goals and hopes for this practice as well as your practical responses. An interdisciplinary approach is also very important for our preaching practice; therefore, consult materials on violence and race, gender, ethnicity, class, religion, and other factors.

CONCLUSION

There will be changes in our preaching if we approach it as a nonviolent spiritual practice. We should not pretend otherwise to ourselves, our colleagues, or our parishes. We are advocating self-education as incarnational practice which transforms preaching about violence against women by focusing on naming, remembering, resisting, metanoia, and active hope.

Our hope as learners of a preaching practice attending to violence against women is to develop the skillful means and wisdom for incarnating God's justice and compassion in solidarity with violated women. We also hope to learn to preach from that practice, those skills and insights, in ways that will effectively and ethically communicate from the pulpit. We want to embrace Christ's ongoing incarnation in ever-deepening ways by practicing a homiletics of risk. We hope to participate in God's ever-present justice and love in the presence of violated women for healing and transformation.

9

Preaching about Sexual and Domestic Violence

John S. McClure

On a Tuesday morning in early autumn, as Rev. Bill Smith sat in the pastor's study look-ing over the lectionary texts for the coming Sunday's sermon, a knock came at the door. He opened the door to a young woman named Jenny. Jenny was visibly shaken. Bill had performed her marriage several years before, and since that time, Jenny and her husband, Shawn, had been very active in the young-couples group. Jenny sat down to tell her story. She began by saying that she feared for her life. Over the past two years, Shawn had be-come more and more protective, even paranoid about Jenny. He wouldn't let her leave the house or have friendships. He was monitoring her mail. He had begun beating her a year ago. She rolled up her long sleeves and showed Bill several recent bruises. After each beating, Shawn would be nice—begging for forgiveness, presenting her with gifts. She said she knew that as a Christian, she was supposed to forgive him, but last week's beating had left her especially frightened. Shawn had purchased a gun, and she wondered if one day he might use it on her. What could she do?

Bill decided to intervene. In the next twenty-four hours, he received a crash course in state and local law, the psychology of victims and perpetrators of abuse, and pastoral care to the families of survivors. It would take nearly a year of learning for him to feel confident to minister effectively to victims and survivors of domestic violence.

Jenny moved out, and a restraining order was issued to keep Shawn away from her. Word of Jenny's situation quickly seeped out into the corridors of conversation within the congregation. Several members of the congregation told Bill that they thought these were "private" matters. They seemed to imply that what goes on behind the closed doors of family life should be protected at all costs. Bill began to wonder if there were other dangerous secrets in the congregation that were being protected by this unwritten policy of silence. He began to speak openly about his concern for victims and survivors of sex-ual and domestic violence. Little by little, those whose lives had been wounded by vio-lence began to seek out opportunities to speak with him—in premarital counseling set-tings, in conversations, after a small-group Bible study meeting, by appointment in his study. They were glad that the silence had been broken. After several months, in spite of the concern expressed by several members that this was a "private" concern, Bill decided that he would preach a sermon about sexual and domestic violence.

Most congregations, left to themselves, prefer silence on issues of sexual and domestic violence. This is not necessarily because of an evil conspiracy. It is often due to a sense of what constitutes good manners, confidentiality, and the general protection of individual lives and families (the private realm) from the encroachment of public scrutiny. In relation to family violence, however, this code of silence can become a blanket of despair and even a malevolent partner in abuse. It betrays victims and survivors and supports a status quo in which abuse and violence are tolerated, if not condoned. Although there are many ways to break the silence in our churches, the most central and pivotal place of all is from the pulpit. Nowhere else can we so clearly communicate that the church does not turn its back on victims and survivors of abuse.

The purpose of this chapter is to set forth a plan of action for breaking the silence from the pulpit. How can preaching become an active component of a broader ministry related to survivors and perpetrators of domestic or sexual violence? How can Bill preach to Jenny, Shawn, and their congregation?

GOALS: WHAT WE'RE TRYING TO DO

Preachers have three goals when speaking out about sexual and domestic violence from the pulpit.

1. To speak a word of hospitality, resistance, and hope to victims and survivors.
2. To send a message that the church will cease to be a place of easy rationalization and cheap grace for abusers.
3. To invite the congregation as a whole to consider how it might become a "safe place" and a force for compassion and resistance in relation to sexual and domestic violence.

GUIDELINES: HOW TO GET THERE

1. Commitment

Commitment is more than an outward display of solidarity, as important as that can be. Commitment is decisive, existential caring.[1] Initially, commitment of this kind may be experienced as *shock.*[2] For Bill and many other pastors, this shock often comes during face-to-face interaction with someone who has been abused within one's circle of friends, family, or community of faith. This shock may also come about from hearing the testimony of someone we barely know—whose experience, passion, and care move us to a deep level of sympathy and caring.

The second level of commitment involves *risk*, the risk of breaking ranks with the status quo.[3] Risk may begin with intervention, with taking sides. When Bill intervened on Jenny's behalf, he began a process of commitment that broke ranks with those who prefer silence and lack of conflict. At a deeper level, for men especially, it is risky to leave the relative ease provided by patriarchy—to venture into an area that will challenge many deeply ingrained assumptions about gender roles in our society.[4]

Next, there is likely to be some *disorientation*.[5] Not only will Bill find himself rethinking stereotypical gender roles and many of his personal relationships, but his language and theology will probably need reexamination as well. It is important during these early stages of commitment that preachers do not go it alone. Bill needs to find one or two others who will embark on this journey with him or who are already involved. As a man, he will need to find a knowledgeable woman or group of women who will partner with him in his pastoral work with women victims and survivors.[6] He will also need help if he is to risk changing. He will want a listening ear as his theology is reformulated. Partners will help him verbalize and deepen his learning and will hold him accountable throughout the process of change. They will give him much-needed feedback on his personal growth, theology, and preaching.

If Bill stays with it, disorientation gives way to *renewal*. He will begin to find new ways to understand himself in relation to others. He will learn new language, rituals, and theology for life and ministry, and a new set of messages for preaching.

As I will suggest later, some of this life-transforming commitment can be shared in sermons. Without turning the pulpit into a confessional, the congregation can be "let in" on the emotional and spiritual struggle that accompanies these new commitments. From the contours of Bill's journey into caring, others can learn that the journey, while difficult, is possible—and ongoing.

2. Education and Involvement

Education is essential. For Bill, education could mean taking classes on the subject of battering or childhood sexual abuse offered at a local hospital, seminary, or college. He could read several outstanding books on pastoral care to victims and survivors.[7] Bill could also find a social worker or psychologist who will be his mentor. Most of all, he will need to learn about the cycle of abuse and the best ways to intervene as a minister. It is important for Bill to become an advocate in his congregation's committees so that sexual and domestic violence become topics for courses taught at the church. He can also help to promote agencies such as shelters for battered women as worthy projects for the congregation's outreach and mission.

3. A Preaching Plan

Preachers committed to this issue should avoid preaching the "one-shot" sermon about sexual and domestic violence. A broader strategy will take planning. Bill should make a list of issues closely related to sexual and domestic violence that can be preached. The list should include human sexuality, creation in the image of God, justice, compassion, family relationships, marriage, forgiveness, judgment, compassion, hope, power, healing, anger, relationships, and violence. If he is a lectionary preacher, Bill can look for opportunities to speak about sexual and domestic violence as they arise. The lectionary provides openings to address all of the theological issues that are crucial for victims, survivors, and perpetrators to hear. Bill can also preach topical sermons that focus directly on sexual and domestic violence. He could make these topical sermons part of a series of sermons on the family, marriage and family, love and sexuality, the Christian home, or violence.

4. Theology

A nonviolent theology can be preached, not only in sermons that treat violence thematically, but in all sermons. There are significant resources in this book to assist preachers
in the development of a nonviolent theology. A nonviolent theology is a theology in
which violence is clearly identified as evil and in which, in the last analysis, neither the
ways of God toward people nor the ways of God's people toward others are implicitly
or explicitly violent. By saying "in the last analysis," I mean to imply that we do not remain unaware and uncritical of the biblical tradition's collusion with the violence that
we, as interpreters, ultimately refute. We cannot avoid the "texts of terror" in the Bible
or the entire violence-laden sacrificial system that undergirds much of the Old and New
Testaments.[8]

In particular, preachers must rethink substitutionary or blood theologies of the atonement. These doctrines can communicate that God is a God of violence.[9] I recently heard
a sermon on John 3:16 in which an old well-used illustration called "the drawbridge"
was used. The story is about a drawbridge operator whose son is playing on the gears of
the drawbridge when suddenly a train appears only a short distance from the bridge. The
drawbridge operator can either keep the drawbridge up, in which case the passengers on
the train will perish, or he can let the drawbridge down, in which case his son will die.
He chooses the latter, of course, and the passengers are saved. The preacher quickly drew
an analogy to God's love(!), which is so deep that God "gave his only [Child] that whoso-
ever believes in [God] should not perish but have everlasting life."

Imagine what such an illustration communicates to a victim or survivor of childhood
sexual abuse or domestic violence. What is Jenny to think of a God who permits—even
perpetrates—such violence? Is the Redeemer that we worship and emulate in the church
merely a passive victim of a God who is essentially both a benevolent and brutal patri-
arch? The preacher I heard did not intend these things to be communicated. But she had
not asked the essential questions: Is violence *anywhere* in the message that I am com-
municating (ideas, illustrations, quotations, language)? How can I say what I really want
to say without conveying this violent subtext?

Other doctrines will need reassessment as well. As Marie Fortune has demonstrated,
we can learn to preach forgiveness in a way that does not condone and support cycles of
violence in human relationships. Jenny needs to hear that her understanding that she
should forgive Shawn regardless of his actions toward her can help to perpetuate the cycle of domestic violence in which she is caught. She needs to hear that forgiveness for
interpersonal violence is the *last* step, not the first step, in a process in which protection,
accountability, restitution, and vindication are first required.

Preaching nonviolently also requires preachers to reassess how God's power is described in their sermons. Bill can help his listeners rethink all of the "omnis" and "su-
pers" that have been traditionally attached to God—in particular: omniscience, omnipresence, and supernaturalism. Sermons can help people change their normative
assumptions about how God relates to the world. As Marjorie Procter-Smith points out:
"Sermons which speak without nuance of the virtue of 'submitting to the will of God,'
for example, or of the way in which 'God sends us suffering to test our faith' may have
critical or even fatal consequences when heard and believed by a woman who may be
considering leaving an abusive husband."[10] Jenny and Shawn both need to hear regu-

larly that God's relationship with the world is (and thus our relationships with one another in Christ should be) noncoercive, nonmanipulative, and grounded in freedom and love.[11]

Nonviolent theologies will actively communicate the message that violence— whether sexual, psychological, social, economic, or physical—is ultimately inconsistent with biblical faith. Jenny must experience her church and its preachers as hospitable friends and allies who understand suffering and injustice in all of its forms. At the same time, Shawn, as a perpetrator of violence, needs to know that the church is prepared to hold him and others accountable for their violent and unjust actions. Their secret is out, and it will not be tolerated.

5. Illustrations

Preachers need to examine all of their illustrations for complicity with ideologies under-girded by violence. Special care is called for when using older illustrations such as "the drawbridge" illustration above. Bill will need to be aware of the *underside* of sermon illustrations—the veneer of cultural assumptions that many seemingly innocent stories or anecdotes carry about relationships, family roles, marriage, gender, and sexuality.[12]

An important part of naming the reality of sexual and domestic violence is to tell the stories of those who have been abused or battered. Victims need to hear their own situation named and held by the preacher. Although it is inappropriate to talk about one's confidential, pastoral practice, it is possible to tell stories from the pulpit in which battering or abuse is disclosed, though carefully disguised.

Bystanders and perpetrators need to experience abuse as their problem—as "in here," not just "out there." Although statistics can provide a jolt from time to time, they have the tendency to keep this issue "out there." Quoting from newspaper articles, television news programs, or magazines can also have this effect. Brief narratives that particular-ize encounters with battering and abuse as an everyday occurrence in a world identical to that of the congregation will underscore that this problem is immediate and "in our midst."

Sunday morning is not the best time for personal testimonials. In a service of healing and wholeness, however, voluntary testimony by survivors can move both victims and friends into direct confrontation with the pain and suffering caused by battering or sex-ual abuse in a holding environment more profoundly capable of supporting the feelings and emotions that are likely to occur.

6. Audience

According to Marie Fortune, there are three audiences for sermons that speak directly about domestic violence: (1) victims and survivors, (2) perpetrators, and (3) bystanders. Bill will need to keep all three audiences in mind when preaching about sexual and do-mestic violence. When addressing either a portion of a sermon or an entire sermon to a particular audience, Bill should mark verbally who the audience is, in order to signal to the hearers who is being addressed. As he shifts from one audience to another, his ser-mon should change tone and shape.

Victims and Survivors. When preaching to victims and survivors, the liturgy and sermon should become a *holding environment* for pain and suffering.[13] Being careful not to break confidence, Bill might use a narrative to mark the reality of domestic violence or childhood sexual abuse. He can frame the experience of sexual or domestic violence in ways that honor the particularity of the experience itself, being careful not to generalize, stereotype, or presume too much identification. Jenny needs to know that the sanctuary (including the sermon) is a "safe place" where God's people can hear and hold pain and suffering of this type. Bill is welcoming strangers into his sanctuary—inner strangers—who have waited, perhaps for years, to hear their names called and their lives addressed from the pulpit.

One way that we as liturgists and preachers can hold the pain of others is through *lament.* As Nancy Ramsay demonstrates, lamentation is more than an expression of sympathy. Lamentation articulates the godforsakenness experienced by victims of violence within the context of remembering and appealing to God's goodness and compassion.[14] Jenny needs to hear her preacher and her congregation cry out to God on her behalf—pleading her case.

Another way that liturgists and preachers can hold the pain of others is through expressions of solidarity and compassion. As Wendy Farley has pointed out, compassion is the "infinitely varied, infinitely patient power" that "ignites the beauty of a soul after suffering has snuffed it out." Jenny needs to hear her preacher express a depth of solidarity and care—God's and her congregation's—that is a steadfast presence, weeping over what has been lost, resisting further destruction of the self, and framing opportunities for renewal or transformation as they emerge.

Perpetrators. When addressing perpetrators, the sermon becomes an exercise in *clarity.* Our goal is to assess with stark clarity the damage that has been done and to show in no uncertain terms that it cannot be undone. Perpetrators like Shawn need to know that nothing that they can ever do will be able to restore fully what their victims have lost. Nothing will suffice to set things right, whether it be asking for forgiveness, giving gifts, mutilating or destroying oneself, or having a dramatic change of heart and soul. The ability to rationalize and deceive oneself about the consequences of abusing another person must be undermined at every corner.

This is not so much the voice of judgment or condemnation as it is the voice of clarity, and it must pervade every sermon that addresses sexual or domestic violence. Even if we hope in our heart of hearts for eventual transformation for perpetrators, there must be no cracks through which they can slip as they listen to these sermons—no escape route from the clear implications of what they have done. Only this kind of preaching brings the possibility of self-confrontation that could, perhaps, lead to change.

Bystanders. The image that the preacher needs to have in mind when preaching to bystanders is the image of *breaking ranks.* The preacher needs to present a positive image of rebellion from the status quo. Marvin Ellison, in his book *Erotic Justice: A Liberating Ethic of Sexuality*, provides a helpful example: "In a famous experiment, a model prison was set up and staffed by volunteers, each assigned to a role as prisoner or guard. Although many of the 'guards' soon displayed acts of brutality toward their 'prisoners,' some men showed moral sensitivity and refrained from any abuse. These 'good guards,' however, never spoke out to reproach any of their comrades for their misconduct. As a consequence, the brutality rapidly escalated."[15]

Much of Bill's audience consists of "good guards," and his task is to help them see that a simple moral consensus against violence toward women is not enough. Bystanders must be challenged to break ranks with the prison guards of brutal patriarchy altogether, so that abusers do not receive even tacit endorsement for their violent behavior. Bill can show that Christians appeal to a deeper authority to order their way of life. A profound allegiance to the God of compassion will require breaking ranks from "father, mother, sister, and brother" in order to condemn violence and bring about change.

7. Exegesis

Part of the preaching task is to learn how to listen to the biblical text from the perspectives of those who have experienced radical evil in the form of sexual or domestic violence. In order to do this, it is necessary to seek out the wisdom of those who interpret the Bible with these concerns in mind.

Commentaries. Bill needs to purchase commentaries written by exegetes who are sensitized to issues of sexual and domestic violence. Most of these will be women. These commentators typically will have an eye to issues of coercive power, domination, and abuse in relation to women and children. It is hard to find these exegetical perspectives in *series* of commentaries. Bill will have better success looking in commentaries that are designed to highlight these and other feminist issues in biblical interpretation. If possible, several helpful resources should be on Bill's bookshelf:

Adams, Carol J., and Marie Fortune, eds. *Violence against Women and Children: A Christian Theological Sourcebook.* New York: Continuum, 1995.

Bach, Alice. *The Pleasure of Her Text: Feminist Readings of Biblical and Historical Texts.* Philadelphia: Trinity Press International, 1990.

Bellis, Alice Ogden. *Helpmates, Harlots, Heroes: Women's Stories in the Hebrew Bible.* Louisville, Ky.: Westminster/John Knox Press, 1994.

Bronner, Leila Leah. *From Eve to Esther: Rabbinic Reconstructions of Biblical Women.* Gender and Biblical Tradition Series. Louisville, Ky.: Westminster/John Knox Press, 1994.

Brown, Cheryl Anne. *No Longer Be Silent: First Century Jewish Portraits of Biblical Women.* Gender and Biblical Tradition Series. Louisville, Ky.: Westminster/John Knox Press, 1992.

Corrington, Gail Paterson. *Her Image of Salvation: Female Saviors and Formative Christianity.* Gender and Biblical Tradition Series. Louisville, Ky.: Westminster/John Knox Press, 1992.

Darr, Katheryn Pfisterer. *Far More Precious Than Jewels: Perspectives on Biblical Women.* Gender and Biblical Tradition Series. Louisville, Ky.: Westminster/John Knox Press, 1991.

Laffey, Alice L. *An Introduction to the Old Testament: A Feminist Perspective.* Philadelphia: Fortress Press, 1988.

Newsom, Carol A., and Sharon H. Ringe, eds. *The Women's Bible Commentary.* Louisville, Ky.: Westminster/John Knox Press, 1992.

Russell, Letty M., ed. *Feminist Interpretation of the Bible.* Philadelphia: Westminster Press, 1985.

Schottroff, Luise. *Let the Oppressed Go Free: Feminist Perspectives on the New Testament.* Trans. Annemarie S. Kidder. Gender and Biblical Tradition Series. Louisville, Ky.: Westminster/John Knox Press, 1993.

————. *Lydia's Impatient Sisters: A Feminist Social History of Early Christianity.* Trans. Barbara Rumscheidt and Martin Rumscheidt. Louisville, Ky.: Westminster/John Knox Press, 1995.

Trible, Phyllis. *Texts of Terror: Literary-Feminist Readings of Biblical Narratives.* Philadelphia: Fortress Press, 1984.

Weems, Renita J. *Just a Sister Away: A Womanist Vision of Women's Relationships in the Bible.* San Diego: LuraMedia, 1988.

Collaborative Exegesis. Scholars and preachers are becoming aware of the impact of social location on biblical interpretation. Where and with whom we interpret the Bible has tremendous influence on how we hear God's Word for preaching. Elsewhere, I have set forth methods for a collaborative practice of sermon brainstorming.[16]

If Bill wants to interpret the Bible in collaboration with women or men who are survivors of domestic violence or sexual abuse, he can gather with a group of four or five persons who are survivors and engage in conversation about the text to be preached. Such a meeting might take place in a shelter for battered women or with a recovery group. The sermon, without betraying confidentiality, can make use of the themes, dynamics, and narrative trajectories expressed in this conversation.

8. Logic and Language

As preachers, we need to be careful that the language used in our sermons is consistent with our nonviolent message. Initially, this means avoiding the language of judgment, command, coercion, or opposition native to some forms of deductive, oratorical, and sovereign styles of preaching.

Inductive and Narrative Preaching. Inductive and narrative sermons invite the hearer to participate in a shared journey with the preacher. Bill's sermons could include the congregation in his wrestling with the implications of a commitment to justice and recovery for women and children victims and survivors. They could share in his struggles with scripture, theology, and life. Along the way, Bill will identify with his hearers, suggesting plateaus of shared knowledge and insight. Without actually hearing every confessional detail, his congregation can be invited to *overhear* Bill's process of encounter, risk, disorientation, and change.[17]

Conversational Preaching. Perhaps an even better and more inclusive model of preaching makes use of the language and forms of logic found in roundtable conversation.[18] Bill can rethink the language of the sermon by reimagining the sermon itself as a roundtable conversation. The conversation is focused on interpreting a biblical text. In this conversation, as the text is interpreted, he gives voice to the interpretations of many who have not been heard but who are in the congregation: the abused, abusers, bystanders, social workers, families, friends, and more. The conversation is not allowed to wander aimlessly. It has a purpose — to articulate emerging congregational and life-style commitments in response to sexual and domestic violence. In the sermon, the congregants hear what is involved personally, communally, and theologically if they are to live into these commitments. Several forms of logic and language are crucial to roundtable communication and can be used in such a sermon.

Following: "Following" is language that acknowledges that the preacher is following someone else's lead in pursuing a topic. This is an excellent way to draw marginalized voices into conversation in preaching. An example of following is "Listen to the voice of . . . "

Repair: "Repair" is language that demonstrates that the preacher, or someone else in the conversation, has revised his or her thinking based on new information. It is a good way for the preacher to let the congregation in on ways that hearts and minds are changing. Repair usually involves some self-disclosure and self-correction. Examples include: "Until recently, I thought that . . . , but after studying this text and listening to . . . , I've decided that . . . "; "I think that many of us are changing . . . "

Frame resistance: It is important when preaching about sexual or domestic violence for the congregation to experience how certain frames of reference are resisted—indeed, must be resisted—by victims and survivors. Frame resistance is sometimes accomplished by *naming* the frame resisted and describing it. According to Carol J. Adams, we need to be careful not to "elide agency" when speaking about abuse. It is important to identify the agents of abuse. We subtly let people off the hook when we speak only about "violent relationships," "incestuous families," or "battering couples."[19] Examples include, "For abusive men . . . "; "When a man batters . . . "

Frame resistance can also be accomplished by naming the frame of reference of the one who is *resisting:* for example, "Women who have been raped, who see life through the eyes of Tamar . . . "; "For a child who has been molested . . . "

Reframing: "Reframing" is the positive process of seeing different connections and meanings that cast new light upon a topic. The preacher can attribute new frames of reference to those who provide it. For example, "Battered women teach us something that is easily missed . . . "; "There's a connection here that we might never have considered if it weren't for . . . "

Storytelling: Storytelling can be a way of empowering our hearers to enter the conversation. Stories should not be sentimental anecdotes illustrating ideas about suffering that are held by those in positions of status and power. Rather, they should be told in such a way that the battered and abused become our teachers. I heard a good example of this in a sermon some time ago:

> A woman in Massachusetts wrote about her experience of being married to a man who battered her and stopped at nothing to control her and isolate her, including manipulating the children to report on her activities. One day in her prayers, this woman was focusing on a mental image of Christ on the cross. Suddenly, the image moved from being in front of her to being beside her. She understood this to mean that Christ was not going to rescue her like a hero. Instead, Christ was suffering alongside of her and wanted her to be healthful and happy. The decision to leave was up to her, and Christ would remain beside her either way. Because her invisible, inner spiritual world was all-encompassing, Christ would be with her wherever she was. Because her life with God was not confined to a place or time of day or marital status, but was her very world, she could leave her tormentor without leaving God.
>
> She did leave, one day when her husband was distracted in the back yard. It takes courage to leave someone who is likely to come after you in a brutal rage. It takes courage to then become an Episcopal priest, as she did. And it takes boldness to speak the good news of God's grace for battered women.[20]

Commitments, Proposals, and Scenarios. Roundtable conversations always have a purpose. Therefore, it is important to suggest the kinds of commitments that are necessary for Christians and congregations to make a difference. Expressing a commitment is more a statement of solidarity than of consensus, an expression of willingness to act in particular ways despite the risks, ambiguities, and uncertainties that accompany such action. Examples of commitments include "Our commitment as the people of God is . . . "; "Here's where our heart can be . . . "

Even more concretely, proposals for concrete action can be offered. Examples of proposals include "One thing we can do is . . . "; "Maybe we could . . . "

It is also possible to project imaginary scenarios into which the congregation can live. These scenarios may begin with "What if . . . ?" or "Imagine . . . "

Inspiring. In roundtable conversations, it is important to generate a certain amount of enthusiasm for the work at hand. Inspirational language is the language of value, energy, anticipation, and hope. Examples include "We can make a difference" and "God's compassion is at work here."

9. Delivery

There is a cartoon in which a preacher is in a tall pulpit hovering over the first few pews, ranting and raving like a barely chained beast. About four pews back, a young child is whispering to his mother: "What are we going to do if he gets out of there?!" The cartoon identifies another way in which the church and its preaching can be unwittingly complicit with violence. Our nonverbal communication often conveys messages that can be abusive and which can prevent those who have been abused from seeking our help. Bill should videotape his preaching from time to time to see how he is coming across. If fingers are pointing, fists are pounding, postures are imposing, and facial expressions are staring or intrusive, he will need to study and practice alternative body language. His goal is to strive for an authentic and conversational pulpit presence.

CONCLUSION

It should be clear by now that for most of us, preaching about sexual and domestic violence involves a rethinking of our identities, relationships, theology, and every aspect of our preaching. It is not an easy commitment, but it is an absolutely necessary one for the sake of so many who are suffering in our midst and for the increasingly violent society in which we live. Preachers have been silent for long enough. The time is right for churches to get involved, and involvement must include the pulpit. We, as preachers, can become agents of resistance, change, and hope. We can and must break the silence and tell the truth about sexual and domestic violence.

Part 4

Model Sermons

10

Whoever Looks Lustfully

J. Mark Barnes

Text: Matthew 5:27–32

Our subject this morning is a difficult one. The text talks about sin as it relates to relationships between men and women. In particular, it addresses adultery, divorce, and lust. It would be more comfortable to keep quiet about such things, and Christians like us usually do—especially in church. But our sexual being is an important part of our lives. Not to acknowledge the joys and the pains of our sexuality would be to present to God and to one another something less than our full humanity.

Jesus speaks to disciples: "You have heard it said, 'You shall not commit adultery,' but I say to you whoever looks at a woman lustfully has already committed adultery in his heart." The first thing to say is that Jesus says "no" to adultery. His words about lust are an extension of the seventh commandment, not a contradiction of it.

As Jesus' followers, we find ourselves in an uncomfortable place, because we live in a society that seems not to mind adultery all that much. It's quite common in the entertainment media: TV soap operas, best-selling novels, videos. Many marriage counselors treat adultery as a symptom of a failing marriage, or a mistake, or an experiment, but certainly not as a sin. Adultery seems to have become more acceptable, something adults can do with no strings attached.

But if we are to stand with Jesus, we'll stand against this trend. Marriage is a holy covenant rooted in our covenant with God; it is a covenant grounded in fidelity. Adultery, infidelity to the covenant, is sin. This means that adultery shoves another person away; and at the same time, shoves God away; and what's more, shoves one away from oneself. Adultery is a three-way shove like any sin. Adultery, of course, is not the only sin, and sometimes Christian people have acted like it was. Furthermore, adultery is a sin for which God offers forgiveness, no less than for any other sin. But adultery is sin nonetheless, and as such, kills community. An affair has ripples that threaten relationships among family, friends, and colleagues. Adultery risks the whole social fabric of a person's life. There are always shock waves of pain and alienation, the hurt of lies and betrayal. We should be clear that adultery is sin. In Christian community, when sexual attraction turns into a brooding and compulsive desire that threatens marriage vows, the appropriate word, the loving word, is "No! Don't." In a spirit of love for persons, remembering that we are all forgiven sinners, we must speak out in Christ's name: "You shall not commit adultery; this is the law of God."

But Jesus goes on to extend the ancient law. "I say to you, whoever looks at a woman lustfully has already committed adultery in his heart." Jesus' words expose those who, while they have never committed adultery, continue to nurse lust under the cover of their outward respectability. In Jesus' day, it was perfectly legal for a husband to divorce his wife for almost any reason. Anything that the husband might construe as bringing some injury to his reputation—things as small as talking too much, being a less-than-satisfactory cook, having warts—any of these could be written down against the wife and processed through the religious authorities, and the wife would be out. The husband then would be free to pursue another woman until he tired of her, and another, and another. This was perfectly legal. Jesus' extension of the law strips this immorality of its pretense. This pretext of using women and discarding them, no less than adultery, is a form of the sin of lust.

It's important to say that lust is not a synonym for sexual desire. In our everyday speech, we sometimes use the word "lust" to mean the feeling of being attracted sexually to another, but this is not how the Scriptures use the word. Lust is abuse of another in pursuit of one's own sexual gratification. Merely having sexual feelings is not sin. Being attracted sexually to others is part of God's design for creation and is an important part of human relationships. How cold and gray life would be without romantic feelings. But the church too often has communicated the message that if you have these feelings, you are bad. And this message has made us feel so awkward around one another. Men and women are afraid sometimes to be alone in the same room together because they're afraid of their feelings of attraction. Let's not be afraid of the wrong thing: sexual feelings are not bad; it's what we choose to do with feelings that matters. When we allow our sexual urges to become focused on hurting, or overpowering, or in any way depersonalizing others, we are guilty of the sin of lust.

The sin of lust is something with which most of us struggle. When President Jimmy Carter confessed in his widely publicized interview, "I have lust in my heart," he might have been speaking for most of us. Sin gets in and twists the way we look at others. We find ourselves daydreaming about using others for our own gratification. We find ourselves treating others as means of pleasing us without much regard for them. Lust is a very real fact about us and is a temptation ever before us. We are still all working on how we give sexual desire an appropriate place in our lives so that we don't run from it, on one hand, or use it as a weapon, on the other. We still struggle with our sexuality. We need understanding, and we need forgiveness. We have a lot of learning to do.

There are a number of fronts on which we have work to do. Lust may wear the face of promiscuity: sex with no real caring or relational aspect; no ties, no hard goodbyes; no commitments. How can we learn to say "no" to promiscuity without condemning persons? One motive for promiscuity is conquest, and that certainly should be rebuked. But we know now that those who have been sexually abused sometimes react to the horrors of the past by acting promiscuously. We cannot rush in with a spirit of condemnation and hope to do anything but add to the brokenness. How do we say "no" to promiscuity and "yes" to persons? How do we say "no" in a spirit of forgiveness?

Lust may wear the face of pornography. Perhaps it is nowhere clearer that lust kills love than in the path of lonely lust. Here lust pulls a person down into the prison of solitary gratification, bleeding off energy for real relationships and killing the possibility of community. The other human being is so thing-i-fied that he or she has, in fact, become an object—a picture, a book, a video. What response are we to make to sexual manipulation in advertising that seems at least to border on the pornographic? More and more, portions of bodies are being shown without faces. Where should the line be drawn? Christian people need to talk about such matters.

Lust may wear the face of sexual abuse. Men and women cause physical and emotional harm in the gratifying of their sexual desires. Adults in families or outside of families use children as sexual objects. What awful pain and ongoing suffering this causes! How can we be a community where victims and perpetrators alike are freed to ask for help?

Lust may wear the face of sexism. Men may use women, or women may use men, for purposes of their own gratification. Jesus extends the commandment against adultery to protect the rights of women. Most of the moral thinking of his time approached the issue of sexual sin assuming the moral culpability of the woman. Women were regarded as the source of temptation to lust. This is nothing that we modern people are beyond. Several months ago, Bacon's Department Store had a full-page ad in the *Courier Journal* touting a new perfume called Poison. There were only three words on the page, in big, bold letters: "woman," "seduction," "poison!" Sexism twists the picture so that women are seen as responsible for the lust of men. Jesus' interpretation of the law protects women from this unjust accusation. Against those in his day who said that a man could divorce a woman for most any reason, Jesus sided with those who said that only adultery was just cause for divorce. In context, it is a protection for women (not an unfair slap at divorced people, which is how many of us have read it). What's more, Jesus' extension of the law literally reads: "Whoever looks at a woman with a desire to injure her adulterously has already committed adultery in his heart." There is no ambiguity about where Jesus is placing blame: it's on the man, who may very well be trying to pin the blame on the woman. Jesus' extension of the commandment protects the rights of women against sexist cultural norms. Jesus' words imply more than they actually say— namely, that sexism is one face of the sin of lust. The sin of sexism is a way of "looking lustfully" at another. Men use women for self-gratification. Sexism can go the other way around, too; women may also use men. But truthfully, this is not as much of a problem. Ours is a culture in which women are still, in many respects, treated as lesser persons. Ours is a church in which women still struggle to be taken seriously. And the reason for this is that men have inherited a way of looking lustfully at women, with the desire to use them as means to their own ends.

Promiscuity, pornography, sexual abuse, and sexism are some of the cruel faces lust wears among us and in us. And how lust hurts: such pain for both men and women, such awkwardness and distrust! How will we ever find a way out of this hellish impulse to use the wonderful gift of sexuality to hurt and destroy?

There is a way. Where the love of Christ rules, lust loses its power. This is the good news! In the community of Christ, our sexuality may enhance the beauty of our relationships without destroying them.

Jesus did not point out the pervasiveness of lust in order to make us feel helpless. His "but I say to you" is delivered in full consciousness that God is doing something new. In Christ, God has broken the compulsive power of sin. Persons can choose not to look at others as means of self-gratification. We can learn to trust one another in the community of faith.

Now this is something really new! Early Christians were accused of being (among others things) sexual libertines. No one could conceive, in the culture of that time, of men and women getting together for anything other than one thing. They couldn't imagine that something new might be happening—that in Christ, men and women could be companions and friends without having to fear sexual manipulation or violence. A wonderful possibility!

We are given the power to trust one another, and we are given the wisdom by the Spirit, if we ask, to find an appropriate place for sexual attraction within the whole mystery and splendor of human relationships. We don't need to repress our sexuality for fear that it will inevitably ruin us. Lust need not rule us. Women and men can care for one another while learning what is in bounds and what is out of bounds for sisters and brothers in Christ. When attraction begins to turn into calculating, brooding desire to possess, or friendship begins to step over appropriate boundaries, we'll know to say "no!" When subtle sexism creeps in, we'll know to confront persons in love and prevent lust from taking root. We will create an environment of grace, so it is possible for us and for others to ask for help when we feel ourselves succumbing to the harmful power of lust. And we'll become a people of prayer who are confident of God's power to heal and make new. In Jesus Christ, we may do this. We may become a new community of men and women who turn from causing harm and are free to explore new depths of friendship without fear. Life in Christ is such good news!

Of course, saying this is easier than living it. Living in Christ means leaving behind old ways; it means change. And we can find many excuses not to change: "Well, we're too old, you know—too set in our ways" or "We're not old enough yet to worry about these matters" or "It's too scary to talk about, or too shameful." But, you know, someone had better speak about sexual matters. Schools have a few courses in how the body works. Parents are bashful. And our young people face a world that doesn't know the difference between sexual attraction and lust, and doesn't acknowledge that lust kills community. Somebody had better speak.

And why wouldn't it be us? We are the ones who know the good news of love's triumph over lust. We can speak. And we can make this congregation a safe place, a place of reverence and wonder, a place sometimes for tears and even great laughter. Laughter of course! After all, when God created human sexuality, male and female persons, on the sixth day, God saw that it was very good. Not just good, mind you, but very good! It can be so now. Why not here and now? Among us?

11

Wings of Eagles and Holes in the Earth

Marie M. Fortune

Texts: Psalms 22, 55

Spirit of the living God, fall afresh on us. Open our ears and eyes, our hearts and minds. Prepare us to hear the truth before us, the truth that makes us flinch before it sets us free. Sit close by us this morning as we continue in our worship together. Amen.

Three days before Christmas, Delia Alaniz, thirty-six, was sentenced to ten years in prison by Judge Harry Follman in Skagit County (Washington) Superior Court. She had pleaded guilty to second-degree murder for hiring a contract killer to kill her husband, who had physically and sexually abused her for seventeen years. He had also beaten and molested their four children, ages eight to sixteen, for years. He threatened to go to their daughter instead; he threatened to rape her daughter in front of her. He held a gun to the children's heads, demanding that they tell him who their mother's lover was; he beat them with a whip. Terrorized for most of their lives, the children now have nightmares about their father coming back and raping their sister.

During the years of her abuse, Alaniz had gone to a shelter in Bellingham; she had had her husband arrested, only to see him released the next day; she had escaped to her sister's house, only to have him physically threaten other family members; she had taken out a protective order against him, and he beat her for it; she had come to Seattle in 1987, only to be turned away from a shelter because she had her fifteen-year-old son with her; she had her sister move into her house to protect her, but her husband's violence continued; she separated from him and tried to live alone, but he would not let her go and kept her under surveillance. She was terrified of him, and she knew there was no place else to go where she and her children could be safe. In desperation, she stopped his violence by having him killed. She is now serving her ten-year sentence in maximum security at Purdy Correctional Center.

If ever there was a woman who knows deep inside what Psalm 55 is talking about, it is Delia Alaniz. Put yourself in her place for a moment and listen to these words:

> Give ear to my prayer, O God;
>   do not hide yourself from my supplication.
> Attend to me, and answer me;
>   I am troubled in my complaint. . . .
> My heart is in anguish within me,

> the terrors of death have fallen upon me.
> Fear and trembling come upon me,
>   and horror overwhelms me.
> And I say, "O that I had wings like a dove!
>   I would fly away and be at rest;
> truly, I would flee far away;
>   I would lodge in the wilderness;
> I would hurry to find a shelter for myself
>   from the raging wind and tempest." (Ps. 55:1–2a, 4–8)

This was the terror that Delia knew for seventeen years. This was the terror that the children knew.

In Psalm 22, we also hear this fear described:

> I am poured out like water,
> and all my bones are out of joint;
> my heart is like wax;
> it is melted within my breast;
> my mouth is dried up like a potsherd,
> and my tongue sticks to my jaws;
> you lay me in the dust of death. (Ps. 22:14–15)

The psalmist knew how it feels to be terrorized.

And the psalmist also knew how it feels to be terrorized by someone very, very close, as did Delia:

> It is not enemies who taunt me—
>   I could bear that;
> it is not adversaries who deal insolently with me—
>   I could hide from them.
> But it is you, my equal,
>   my companion, my familiar friend,
> with whom I kept pleasant company;
>   we walked in the house of God with the throng. (Ps. 55:12–14)

It was not an enemy; it was her husband, the father of her children. One might expect this assaultive behavior from a stranger or an adversary, but one does not expect and should not expect such things from the one to whom one is joined in the covenant of marriage.

Then the psalmist goes on and offers a promise:

> But I call upon God
>   and God will save me. . . .
> Evening and morning and at noon
>   I utter my complaint and moan,
> and God will hear my voice.
>   God will redeem me unharmed
> from the battle that I wage,

for many are arrayed against me. (Ps. 55:16, 18)
For God did not despise or abhor
 the affliction of the afflicted;
God did not hide God's face from [her]
 but heard when [she] cried to God. (Ps. 22:24)

The psalmist is telling us God has promised to be there, to hear our cry, not to desert us, no matter what. Can this be true?

Not only will God be present, says the psalmist, but there is judgment on those who bring terror and suffering, who break their covenants—and a word of prediction:

But you, Oh God, will chase them down
 into the lowest pit;
the bloodthirsty and treacherous
 shall not live out half their days. (Ps. 55:23)

So it was with Roy Alaniz, a man of blood and treachery. He did not live out half his days.

We have here a tragedy, lived out for seventeen years and extended for perhaps another ten—even unto the next generation, as the Alaniz children are now deprived of their mother.

Delia and her children lived with fear every day in their home. Some of us have some idea of what Delia has lived through, although few of us could compare our experiences to hers. For those of us who, because of gender, race, class, sexual orientation, or age, are vulnerable to violence, fear is a constant companion.

It is safe to assume that every woman here today has felt the fear of physical or sexual attack; some carry the memory as well. There are many of us who as children felt fear in the threat of a bigger, older child or of an abusive parent. For a person of color, the fear that grips one's stomach when walking down the street and encountering a group of young white skinheads is very real.

Fear is especially intense for some of us because we know that we are at a disadvantage. While anyone can be the target of violence, some of us are much more likely to have this experience simply because of who we are.

Howard Thurman, the black pastor and theologian whose writings convey profound insight into the human condition, observed: "When the power and tools of violence are on one side, the fact that there is no available and recognized protection from violence makes the resulting fear deeply terrifying." Again Thurman: "Physical violence . . . need not fulfill itself in order to work its perfect havoc in [our] souls. . . . Fear, then, becomes the safety device with which the oppressed surround themselves in order to give some measure of protection from complete nervous collapse."[1]

How do we protect ourselves? By accommodating our behavior in order to reduce our vulnerability to violence.

As women, it is second nature to us to check the back seat of our car before we get in; it is second nature to feel our heart race when we hear footsteps behind us; it is second nature to decline an invitation to an evening meeting because we are afraid to go out at night; it was second nature for Delia to feel her neck muscles tighten whenever Roy walked into the room.

We agree to limit our lives as an accommodation to fear. Not only did Delia limit her life, she tried every means available to protect herself. Leaving him, seeking shelter, calling the police, having him arrested, not having him arrested, getting a restraining order, calling on her family for support—you name it, she tried it. But still he came after her.

It is very easy in response to Delia's case to conclude that it is an extraordinary situation, a rare occurrence. And yes, it is tragic, but she knew before she had him killed that there would be serious consequences.

Well, it is not so extraordinary; there are many women facing the choice that Delia faced every day. There are many women who have tried every available means to stop the violence in their lives, and yet it goes on. There are many women who have chosen to defend themselves and are serving life sentences in prison.

In fact, this could easily be you or I locked in maximum security at Purdy. If any one of us had chosen to defend herself and her children from an attacker, she could be serving a long sentence for that choice—you or I.

So where is God's promise to us? Where is God's promise to Delia? Where is God's promise to those who choose to protect themselves in the face of violence? The book of Revelation is a somewhat peculiar place to look for God's word in all this, yet here we do find it.

In Revelation, we are given this powerful image of the great dragon pursuing the woman who had recently given birth; she is obviously very vulnerable. But God gives her the wings of a great eagle in order to escape the serpent who pursued her and poured forth water by which to drown her. The earth, scripture says, opens its mouth and swallows the flood. The woman is safe; the dragon is angry and goes off to continue its attack on those who bear witness to Jesus. It is a very powerful image: God sends the woman the means to protect herself from the power of evil. And the earth itself is her mainstay, her protector.

Traditionally, this passage has been interpreted as a grand metaphor of the church in its struggle with the devil. The woman represents the church with the Christ child, and the devil represents the dragon. God finally saves the church.

Let me suggest a slightly different metaphor here: I suggest that the woman represents women and the dragon represents violence against us. As we know very well, this dragon persists in brutalizing those who are seen as most vulnerable in our society—women and children.

Of course, we must realize that the eagle's wings and the hole in the earth that save the woman do not defeat the dragon so that everyone lives happily ever after. The dragon goes elsewhere and directs his venom and misogyny at others. But God is very clear about where God stands in all of this.

God offers sanctuary to those who are vulnerable. God offers a safe place, a respite. God gives us the wings of an eagle, and the earth swallows up the efforts of our assailants to destroy us.

Perhaps we should pray for these: pray for an eagle's wings for Delia; pray for a great hole in the earth to swallow the system that continues to punish her for trying to protect herself and her children.

The role that God takes and the role that God expects of all of us is clear: It is to stand with, to be in solidarity with, those who are vulnerable and threatened by violence and harm. It is to provide sanctuary and to seek justice.

What justice is served by a ten-year sentence for Delia? When she is released, her youngest child will be an adult. Her husband's violence deprived her children of a home free from fear; now the state will deprive these children of their mother, the one person who could help them heal from this trauma.

Now I am sure that some of you are uncomfortable with the implications of what I am saying. I appreciate that. Ethically, this case raises the larger issue of self-defense. Whenever any one of us takes the life of another human being, we should be called to account for our actions. It is the accounting we give that matters. Self-defense is the accounting to be given in this case.

But there are two aspects of this as a self-defense case that are ethically troublesome for some people and involve subtleties that the law has difficulty grasping: premeditation and hiring a contract killer.

Supposedly, premeditation precludes self-defense. Legally, one can only defend oneself if *in the midst of being attacked,* one chooses to strike back, and in doing so, injures or kills the attacker. This may be a reasonable view of an attack by a stranger, but it is unreasonable in understanding an attack by a husband.

The thing about wife-abuse is that it is a series of assaults that take place over time, often increasing in severity. The victim knows the pattern well and knows the terrorism of which her partner is capable. She also knows that given her lesser physical strength and her fear of what her partner will do to her and her children, she is very unlikely to be able to stop him in the midst of an attack. The only way to stop his terrorism is to pre-empt his violence by striking before he can attack again.

And why didn't she do it herself? Most likely because she was so terrified of him that she knew she could never face him, even with a weapon in her hand. She agreed that someone who could do it would do it. An agent acted on her behalf.

In sentencing Alaniz, the judge lectured her: "Our criminal justice system is not perfect, but it works." He told her that she should have used it. Of course, she had used it, and it had not protected her. Now the system is punishing her for its own failings.

The killing of Roy Alaniz was not the failure of Delia Alaniz's moral character; it was the failure of our community. We, the community and the legal system, did not protect her from him. Even here, with the Domestic Violence Act, inadequate enforcement and too few social services to support victims mean that we cannot, in fact, guarantee the protection of battered women and their children from their batterers. Until we can, women will choose this last resort to end the violence in their lives.

They should be called to account for this choice. But they should not be punished for it.

There is something we can do for Delia Alaniz. We can ask the governor for clemency; we can ask that her sentence be commuted to time already served. If you would like more information, see me after the service.

The prophet John believed that ultimately God would set things perfectly right; evil would be dethroned and righteousness exalted. As part of this process, God asks for our help. We are the eagles' wings; we are the holes in the earth. It is for us to provide sanctuary, protection, and justice. May God give us the love, the concern, and the means that we will need.

Let us pray: Spirit of the living God, who moves across the face of our hearts, open us to one another so that we might fully comprehend that when one of us suffers injustice, we all suffer injustice.

Make your presence real to us here today; may we taste it and feel it and hear it as it binds us one to the other. Move us and shake us to help bring an end to the affliction of the afflicted.

Use us as eagles' wings, as great holes in the earth, to bring safety and solace to those who live in fear.

Grant us courage and strength. Grant us your peace. Now and always.
Amen.

12

When Will We Hear Her "No!"?

Karen Brau

Text: 2 Samuel 13:1–22

This week's *Baltimore Sun* carried a small article about a woman who was raped under a bridge in the city. She was threatened with a knife and then assaulted. After the attack, her screams were heard by the police. She was six months pregnant.

If this were a unique story, its horror alone would be upsetting. But in city after city, and in community after community, women are raped each day. Over and over, women who cry "no!" are ignored.

How do we respond to this newspaper story? How do we respond to the many unreported rapes that happen each day? How do we deal with our own rage and anguish at the ongoing incidence of violence toward women?

Yet none of this violence is new. In 2 Samuel, 13:1–22, a story of royal rape is recorded. It is a story of desire, a story of deception, a story of degradation. And the question becomes, is it a story with any hope?

This text is in the midst of the story of King David and his family. In chapter 13, we hear about David's daughter Tamar, who is described as a beautiful young woman and the sister of Amnon and Absalom. Then we hear that her brother Amnon has fallen in love with her. In fact, Amnon is so taken by Tamar and so wants to have her as his own that he becomes lovesick.

Now Amnon has a friend named Jonadab, who is known as a very crafty person. When Jonadab sees that Amnon is so upset, he asks what is going on. Amnon confesses that he is in love with his sister Tamar, and crafty Jonadab has an immediate suggestion. He tells Amnon to pretend that he is ill and to request that his father send Tamar to his room so that she can make him some cakes. And wouldn't it be lovely to eat from her hand?

Amnon follows Jonadab's plan, and sure enough, King David complies. Soon we hear that Tamar is in Amnon's room making cakes for him. Yet Amnon desires more than cakes from Tamar, so he sends everyone else away. When Tamar finishes the cakes and brings them to Amnon, he grabs her by the arm and says he wants to lie with her. She pulls away and says "no!" She protests, saying that this is wrong. Tamar attempts to reason with Amnon and suggests that he just ask King David for her. But Amnon does not listen to Tamar's "no!" He doesn't listen to her reason. And because he is physically stronger than she is, he rapes her.

After the deed is done, the love that Amnon supposedly had for Tamar is replaced by revulsion for his victim. And a disgusted Amnon demands that Tamar leave immediately. Again Tamar says, "no!" She explains that sending her away after raping her would be worse than the rape itself. But Amnon still can't hear her, so he sends her away.

A devastated Tamar rushes out of the room, puts ashes on her head, tears her long robe, and weeps loudly. Her cries are heard by her brother Absalom, who comforts Tamar and who takes her into his household, where she lives out the remainder of her broken life.

In this sad story, we wonder, "Where is God?"—the Sovereign God, the one who gives strength to David to defeat Goliath; the Sovereign God, the one who parts the Red Sea and leads the people out of Egypt; the Sovereign God, the one who brings down Israel's enemies in a moment. Why is there no one to rescue Tamar? Why is there no one to intervene on the side of justice? Why is there no one to give Tamar the strength to resist someone who is physically stronger than she? Or is there a divine presence in this story? Is the Holy One in Amnon's chamber?

Initially, Tamar is silent when she is summoned to minister to her brother's needs. She is silent as she prepares cakes for him to eat. She is silent as Amnon clears the room of everyone. She is silent as Amnon commands her to come to his side and to feed him.

But Tamar does find her voice, and she finds it when Amnon says, "Come lie with me, my sister." Tamar finds her voice when her brother grabs hold of her arm in an unbrotherly fashion. Tamar finds her voice when her brother demands that she give him her body. Tamar finds her voice in the face of her attacker and cries out, "No, brother, do not force me; for such a thing is not done in Israel, do not do anything so vile!"

And I think it is there—where Tamar speaks for herself with a mighty "no!"—that God is profoundly present. For the God of love, who says "yes" to hope and wholeness and who says "yes" to life also says "no!" to death, "no!" to violation, and "no!" to rape.

But Amnon cannot hear Tamar's "no!" And by ignoring Tamar's strong resistance, Amnon ignores God's resistance, coming through the voice of a young woman. Yet, in many ways, that's not surprising. For over and over it's the mighty and the strong that triumph and have their way.

But remember Mary's words in Luke: "My soul magnifies God, and my spirit rejoices in God my savior, for God has looked with favor on the lowliness of God's servant." It goes on: God "has brought the powerful down from their thrones, and lifted up the lowly."

And the lowly child of Mary, when he walked the earth, preached and lived a life that valued all of God's children. And when Jesus was crucified and hung on the cross to die, he seemed to be defeated. But it was early Easter morning that it became apparent that Jesus Christ was saying "no!" to death and "yes!" to life.

The power of God does come through in big battles and dramatic encounters, yet it also comes through in the lives and the voices of women: young women, older women, daughters of kings, daughters of the poor.

Women who over and over say "no" to death and "yes" to life. And God continues to speak through women today: women in Bosnia who say "no!" to rape as a method of war, women in El Salvador who say "no!" to rape as a way of political control, a woman in Baltimore who says "no!" to rape and the damage it might do her unborn child.

God continues to speak through the voices of women who resist the notion that women's bodies are a commodity that can be taken and used for violent purposes. God continues to speak through the voice of women and men who understand that the community of God calls us to respect the value of each individual and who acknowledge that when one sister is hurt, we are all hurt.

So is there any wholeness in the midst of ongoing violence toward women? Is there any hope? I believe hope comes as we strive to hear the word of God—the holy "no!"— and as we respect the "no!" that means a resistance to violence toward women.

I believe hope comes when we support the victims of rape, just as Absalom took his sister Tamar into his household and cared for her. We need to find ways to care for victims of rape who are members of God's household.

I believe hope comes when we hold rapists accountable for their actions, making certain that justice is carried out. In the sadness in the story of Tamar, we strive to find hope.

And later on in 2 Samuel, we hear that Tamar's brother Absalom has a child, a girl child who is beautiful and who is named Tamar. A strong woman who seems to be defeated by violence lives on in a child.

And in the newspaper article in Baltimore, I read that the pregnant woman who was raped was rushed to the hospital, where she gave birth to a healthy child.

There are signs of hope in the midst of sadness. And this hope will grow when we find ways to teach all of our children that our bodies are to be respected and cherished— not used or abused; and that over and over, our loving God says "yes" to life and "no" to death; "yes" to dignity and "no" to degradation; "yes" to respect and "no" to rape.

May we not only hear the Word of God, but may our lives show that we're actually listening. Amen.

13

Manna in the Wilderness

Anne Marie Hunter

Texts: Exodus 16:1–12, 17:5–7; Psalm 105

I have been a battered woman.
I have known the church to be hurtful.
I have known the church to be helpful.
I have been an advocate for battered women in a battered women's shelter.
I have been a pastor in a local church and have struggled between being helpful and being hurtful.
So I have seen the problem of domestic violence from many different perspectives.

Domestic violence has been talked about a lot lately. But what is domestic violence, really? As you know, domestic violence is an "equal-opportunity employer"—that is, it crosses all levels of income and education, all colors, classes, creeds. It is in our neighborhoods, our homes, our schools, and our churches.

Domestic violence often has a physical component, with which we are most familiar. It is kicking, hitting, dragging, punching, shooting, knifing, bludgeoning. Domestic violence is the black eyes, the chipped teeth, the broken bones, the hospital visits that are a part of so many women's lives.

But domestic violence can also be verbal. It can be name-calling and constant accusations (that you are having an affair, spending too much money, not taking good enough care of the kids, not keeping the house clean enough, and so forth). When I was in an abusive relationship, I was told that I was stupid, fat, ugly, lazy, irresponsible, and childish. In the mind of my abuser, these accusations justified the abuse and control.

Domestic violence is also isolation. Victims are systematically distanced from friends and family, so that their dependence on the abuser is maximized. I was not allowed to talk to my friends or visit my family. Phone calls home were monitored and actively discouraged. My husband once commented, "I hate it when you see your family. It takes me a week afterward to get you back under control."

Verbal abuse and isolation work together to form another important component of domestic violence—mind control or brainwashing. Because it is humanly impossible to maintain your sense of what's "real" and "true" all by yourself, a battered woman, like a prisoner of war, comes to believe that the "reality" framed by her oppressor is true. Isolation and verbal abuse are powerful tools in the batterer's attempts to make the victim believe all the accusations, threats, and justifications for the abuse. Even though I only weighed ninety-eight pounds, I really did believe that I was fat. I really did believe that I was stupid, childish, and generally pretty worthless.

Domestic violence is also emotional abuse. It is constant surveillance, constant undermining of your self-image. It is threats to children, family members, and pets. It is love that is always conditional, always scarce, always unpredictable. It is spending your life "walking on eggshells," monitoring everything you do to try to avoid further abuse. It is abuse which is followed by contrition, apologies, tears, and promises to change that never materialize. Domestic violence is all the "mind games" that make you feel like you are losing your grip on reality.

Domestic violence is also financial abuse. Victims are kept from spending money that they earned, or they are not allowed to work outside the home. Victims have to beg for enough money to buy a carton of milk for their children, and then they have to bring back a receipt and change. Victims are kept from using financial resources that belong to the family unless they have gotten "approval" from their partner. Many women with whom I have worked have money for clothes, make-up, and new tea towels, but can't get their hands on money for a lawyer or another place to live. I was not allowed to handle money, and I had no checkbook or credit cards.

Domestic violence is also sexual abuse. It includes sex that is rapid-fire, abrupt, and unloving, sex without warmth or love or affirmation, sex that makes you feel used, sexual acts that you are forced to participate in, or rape. Many women have told me about being beaten severely, then immediately forced to have sex.

In the final analysis, domestic violence is *control*. It's a very effective way for the abuser to get the victim to do what he wants, or give him what he wants, or act the way he wants. It's a very effective way for the abuser to keep the victim down, to get his own way, or to win every argument. Domestic violence *works*. That's why abusers use it.

When you add up all these components of domestic violence—physical, emotional, verbal, sexual, and financial abuse—you begin to appreciate that domestic violence is also spiritual abuse. There is no way that you can beat up on someone's mind and body without also affecting her soul. Domestic violence bruised my body, undermined my self-image, deprived me of my family and friends, separated me from my identity. But it also shriveled my soul and starved that part of me that is most fully "me."

I was in an abusive marriage for four years. I stayed because I had made a vow before God; I had been taught to forgive seven times seventy; I had been told to turn the other cheek; I had learned to forgive and forget. I stayed because of some of my best qualities: I am loyal, hard-working, determined, and persistent. I do not easily break commitments. I take responsibility for making my relationships work. When you are a victim of domestic violence, even your own best qualities will be used as weapons against you.

When I finally left the relationship, I wandered. I didn't know where to turn. I didn't know what I wanted. I didn't know what to do. I didn't know where I was. I didn't know who I was. And, most important, I didn't know who God was. I wandered for two and a half years before I got my feet on the ground again.

As I work with other battered women, in the shelter and in my church, I notice that they do a lot of wandering, too. Domestic violence seems to steal your soul and your identity so much that it's hard to know where to turn as you try to make major decisions and "do the right thing." It reminds me of the Israelites leaving Egypt and how they wandered in the wilderness for forty years. The story of the Exodus expresses for me the panic and the pitfalls of that wandering.

For example, recent studies have shown that battered women leave their batterers an average of six times before they are able to make the final break. There are many reasons for this. One is the lack of support that battered women find in the larger community. Often communities fail to provide the safety and support that women need to live "in the wilderness." Many battered women are homeless and hungry after they leave.

But remember, even the Israelites wanted to return to Egypt. On the brink of the Red Sea, they panicked and cried out to Moses, "Was it because there were no graves in Egypt that you have taken us away to die in the wilderness?" (Exod. 14:11). And again, when they were hungry, they complained, "If only we had died by the hand of God in the land of Egypt, when we sat by the fleshpots and ate our fill of bread; for you have brought us out into this wilderness to kill this whole assembly with hunger" (Exod. 16:3).

It is important, as we in the religious community work with victims of abuse, not to lose patience with battered women who return to the batterer. It is only human to want to return to what is known when faced with a vast and terrifying unknown. Even the chosen people of God wanted to return to Egypt, where at least they had food and shelter.

When the Israelites threatened to return to Egypt, God provided them with manna in the wilderness—that is, with sustenance for their journey. We, as the church community, need to be manna in the wilderness to battered women. Every pastor should know how to make a safety plan and how to refer a victim to local battered women's services and to the local domestic violence police officers. Every pastor should be able to address the faith issues with which battered women struggle: forgiveness, suffering, and the nature of covenant, for example. Every pastor should preach about domestic violence and include domestic violence in premarital counseling and in pastoral prayers. Every pastor should be able to respond to the perennial "wilderness" question: "Is God with me or not?" When battered women are struggling with whether they are making the right choices or doing the right thing, they need to know: "Is God with me or not?"

It is important, too, that we not lose patience with victims of abuse when they seem to go off on a tangent. As we see in the Exodus story, leaving oppression and moving toward freedom is a process, not a one-time event. Even with God's guidance, it took the Israelites forty years to reach the Promised Land. I know that in my own life, this "wandering" time was one of trial and error and searching. I had trouble keeping relationships on an even keel. I hopped from one interest to another. I wasn't sure what was important in my life. Remember that even the followers of Moses worshiped false gods in the wilderness.

When the Israelites lost their sense of who they were and where they were going, God reminded them of how far they had come, and helped them to envision the Promised Land. We in the church community need to model a "Promised Land" that victims of domestic violence can see and feel and touch. We need to model relationships that are based on mutuality and equality. We need to model what it is to share power across gender, race, class, and age lines. We need to model respect and appropriate boundaries in our family relationships as well as in our parish relationships. The battered women in our parishes need the church's help to see the Promised Land.

In today's world, battered women are the ones who are wandering in the wilderness, with their souls shriveled by oppression. For women of faith, the church, the Bible, the faith community, and the pastor can be stumbling blocks or support. It's up to us to decide to be the manna that battered women need in the wilderness.

Shortly after I left my abusive marriage, my priest called me in to talk to him. I had not told him what was going on because no one in my church had ever talked about domestic violence, so I assumed that I was the first one this had ever happened to. I gladly went in to talk to the priest because I knew that I needed the support of my religious community.

It turned out that my husband had called the priest and "filled him in" on the situation. So the priest started our meeting by asking me why I had abandoned my marriage. Already upset at the word "abandoned," I stammered out that when I tried to be myself in this marriage, my partner would get violent. That was the opening the priest needed. "All you people in the younger generation think about is me, me, me," he shouted at me. "You are always abandoning your commitments to other people in order to be yourself or find yourself." He then told me that my husband had had a religious conversion and was in the chapel on his knees at that very moment, praying for me to come back. "Now it's your turn to forgive and forget."

I had been raised in the church and taught to respect priestly pronouncements. But I just couldn't "forgive and forget." There had been too many promises to change. I just couldn't trust my husband, and I told the priest that. He said to me, "You must not be a Christian, because you obviously don't believe in the power of the Holy Spirit to change a person."

I felt as though God had turned God's back on me. I had been declared unfaithful, un-Christian, beyond the pale. I walked out of the interview and out of that church. If it hadn't been for my very level-headed mother, I would have returned to the abuse that day.

Not long after that, I went to talk to a clergywoman I had met in town. Her name was Barbara. I told her my story, and she listened to me and believed me. She was helpful, patient, and concerned. She didn't try to tell me what to do, but she helped me to focus. I was struggling so hard to do what God would have me do. But Barbara said: "I just don't see how it can be God's will that someone be beaten up in a marriage. I just don't think God would do that." That comment helped to free me from my concern about breaking my marriage covenant, and helped me to see that the covenant was broken by the abuser's violence, not by my leaving.

I began to attend a local United Methodist church, where two wonderful pastors helped me to put myself back together and sort through my guilt, humiliation, and confusion. I began to understand forgiveness and suffering in a new way. I began to see the Promised Land where relationships that empower rather than suppress are the norm. I received manna in my wilderness from that church, from my pastors, and from my friends and family. Without that manna, I would be in Egypt today.

For the church, being manna means that we nurture, support, and sustain a person who is experiencing violence in her home. It does not mean that we tell her what to do—remember that the people wandering in the wilderness have the pillar of fire sent by God to show them the way. Manna is meant to nourish and nurture people on the way.

Being manna in the wilderness for battered women means that we have to be willing to walk in the wilderness. It is a wilderness of fear and disorientation. It is a wilderness of struggle and confusion. It is a dry, deathly place.

Being manna in the wilderness means that we have to be willing to stand with battered women as they ask the tough questions:

Who is God?
What does "suffering" mean?
Does God want me to suffer?
Does suffering lead to salvation?
If Christ suffered for me, does that mean I should suffer to be more Christlike?
Is this my cross to bear?
Am I supposed to forgive seven times seventy?
Am I supposed to turn the other cheek?

It has been sixteen years since I left my abuser. I have gone to seminary and become a pastor. I am happily married with two young children, and I take great delight in my family. I have lived the tough questions for a long time, and I relive those tough questions whenever I work with a battered woman of faith.

I have begun to live the answers, too. I believe in a God who stands with the oppressed, who hears their cries, and who moves in human history to end oppression and establish justice. I believe that Jesus suffered because he opposed institutionalized injustice and oppression. He was crucified by the people whose abusive power he undermined. Salvation came not because of Jesus' suffering and crucifixion, but because of God's decision to answer injustice, suffering, and death with new life. Our job as Christians is not to continue suffering and crucifixion but to establish new life, wholeness, and resurrection.

I believe that, like Jesus, we are called to hold people who abuse power to accountability. As the Jesus story tells us, it is a difficult and dangerous undertaking. That is why we need a community, the church, to move and work with us. For batterers, "accountability" means taking responsibility for past abusive behavior and getting long-term help from people who are trained and experienced in dealing with abusive behaviors. I believe that abusive people must change their behavior. Then and only then is forgiveness appropriate or possible.

I believe that all of us abuse power in some way across lines of race, faith, age, class, gender, education, sexual orientation, and physical ability. All of us must choose, every day, to change abusive behaviors and to end the suffering caused by our own abuses of power.

I know that I am called to be manna in the wilderness for battered women, but I believe that the church is also called: to stop crucifixion, to live resurrection, to be manna for those who are called out of oppression, to ask the wilderness questions.

The wilderness is one of the toughest places you will ever be, but it is also, for me, the place of most-profound ministry, the place of most-profound renewal, the place of most-profound questioning, the place of most-profound relationship to God. It is a place of resurrection. Not for nothing did Jesus' ministry begin with forty days in the desert.

See you there?!

14

Amnon's Folly

W. Eugene March

Text: 2 Samuel 13:7–19

This is not the usual lectionary text, nor is it an example of how to resolve conflict. And least of all is it a Dan Quayle family-values text. It is a sober, honest glimpse into a dysfunctional family. It is a terrible, terrifying account of an attempted seduction that turns into a forceful rape. The language of the New Revised Standard Version isn't quite strong enough to say either what Amnon said to Tamar or what she said back. "Come lie with me, my sister," doesn't quite catch the force of what is going on. He grabs her and throws her down and says, "I'm going to have you!" It is a terrible story, a story of a violent rape. It is an important portrayal of how one can be captivated and destroyed by lust.

This is an important story for us to consider. What's more, it is a story about Jesus' family—yes, Jesus, the one who hosts us at this table. This is his family. These are his forebears. He springs from the same King David as did Amnon. And because it is Jesus' story, or part of that story, it is our story. It is our family story and all the more reason to listen and to listen closely.

Amnon was probably intended to be successor to the throne. He was firstborn. He had all of the opportunities of privilege, the advantages of privilege. He was first among his peers, we assume as we look at the text. But he, as an individual, becomes completely incapacitated by his lust for his beautiful half-sister, Tamar. He tries in the verses immediately preceding, where we began, to cover up his lust by saying that he is in love with his sister. He pictures himself rather as a poor Romeo, separated from his Juliet by a family structure. But that is just a self-deception, and as we see the story unfold, it becomes clear that he is expert at deceiving himself.

I know a man who has been married ten times. His good friends quit giving gifts after the third. He loves romance; he just doesn't care for marriage. He is an expert at deceiving himself, apparently, in terms of what is really going on. He won't face the responsibility. He is unwilling to join into a marriage relationship in a significant way, and he won't get help. He doesn't think he has a problem. Maybe he doesn't, but it seems to me that is a strange way to have a harem. King David might have had ten wives or twenty, but that was a different time and a different place.

Self-deception is at the very heart of sin. That is what we do, mainly, when we sin in radical fashions: we deceive ourselves. We explain it away; we say, "Oh, it really doesn't matter" or "I made an error of judgment" or "I won't do it again," when we know full well that we will. It is also self-centered; it is absolute unconcern for the other. It is "What can I get that I want now?" In this particular text, there is a play between what is wise and what is foolish. And Amnon is pictured in a particular way. The text says, "He would not listen to her." It says it a couple of times: he wouldn't listen. The heart of being wise is the capacity to listen, to hear, to learn. But in his self-centeredness and his self-deception, he got his way. He didn't listen, but he was stronger, and he forced her. He raped her!

The consequences of that sin were quite destructive—destructive for him, destructive for Tamar, destructive for the family. Because it is so graphic, it is sometimes hard to listen to. I remember the first time I preached this text some twenty years ago, I warned the average Houston congregation to which I was about to address myself that if they had small children whom they didn't want to hear a hard story, they had better take them out. But just because it is so bold and so clear, we need all the more to listen to it, to learn from it.

Amnon is only one of the characters. The other character in the story is Tamar, his half-sister—beautiful, dutiful, capable, all traits that are valued. She turns out to be the only one of David's daughters who is remembered by name in Scripture. Beyond the qualities that I just mentioned, she also has wisdom. She demonstrates what it means to be wise. She tries to make her brother see a better way. She tries to reason with him. She says, "No, don't do this, this thing that you are about to do. Don't do it! Ask David, our father, he will let me marry you." It was a possibility within the social structure of their time.

Of course, we know that Amnon would not listen. He could not hear her. And even after he has raped her and is about to push her out the door, she says, "No, no. What you are doing now is even worse. You can still amend the picture some by not forcing me away, not turning me out." But again, he would not listen. Though wise counsel was offered him, he could not hear it.

Tamar, in her discussion with him, does something else. She names the act that he is about to commit. We would call it "rape," and certainly it was, but she calls it in Hebrew something else which gives it an even deeper significance. I don't know that we can say it in a single word in English. To say it is a "vile thing," as the NRSV does, is true; it is certainly a vile thing! But that doesn't touch it. It is *nebalah*. It is *stupidity*! It is *wanton stupidity* that he is about to do. It is something that is so foreign to what God wants that only a *fool* would do that. Tamar further says in the NRSV, "You will be counted as one of the scoundrels in Israel." I don't know how often you have used the word "scoundrel." I don't use it very much, and it doesn't do much for me. I'd prefer an earlier translation, "You will be among the *fools* of Israel." A fool, the psalmist reminds us, is one who says in his or her heart, "There is no God. I can do what I please." Whenever one of us is tempted to feel that way, we become one of the fools of Israel and we do the acts of fools, utter folly.

One final thing about Tamar: she is also a victim. We know she is a victim. Even in the midst of her dilemma, she offers wise counsel. She tries to persuade her brother. She tries to go a different direction. But, having said all, she is victimized. She leaves that chamber a different person, and we should never forget it. One little word, however, at the end of what I read at least gives us some clue as to what we should do when we are victims and how we should hear those who are victims. It says, "She went out [and the Hebrew would have this word the last in the sentence] crying aloud." The verb in Hebrew is *za'aq*. She is not just sobbing quietly to herself in her pain. She is crying out for justice. This is the word used in the Psalms, "O, God hear us!" This is the word that provoked God to respond at Exodus. God heard the people *za'aq*. They cried out in the midst of their oppression. She's not a quiet victim. She ruins her garments so that everybody can see that she has been violated, and she walks out crying for God's justice.

Victims of family violence have for too long been counseled, "Be quiet. It will take care of itself. Don't upset the family. My gosh, what would Thanksgiving be?" It is not easy for a victim to cry out. That's where the community has to offer all the more support, but we are right to do so. We must help the victims regain their voices.

We listen to this family story and think about it. We learn about sin, the dynamics of sin, the consequences of sin. In this sense, "sin" can be defined as self-centered, self-serving stupidity, and its consequences are pain and shame and separation. We come to God's table as family, having heard a part of our family story. We come to our brother Jesus' table, and we come for a variety of purposes. But among them, I'm sure, some come to receive forgiveness for what we know we have done wrongly to others. Others come this day for healing, healing for wrongs done to them. We come for encouragement, for empowerment. We come that we may be more faithfully the family of God.

So, let us come. Let us come to the table and receive from our very present brother Jesus the gift of life. Amen.

15

If It Had Not Been for God on Our Side

Aubra Love

Text: Genesis 21:8–20

As a global community, our effectiveness toward ending domestic violence is largely contingent upon how we choose to understand this social aberration. Several years ago, when I first entered seminary, one of my professors, who had the reputation of being a great ponderer of profound notions, posed a question to me. With a concerned, searching look on his face, he asked me, "Sister Love, why is God calling so many women to the ministry now? Do you think it's the end times?" After I looked him in the eye, I discerned that he was sincerely seeking a way that he might choose to understand the significant increase of women in ordained ministry. And the way he posed the question clued me in that he did not want the oppression of women, the blatant sexism, the misogyny, to be a part of this understanding.

So, as gently as I could manage, I told him that I suspected that it was for the same reason that God was calling men and women of color to the professions. Is it the end times because we see an increase in middle-income professionals among people of color? Are people of color becoming more professionally competent? If this were so, then racism would not have to be part of our understanding. I believe that we choose the way in which we make sense of those matters that seem, at first glance, to be complex. The dynamics of institutional oppression that would prevent women of faith from being credentialed as ordained ministers of the gospel and people of color from fully actualizing in the professional arena—these dynamics of institutional oppression can seem very complex, at first glance. And the way we choose to understand these matters can move us toward peace and healing—or it can move us toward eternal suffering, oppression, and chaos.

So what does all of this have to do with domestic violence? Only everything. Let me share one more story with you about a question I was asked recently at a women's national religious conference. A mature, apparently good-natured woman asked me, "Why do we hear so much about this domestic violence nowadays? Years ago, a man and a woman got together, and if they had any differences, they worked them out." She didn't want gender-role stereotyping or heterosexism to be a part of her understanding.

Many of you know that God has always called women to ministry and accomplished great works of faith through them. Some of you even realize that people of color have always made valuable contributions whenever the threat of violence was not imminent and the opportunity was present. The safer we make it for people to be themselves and tell the whole truth, the more we will learn about the human condition. As we relent in our oppression of others, we will see all that God is doing and all that God intends for us as God's people. If we choose to rationalize and explain away oppression, this will negatively impact what our experience of God is like.

I have chosen the Old Testament sister Hagar for our case study this evening. Most of us here know Hagar. Well, let's get in her business for a better understanding. Let's take a look at the story in Genesis 21:8–20, where Hagar and Ishmael are sent away.

Some people have difficulty seeing that Hagar is a woman suffering abuse. They dismiss her suffering by quickly reminding us that she was Abraham's and Sarah's slave. That assertion never really seemed relevant to me. Earlier texts around Genesis 16 tell us very plainly that Hagar was given to Abraham as a wife. And for that matter, all women were considered property during these times.

Let us weigh the words. Slave/ancient wife, ancient wife/slave. The conclusion of the whole matter is that they both belonged to Abraham to do with as he pleased—up to and including the expulsion of Hagar and their firstborn son. Something very important is going in this Genesis story. In this story, the ancient Hebrew community has encountered a situation of domestic abuse. The text gives us no account of a community response, appropriate or otherwise. With little or no training in domestic violence, our Christian education sometimes explains this lack of response to Hagar and the child by teaching that "God told Abraham not to concern himself with that."

Something awfully important is happening in this Genesis story. Our Christian teachings have too often dismissed the abuse by saying, "Well, Ishmael wasn't really the son of the promise, so this isn't really child abuse." To ignore the suffering of Hagar is to miss a valuable teaching opportunity around family violence that would implore any community of faith to consider the appropriate human response to this set of circumstances.

Instead of hearing a victim's cries for help, some of our contemporary faith communities are guilty of rationalizing, minimizing, and dismissing the suffering of those most vulnerable by craftily justifying the abuse.

If we allow ourselves to be those human beings made in the image of God, we have to notice that Hagar's story is full of unjust suffering. Here is Hagar wandering through the deserts of Beersheba with a child, after being kicked out of her home with only some bread and water. This is emotional abuse, compounded by physical abuse. Surely, this is a blow to the spirit of Hagar, who was strongly persuaded to give birth to this child. Ishmael's birth was eagerly anticipated by both Sarah and Abraham. But a change of circumstances has resulted in Hagar being a homeless, single mother of African heritage. So it's difficult for some to remember that she is indeed a person of worth.

Many of the details of her home life, we don't know. We don't know if she was ever shoved or slapped or kicked, because domestic violence often occurs in private, and what we usually see is the devastating end result—the woman, the children in crisis. Or perhaps even murdered. Our text tells us that Hagar was of a different race and culture from those with whom she shared community. And the societal oppression complicated her predicament so much that she was unable to find shelter from the elements as she wandered about in the desert. She was fleeing with her sixteen-year-old son, who we know was too old for acceptance into most of today's battered women's shelters—and I don't believe she could have handled sending him to a county shelter for homeless adult men.

We don't have conclusive evidence of the severity of her abuse or why she had no child support. But we do know that all the nurturing attention had been shifted to the other wife and their new son. And this was not the first time that Hagar had to leave the home due to hostile circumstances.

We know that she was economically dependent. And that there was no community response on her behalf. And if it had not been for God on her side, where would she be?

It grieves me that our Old Testament sister wasn't among people who shared a common position against family violence. The Seventh-Day Adventists' position on family violence states explicitly that the church has a responsibility to care for those involved in family violence and to respond to their needs by highlighting the injustices of abuse, and speaking out in defense of victims—both within the community of faith and in society.[1]

This implies that it is of little consequence when an abused woman is of a different faith: the charge to call out abusive behavior and defend the victims extends beyond our churches and into the broader society. This statement regards those suffering from abuse as persons of value, who are worthy of our love, affirmation, and protection.

And I don't have to tell you that saying it and doing it are two different things. Can we make that talk, walk?

In our reading, Hagar is out in the desert by herself with a nearly dehydrated child, whom she lays in the coolness of a shrub as she goes off to petition God. She is of a different faith from those with whom she shared community. So nobody was too concerned about her welfare. And even in the midst of all of her own suffering, it is the fate of her child that concerns Hagar most. "Look!" Hagar cries out to God, "Do not let me look on the death of the child." And if it had not been for God on her side, where would she be, people?

If Hagar were in this situation tonight, some conscious religious community would provide a safe haven for her and her son while they were in need. A conscious religious community would exhort society to share compassion and comfort with this woman and child who were afflicted by the tragedy of domestic violence. The leaders of communities of faith would be identifying some actions to create a unified response to violence against women. Among these actions would be:

1. Displays of family-violence brochures in the entrance of all churches and all women's rest rooms.
2. Education of the congregation through all monthly newsletters and weekly announcements in church bulletins and in all marriage-preparation classes.
3. Speak-outs against domestic violence from every pulpit. People's attitudes and beliefs would be profoundly and powerfully impacted by their faith leaders.
4. Leadership by example. All clergy would be serving on the board of directors of their local domestic violence agencies or receiving training to become acquainted with community resources.
5. Every church would be offering space for meetings or weekly domestic violence support groups; and serving as supervised visitation sites when parents needed to visit safely with their children.

6. Clergy and lay leaders would be actively doing the theological and scriptural homework necessary in order to understand and respond better to family violence, and they would be receiving training from professionals in the field.
7. Intervention would be occurring whenever anyone suspected violence in a relationship. We would be speaking to each member of the couple separately; and helping the victims to plan for safety. We would know, without a doubt, that couples-counseling is unsafe for victims and can result in death from an abuser's retaliation for the victim's disclosure to any outsider.

It grieves me to think that there was no law enforcement support available to Hagar. If this were happening tonight, law enforcement would be employing their innovative strategies to prevent and prosecute violence against women more effectively. Law enforcement leaders would be using these strategies consistently, thereby reducing the incidence of violence against women. Among these innovative strategies would be:

1. Recording each domestic violence incident on a uniform domestic violence reporting form, which includes an investigative checklist for use in every incident.
2. Creating a unit of employees with special expertise to handle domestic violence cases.
3. Meeting with staff and residents of local battered women's shelters to receive suggestions for improving response to these crimes.

If this terrible thing were happening to Hagar this evening, health-care professionals might be her first point of contact. And they would be recognizing the nature of the problem and providing medical care, even if she had no proof of insurance or was too afraid to give the name of her insurance carrier.

If it were happening on this night, the media coverage would read differently from this account in Genesis. The media industry would be influencing and garnering the support of millions of Americans by changing attitudes about violence against women. Members of the media who report on domestic violence would be eagerly pursuing education about the oppressive dynamics of power and control operating in domestic violence incidents. They would be monitoring for gender stereotyping that reinforces and excuses abusive acting out.

This evening, men and women in the workplace would be very sympathetic to what was happening to Hagar. We would all know that domestic violence is a workplace issue that affects the safety, health, and productivity of all workers.

If this kind of thing were happening to this woman and child today, professional, college, and Olympic athletes would be participating in any rally or event to bring attention to the problem of violence against women. Renowned athletes would be making public-service announcements during the Super Bowl and the broadcast of all major sporting events. The sports industry would be characterized by strict disciplinary policies for players with regard to domestic violence and violence against women, similar to drug policies.

If this outrageous, horrible thing were happening tonight, things would be so different for this woman and this child. Wouldn't they?[2]

In this desperate story of Hagar and Ishmael, there is no community response. The angel of God alone is responsive to the suffering of Hagar and Ishmael. Now I know it's God who sees her crying in the desert, and the angel says, "Go get your child out of that bush, because God is getting ready to supply your needs." Are you out of water, this evening? I come to tell you that God says, "I've got a well for you!" And God blessed Hagar, and God blessed Ishmael. And God opened Hagar's eyes to see her resources when she wandered through the wilderness thinking that everybody had deserted her. When she was way out there in the middle of the desert and she couldn't hear anybody pray. But if it had not been for God . . . my, my, my!

Whenever we come together to talk about domestic violence, there are always victims and perpetrators seated together. There are always those who suffered abuse as children and those who inflict abuse upon children.

Whenever we come together like this, there are even those who have made light of the suffering by minimizing the stories of those most vulnerable to abuse.

When we get together like this, someone is reminded of families that were devastated and lives that were lost due to male violence perpetrated upon women and children. Oh, you and I are so fortunate tonight! We are so fortunate that during this time, we get to be the ones who sit together and study the problem and offer the solutions.

We are so blessed that for these moments together, we are the ones who get to make our own decisions, and come and go as we please. We are just so blessed to rest tonight with no fear of awakening to battery and rape.

I have been talking about Hagar and Ishmael this evening, but we could have been talking about your child's teacher or your dentist. We could have been talking about the woman who played the piano in the last worship service. In some cases, we could have been talking about your aunt or your very own daughter. Or perhaps, but for the grace of God, we could be talking about you. And if it had not been for God on our side, where would we be?

Notes

Introduction: Poured Out like Water

1. Most of this information can be found in *Domestic and Sexual Violence Data Collection: A Report to Congress under the Violence against Women Act* (Washington, D.C.: U.S. Dept. of Justice, Office of Justice Programs, National Institute of Justice, n.d.). See also Carol J. Adams, "Toward a Feminist Theology of Religion and the State," in *Violence against Women and Children: A Christian Theological Sourcebook,* ed. Carol J. Adams and Marie M. Fortune (New York: Continuum, 1995), 15–17.

2. John M. Johnson and Denise M. Bondurant, "Revisiting the 1982 Church Response Survey," in *Violence against Women and Children,* ed. Adams and Fortune, 423.

1. Evil, Violence, and the Practice of Theodicy

1. Chan Khong (Cao Ngoc Phuong), *Learning True Love: How I Learned and Practiced Social Change in Viet Nam* (Berkeley, Calif.: Parallax Press, 1993), 6.

2. Notice that another chapter in this collection, that of Barbara Patterson, emphasizes the connections between experience and practice as well. My chapter emphasizes the dependence of practice on theology; hers emphasizes the dependence of theology on practice. The two chapters should be understood as interdependent perspectives.

3. Simone Weil, "The *Iliad,* Poem of Might," *The Simone Weil Reader,* ed. George A. Panichas (New York: McKay, 1977), 155. The philosopher Emmanuel Levinas, too, is aware that the power of evil is not only to kill but to create what he calls the "servile soul." Socrates' death is a fine death—unjust but fine.

> Yet we know the possibilities of tyranny are much more extensive. It has unlimited resources at its disposal, those of love and wealth, torture and hunger, silence and rhetoric. It can exterminate in the tyrannized soul even the very capacity to be struck, that is, even the ability to obey on command. . . . That one can create a servile soul is not only the most painful experience of modern man, but perhaps the very refutation of human freedom. (Emmanuel Levinas, "Freedom and Command," *Collected Philosophical Papers,* trans. Alphonso Lingis [Dordrecht: Martinus Nijhoff, 1987], 16)

(As an aside, some of my intellectual companions here wrote before the idea of inclusive language had arisen. In a paper like this, gendered language is more jarring, and yet I cannot change the fact that fifty years ago a great thinker like Weil used masculine language as if it were generic for human experience.)

4. Simone Weil, "Love of God and Affliction," *Simone Weil Reader,* 441.

5. Ibid., 442.

6. Cf. Societal Violence Initiative Team, "Information Packet" (Louisville, Ky.: National Ministries Division, Presbyterian Church [USA]); and Mary D. Pellauer, "Violence against Women: The Theological Dimension," in *Sexual Assault and Abuse,* ed. Mary Pellauer, Barbara Chester, and Jane Boyajian (San Francisco: Harper & Row, 1987), 50–52.

7. Fyodor Dostoevsky, *The Brothers Karamazov,* trans. Andrew H. MacAndrew (New York: Bantam Books, 1970), 293.

8. The gnostics had a very reasonable solution to this: God did not make the world; no good God could possibly have had anything to do with this world. Our job is to get the hell out of Dodge—to refuse the conditions of the world and our bodies and to direct ourselves to a deity beyond these conditions. The virtue of this response to evil is that it recognizes evil as real and as ubiquitous. Orthodoxy resisted this solution. Its reasons were not always good and its methods not always admirable, but there is an insightfulness about resisting this tempting and sensible solution. Christianity, for all its failures in actually doing so, has always wanted to affirm the goodness of creation, of embodiment, of human life. It also has wanted always to affirm an intimacy between human being and God which is established within the conditions of creation and not in spite of them. Trying to hold these insights together—the reality of evil, the goodness of creation, the power and goodness of God—is quite difficult. It is the genius of Christian theology to be aware of the complexity of existence, a complexity that approaches the paradoxical.

9. See Weil, "Human Personality," *Simone Weil Reader*, 335:

> To maintain justice and preserve [human beings] from all harm means first of all to prevent harm being done to them. For those to whom harm has been done, it means to efface the material consequences by putting them in a place where the wound, if it is not too deep, may be cured naturally by a spell of well-being. But for those in whom the wound is a laceration of the soul it means further, and above all, to offer them good in its purest form to assuage their thirst.

10. Likewise, Ivan, in presenting his case against God to Alyosha, restricts himself to the suffering of children. "In the second place, I also will not speak of adults at the moment, because, besides being disgusting and undeserving of love, they have something to compensate them for their suffering: they have eaten their apple of knowledge, they know about good and evil and are like gods themselves. And they keep eating the apple" (Dostoevsky, *Brothers Karamazov*, 285).

11. See Karl Rahner, *Foundations of Christian Faith* (1978; reprint, New York: Crossroad, 1982), 96:

> But freedom is not the capacity to go on eternally in an eternally new process of disposing and redisposing. Freedom has rather a necessity about it which is not connected with physical necessity in the usual sense. For freedom is a capacity of subjectivity, and hence of a subject who is not an accidental point of intersection in a chain of causes extending indefinitely forward and backward, but is rather what cannot be so derived. Freedom therefore is not the capacity to do something which is always able to be revised but the capacity to do something final and definitive.

12. Simone Weil makes a similar point in "Human Personality" (*Simone Weil Reader*, 335):

> Sometimes it may be necessary to inflict harm in order to stimulate this thirst [for good] before assuaging it, and that is what punishment is for. [Those] who are so estranged from the good that they seek to spread evil everywhere can only be reintegrated with the good by having harm inflicted upon them. . . . The innocent part of the criminal's soul must then be fed to make it grow until it becomes able to judge and condemn his [or her] past crimes and at last, by the help of grace, to forgive them. With this the punishment is completed.

2. Violence and the Bible

1. The role of aggressor for the ancient faith community is limited to the time of the entry into the land of Canaan. Even in this period, reflected in the biblical book Joshua, it is difficult to estimate the scope of the aggression since the accounts are contradictory and, in places, certainly embellished.

2. One of the difficulties for students of the biblical era lies in grasping the extent of the political turmoil that beset the geographical area where the texts of the Bible were composed and col-

lected. From 1200 B.C.E. until the first century C.E., I would characterize only the latter part of the tenth century, under King Solomon, as a time of relative stability.

3. Studies of this type are available for the interested reader. See, for example, Walter Brueggemann, "Revelation and Violence: A Study in Contextualization," in *A Social Reading of the Old Testament: Prophetic Approaches to Israel's Communal Life,* ed. Patrick D. Miller (Minneapolis: Fortress Press, 1994), 285–318.

4. Subjectivity in reading texts is today recognized as an essential factor in the interpretive process. For a recent contribution on the role of the interpreter in reading the biblical text, see for example, Fernando F. Segovia and Mary Ann Tolbert, eds., *Reading from This Place,* vol. 1: *Social Location and Biblical Interpretation in the United States* (Minneapolis: Fortress Press, 1995).

5. George R. Edwards, "A Biblical View of Gay/Lesbian Liberation," speech presented at Louisville Presbyterian Theological Seminary, Louisville, Ky., December 1, 1992.

6. This observation is reflected in the epigraph to this chapter; see James W. Douglass, *The Nonviolent Coming of God* (New York: Orbis Books, 1992), 148.

7. Elisabeth Schüssler Fiorenza, *But She Said: Feminist Practices of Biblical Interpretation* (Boston: Beacon, 1992), 114–18. For a similar broad framework for a feminist theological perspective, see also Elizabeth A. Johnson, *She Who Is: The Mystery of God in Feminist Theological Discourse* (New York: Crossroad, 1992). I think especially of her pertinent remark in this volume, that "the goal of feminist religious discourse pivots in its fullness around the flourishing of poor women of color in violent situations" (11).

8. Thus observes Elisabeth Schüssler Fiorenza in the introduction to Elisabeth Schüssler Fiorenza and M. Shawn Copeland, eds., *Violence against Women* (London: SCM Press, and Maryknoll, N.Y.: Orbis Books, 1994), x. This introduction presents a list of abuses that rage against women across the globe as well as a systemic analysis of these practices. See also Miranda Davies, ed., *Women and Violence: Realities and Responses Worldwide* (London: Zed Books, 1994), for a presentation and analysis of the problem in its entire scope.

9. See Jacques Pons, *L'Oppression dans l'Ancien Testament* (Paris: Letouzey et Ane, 1981), 29.

10. For a study of rape as a part of patriarchal culture, see Susan Brownmiller, *Against Our Will: Men, Women, and Rape* (New York: Bantam Books, 1975).

11. A detailed and provocative analysis of the story of Dinah and its possible background in Haran is provided by Ita Sheres, *Dinah's Rebellion: A Biblical Parable for Our Time* (New York: Crossroad, 1990).

12. See the extensive network of skills and occupations practiced by the woman who is the focus of praise in Proverbs 31:10–31. For a detailed analysis of the function and the roles of women in ancient Israel, see Carol Meyers, *Discovering Eve: Ancient Israelite Women in Context* (New York and Oxford: Oxford University Press, 1988).

13. Adams, "Toward a Feminist Theology of Religion and State," 15.

14. Archaeological research has uncovered this greater vulnerability of women in the premonarchical period of ancient Israel by investigating skeletal remains in tomb groups. See Carol Meyers, "Roots of Restriction: Women in Early Israel," in *The Bible and Liberation: Political and Social Hermeneutics,* ed. Norman K. Gottwald (Maryknoll, N.Y.: Orbis Books, 1983), 289–306.

15. As Phyllis Trible observes (*Texts of Terror: Literary Feminist Readings of Biblical Narratives* [Philadelphia: Fortress Press, 1984], 87): "Woman as object is still captured, betrayed, raped, tortured, murdered, dismembered, and scattered. To take to heart this ancient story, then, is to confess its present reality. The story is alive, and all is not well."

3. The Wounds of Jesus, the Wounds of My People

1. For some theological discussions of Christian ministry in the context of urban social dislocation, see James H. Evans Jr., *We Shall All Be Changed: Social Problems and Theological Renewal*

(Minneapolis: Fortress Press, 1997); Forrest E. Harris Sr., *Ministry for Social Crisis: Theology and Praxis in the Black Church Tradition* (Macon, Ga.: Mercer University Press, 1993); Dieter T. Hessel, *Social Ministry,* rev. ed. (Louisville, Ky.: Westminster/John Knox, 1992); Eleanor Scott Meyers, ed., *Envisioning the New City: A Reader on Urban Ministry* (Louisville, Ky.: Westminster/John Knox, 1992); Paul Plenge Parker, ed., *Standing with the Poor: Theological Reflections on Economic Reality* (Cleveland: Pilgrim Press, 1992); Jamie T. Phelps, "Mission in Situations of Conflict and Violence in the United States of America," *Missiology: An International Review* 20, no. 1 (Jan. 1992): 21–31; J. Deotis Roberts, *The Roots of a Black Future: Family and Church* (Philadelphia: Westminister Press, 1980); J. Deotis Roberts, *The Prophethood of Believers: An African American Political Theology for Ministry* (Maryknoll, N.Y.: Orbis Books, 1995).

2. William Stringfellow, "Violence in the Technocratic Society," *Sojourners* (22 Oct. 1984): 22.

3. A large body of literature has developed on the painful realities of sexual and physical violence against women and children. Some important contributions include Carol J. Adams, *Woman Battering* (Minneapolis: Fortress Press, 1994); Marie M. Fortune, *Sexual Violence: The Unmentionable Sin* (New York: Pilgrim Press, 1983); and Carolyn H. Heggen, *Sexual Abuse in Christian Homes and Churches* (Scottdale, Pa.: Herald Press, 1993).

4. Deborah Prothrow-Stith, *Deadly Consequences: How Violence Is Destroying Our Teenage Population and a Plan to Begin Solving the Problem* (1991; reprint, New York: Harper Perennial, 1993), 184.

5. *New York Times,* 26 Nov. 1996, Section B, 15.

6. bell hooks, "Violence in Intimate Relationships: A Feminist Perspective," in *Talking Back: Thinking Feminist, Thinking Black,* ed. bell hooks (Boston: South End Press, 1989), 84.

7. Dorothy Gilliam, cited in Ellis Cose, *The Rage of a Privileged Class* (New York: HarperCollins, 1993), 5.

8. *The Random House Dictionary of the English Language* (New York: Random House, 1973), 1594–95

9. Felipe E. MacGregor, S.J., and Marcial Rubio Correa, "Rejoinder to the Theory of Structural Violence," in *The Culture of Violence,* ed. Kumar Rupesinghe and Marcial Rubio Correa (New York: United Nations University Press, 1994), 46.

10. For a fuller discussion, see Judith Lewis Human, *Trauma and Recovery* (New York: Basic Books, 1992).

11. Ibid., 48–49.

12. Iris Marion Young, *Justice and the Politics of Difference* (Princeton, N.J.: Princeton University Press, 1990), 41. Young defines a "social group" thus:

> a collective of persons differentiated from at least one other group by cultural forms, practices, or a way of life. Members of a group have a specific affinity with one another because of their similar experience or way of life, which prompts them to associate with one another more than with those not identified with the group, or in a different way. Groups are an expression of social relations: a group exists only in relation to at least one other group. (43)

13. Ibid., 62, 63.

14. For some analyses of structural oppression in U.S. cities (especially in core or inner-city areas populated by black and brown peoples), see David Harvey, *Social Justice and the City* (Oxford: Basil Blackwell, 1988); Herbert J. Gans, *The War against the Poor, The Underclass and Antipoverty Policy* (New York: Basic Books, 1995); John Mollenkopf and Manuel Castells, eds., *Dual City: Restructuring New York* (New York: Russell Sage Foundation, 1991); Frances Fox Piven and Richard A. Cloward, *Regulating the Poor: The Functions of Welfare* (New York: Vintage Books, 1971); Cornel West, "The New Cultural Politics of Difference," in *Out There: Marginalization and Contemporary Cultures,* ed. Russell Ferguson et al. (New York and Cambridge,

Mass.: The New Museum of Contemporary Art and MIT Press, 1990),19–36; Cornel West, "Nihilism in Black America," *Dissent* (spring 1991): 221–26; Cornel West, *Race Matters* (Boston: Beacon Press, 1993); William Julius Wilson, *The Truly Disadvantaged: The Inner City, the Underclass, and Public Policy* (Chicago: University of Chicago Press, 1987); William Julius Wilson, *When Work Disappears: The World of the New Urban Poor* (New York: Alfred A. Knopf, 1996).

15. Andrew Hacker, *Two Nations: Black and White, Separate, Hostile, and Unequal* (New York: Charles Scribner's Sons, 1992), 73; also Young, *Justice and the Politics of Difference*, 122–55.

16. Eugene F. Rivers III, "Beyond the Nationalism of Fools: Toward an Agenda for Black Intellectuals," *Boston Review* 20, no. 3 (summer 1995): 16.

17. Alan Durning, "Ending Poverty," in *State of the World 1990: A Worldwatch Institute Report on Progress toward a Sustainable Society* (New York: W. W. Norton, 1990), 137–38.

18. Prothrow-Stith, *Deadly Consequences*, 16–17.

19. Hacker, *Two Nations*, 189.

20. Holly Sklar, "Young and Guilty by Stereotype," *Z Magazine* 6, 7/8 (July/Aug. 1993): 60.

21. Hacker, *Two Nations*, 78.

22. Henry Louis Taylor Jr., "Violence, the Black Community, and the Role of Religious Institutions," paper presented at the Church, Theology, and Violence Conference, 20–22 Oct. 1994, New York, typescript, 6.

23. Ibid., 4.

24. See Schüssler Fiorenza, Introduction to *Violence against Women,* ed. Schüssler Fiorenza and Copeland, viii; also see M. Shawn Copeland, "Editorial Reflections," 119–22, in the same volume.

25. Bernard Lonergan, *Method in Theology* (New York: Herder & Herder, 1972), xi.

26. Imagination can be defined as the "sum total of all the forces and faculties in [the human person] that are brought to bear upon our concrete world to form proper images of it" (William F. Lynch, *Images of Hope: Imagination as Healer of the Hopeless* [1965; Notre Dame: University of Notre Dame Press, 1974], 243). Or imagination may be apprehended as "a faculty or power of reproducing images stored in the memory under the suggestion of associated (reproductive imagination) images or of recombining former experiences in the creation of new images directed at a specific goal or aiding in the solution of problems (creative imagination)" (*Random House Dictionary of the English Language*, 711).

27. MacGregor and Correa, "Rejoinder," 51, 52.

28. T. J. Jackson Lears, *No Place of Grace* (New York: Pantheon Books, 1981), 300.

29. Taylor, "Violence, the Black Community," 8. The term "outlaw culture" was coined by Mark Naison in "Outlaw Culture and Black Neighborhoods," *Reconstruction* 1, no. 4 (1992): 128–31. For a similar negative apprehension of outlaw culture, see West, *Race Matters*; for a different and problematizing usage (i.e., outlaw culture as resistive and creative culture of the marginalized, of women, of racial and other so-called minorities), see bell hooks, *Outlaw Culture: Resisting Representation* (New York: Routledge, 1994).

30. Tricia Rose, *Black Noise: Rap Music and Black Culture in Contemporary America* (Hanover, N.H., and London: Wesleyan University Press, 1994), 18. For some other discussions of hip-hop culture and rap, see Houston A. Baker Jr., *Black Studies, Rap, and the Academy* (Chicago: University of Chicago Press, 1993); Michael Eric Dyson, *Between God and Gangsta Rap: Bearing Witness to Black Culture* (New York: Oxford University Press, 1996); Garth Kasimu Baker-Fletcher, *Xodus: An African American Male Journey* (Minneapolis: Fortress Press, 1996), esp. 131–94.

31. Rose, *Black Noise,* 21.

32. Ibid., 40.

33. bell hooks, *Outlaw Culture,* 120–21.

34. Rob Marriott, "All That Glitters," *Vibe Magazine* 5, no. 4 (May 1997): 59.

35. Rose, *Black Noise*, 21. Rose borrows the phrasing "crossroads of lack and desire" from Houston A. Baker Jr., *Blues, Ideology, and Afro-American Literature* (Chicago: University of Chicago Press, 1984), 7, 11, 150. Baker uses the phrase to reference the blues tradition, Rose to reference hip-hop. I extend it to signal the disordered desire of violence.

36. J. Deotis Roberts, "Victory over Violence: A Theological Perspective," paper delivered at the Church, Theology, and Violence Conference, 20–22 Oct. 1994, New York, typescript, 4.

37. Ibid., 5.

38. MacGregor and Correa, "Rejoinder," 54.

39. bell hooks, *Outlaw Culture*, 120.

40. Emilie M. Townes, "Washed in the Grace of God," in *Violence against Women and Children*, ed. Adams and Fortune, 69.

41. Rose, *Black Noise,* 169.

42. Young, *Justice and the Politics of Difference*, 148.

43. Roberts, "Victory over Violence," 4.

44. I have borrowed the term "counterimagination" from Walter Brueggemann, *Texts under Negotiation: The Bible and Postmodern Imagination* (Minneapolis: Fortress Press, 1993). For some studies of black preaching, see Charles V. Hamilton, *The Black Preacher in America* (New York: William Morrow, 1972); Gerald L. Davis, *I Got the Word in Me and I Can Sing It, You Know: A Study of the Performed African American Sermon* (Philadelphia: University of Pennsylvania Press, 1985); Henry H. Mitchell, *Black Preaching: The Recovery of a Powerful Art* (Nashville: Abingdon Press, 1990); James Henry Harris, "Preaching Liberation: The Afro-American Sermon and the Quest for Social Change," *Journal of Religious Thought* 46 (winter–spring 1989–90): 72–89.

45. See Albert J. Raboteau, *Slave Religion: The "Invisible Institution" in the Antebellum South* (New York: Oxford University Press, 1978); Mechal Sobel, *Trabelin' On: The Slave Journey to an Afro-Baptist Faith* (Westport, Conn.: Greenwood Press, 1979); C. Eric Lincoln and Lawrence H. Mamiya, *The Black Church in the African American Experience* (Durham, N.C., and London: Duke University Press, 1990). Lincoln and Mamiya contend that the health, vibrancy, and potent sway of the historic black churches were uncontested for more than two hundred years. However, the forces of modernity (secularization with the accompanying processes of complex class and social stratification and differentiation, increasing tolerance for social and cultural pluralism in the larger U.S. society, and, I believe, the more-or-less end of de jure and de facto segregation) have tended "to diminish the cultural unity provided by the black sacred cosmos" (383).

46. For some discussions of Africanisms or the retentions of personal, religious, cultural, social West African traditions, patterns, and practices see Molefi Kete Asante, *The Afrocentric Idea* (Philadelphia: Temple University Press, 1987), esp. 34–39; Molefi Kete Asante and Kariamu Welsh Asante, eds., *African Culture: The Rhythms of Unity* (1985; reprint, Trenton, N.J.: African Third World Press, 1990); Joseph E. Holloway, ed., *Africanisms in American Culture* (Bloomington: Indiana University Press, 1990); Marimba Ani, *Yurugu: An African-Centered Critique of European Cultural Thought and Behavior* (Trenton, N.J.: African Third World Press, 1994); and Vernon Dixon and Badi Foster, *Beyond Black or White* (Boston: Little, Brown, 1971).

47. Dolan Hubbard, *The Sermon and the African America Literary Imagination* (Columbia: University of Missouri Press, 1994), 5.

48. Stephen Henderson, *Understanding the New Black Poetry: Black Speech and Black Music as Poetic References* (New York: William Morrow, 1973), 44.

49. Ibid. 41.

50. Roberta Flack, *Quiet Fire*, Atlantic Records, 1971. For two very good general treatments of the history of African American music, see Eileen Southern, *The Music of Black Americans: A History,* 2d ed. (New York: W. W. Norton, 1983); and Samuel A. Floyd Jr., *The Power of Black*

Music (New York: Oxford University Press, 1995). The classic treatment of the spiritual is offered by John Lovell Jr., *Black Song: The Forge and the Flame—The Story of How the Afro-American Spiritual Was Hammered Out* (1972; reprint, New York: Paragon, 1986). See also Howard Thurman, *Deep River and the Negro Spiritual Speaks of Life and Death* (Richmond, Ind.: Friends United Press, 1975). Some important discussions of the sacred and blues traditions in African American music include those by LeRoi Jones, *Blues People: The Negro Experience in White America and the Music That Developed from It* (New York: William Morrow, 1963); James H. Cone, *The Spirituals and the Blues: An Interpretation* (Westport, Conn.: Greenwood Press, 1972); Jon Michael Spencer, *Protest and Praise: Sacred Music of Black Religion* (Minneapolis: Fortress Press, 1990); Jon Michael Spencer, *Black Hymnody: A Hymnological History of the African-American Church* (Knoxville: University of Tennessee Press, 1992); Jon Michael Spencer, *Blues and Evil* (Knoxville: University of Tennessee Press, 1993); and Alan Lomax, *The Land Where the Blues Began* (New York: Delta Publishing, 1993).

51. Clarence Joseph Rivers, *The Spirit in Worship* (Cincinnati: Stimuli, 1978), 199.

52. Katie Geneva Cannon, *Katie's Canon: Womanism and the Soul of the Black Community* (New York: Continuum Books, 1995), 113.

53. Baker-Fletcher, *Xodus*, 327–28.

54. Cannon, *Katie's Canon*, 114.

55. Ibid., 121.

56. Margaret A. Farley, "Sources of Sexual Inequality in the History of Christian Thought," *The Journal of Religion* 56, no. 2 (April 1976): 37.

57. Cannon, *Katie's Canon*, 114.

58. Ibid., 116.

59. Ibid., 117, 119.

60. Hubbard, *The Sermon*, 11.

61. Davis, *I Got the Word in Me*, 94.

62. Hortense Spillers, "Fabrics of History: Essays on the Black Sermon," 4, cited in Hubbard, *The Sermon*, 7.

63. Cannon, *Katie's Canon*, 118.

64. Baker-Fletcher, *Xodus*, 190.

65. The cultural and social situation of African Americans is confounding to all African American Christian churches, Protestant and Catholic alike. What is required is a critical, prophetic mediation of the gospel that takes into full and serious account racism, sexism and misogyny, homophobia, economic exploitation and joblessness in the midst of postindustrial meltdown, as well as the existential realities of suffering, dread, disappointment, death. To this end, political scientist Manning Marable raises several challenges that expose the ambivalent posture of African American Christian churches toward this situation. Marable directs his critique specifically at the historic black church; however, it seems to me that this challenge ought to be leveled at all those engaged in forms of Christian ministry: Why, Marable asks (in *How Capitalism Underdeveloped Black America* (Boston: South End Press, 1983], 211), has African American Christianity

> failed repeatedly to evolve into a coherent agency promoting the liberation of African-American people, and why has it succeeded to reveal itself as an essential factor in Black struggles at certain difficult historical periods? Why is the stereotypical Black preacher the frequent object of embarrassment, ridicule, scorn for the Black petty bourgeoisie and to much of the Black working class, yet simultaneously [the preacher] continues to be a critically important contributor to the total sum of Black social, cultural, economic, and political life?

Also see Charles P. Henry, *Culture and African American Politics* (Bloomington and Indianapolis: Indiana University Press, 1992).

4. Preaching Forgiveness?

1. Richard P. Lord, "Do I Have to Forgive?", *Christian Century* 108, no. 28 (Oct. 9, 1991).

2. Alan Reid, *Seeing Law Differently: Views from a Spiritual Path* (N.p.: Borderland Publishing, n.d.), 139.

3. Moses Maimonides, *Mishnah Torah, Book One: Knowledge: Repentance*, ed. Philip Birnbaum (New York: Hebrew Publishing Co., 1967).

4. Berel Lang, "The Holocaust and Two Views of Forgiveness," *Tikkun* 11, no. 2 (March–April 1996): 43.

5. Tina Rosenberg, "Recovering from Apartheid," *The New Yorker*, Nov. 18, 1996, 88.

6. Ibid., 90.

7. Lang, "The Holocaust," 45.

8. Ibid.

9. *Seattle Times*, Feb. 5, 1997.

10. Fred Keene, "Structures of Forgiveness in the New Testament," in *Violence against Women and Children*, ed. Adams and Fortune, 121–34.

5. Preaching to Survivors of Child Sexual Abuse

1. Nancy Ramsay, "Sexual Abuse and Shame: The Travail of Recovery," in *Women in Travail and Transition: A New Pastoral Care*, ed. Maxine Glaz and Jeanne Stevenson Moessner (Minneapolis: Fortress Press, 1991), 110.

2. See especially Robert Kegan, *The Evolving Self* (Cambridge, Mass.: Harvard University Press, 1982), and Judith Jordan et al., *Women's Growth in Connection* (New York: Guilford Press, 1991), for discussions of development within a relational context.

3. Alex Kotlowitz, *There Are No Children Here* (New York: Doubleday, 1991).

4. Gershen Kaufman, *Shame*, 2d ed., rev. (Rochester, Vt.: Schenkman Books, 1985), 10, 7.

5. Ramsay, "Sexual Abuse and Shame," 113.

6. Elaine Westerlund, *Women's Sexuality after Childhood Incest* (New York: W. W. Norton, 1992), 52–55.

7. Erik Erikson, *Childhood and Society,* 2d ed., revised and enlarged (New York: W. W. Norton, 1963), 250.

8. Wendy Farley, *Tragic Vision and Divine Compassion* (Louisville, Ky.: Westminster/John Knox Press, 1990), 53.

9. Toinette Eugene, "'If You Get There before I Do': A Womanist Ethical Response to Sexual Violence and Abuse," in *Perspectives on Womanist Theology*, ed. Jacquelyn Grant (Atlanta: ITC Press, 1995), 105.

10. William Placher, *The Vulnerable God* (Louisville, Ky.: Westminster/John Knox Press, 1994), 17.

11. Patrick Miller, *Interpreting the Psalms* (Minneapolis: Fortress, 1986), 100–119. This is a very helpful resource for considering the role of the psalms of lament, and Psalms 22 and 23 in particular.

12. Walter Brueggemann, *The Message of the Psalms* (Minneapolis: Augsburg, 1984), 51–122.

13. Farley, *Tragic Vision*, 95–114.

14. Elaine Ramshaw, *Ritual and Pastoral Care* (Minneapolis: Fortress, 1987).

15. Gene Outka, "Universal Love and Impartiality," in *The Love Commandments*, ed. Edmund N. Santurri and William Werpehowski (Washington, D.C.: Georgetown University Press, 1992), 2.

16. Marie McCarthy, "The Role of Mutuality in Family Structures and Relationships: A Critical Examination of Select Systems of Family Therapy from the Perspective of Selected Options in Contemporary Theological Ethics" (Ph.D. diss., University of Chicago, 1985), 230.

17. Daniel Day Williams, *The Spirit and the Forms of Love* (New York: Harper & Row, 1968), 3.

18. Valerie Saiving, "The Human Situation: A Feminine View," *Journal of Religion* 40 (April 1960): 108.

19. Marie Fortune, "Forgiveness: The Last Step," in *Violence in the Family*, ed. Marie Fortune (Cleveland: Pilgrim Press, 1991), 173–78.

20. Keene, "Structures of Forgiveness," 121–34.

21. Ibid., 128; see Keene's discussion of this important illustration of the balance of power forgiveness presumes in the New Testament.

22. Martin Luther, *Lectures on Romans,* trans. and ed. Wilhelm Pauck (Philadelphia: Westminster Press, 1961), 366–67.

23. James Nelson, *Between Two Gardens* (Cleveland: Pilgrim Press, 1983), 18.

6. Preaching to Perpetrators of Violence

1. James N. Poling and Christie Neuger, eds., *The Care of Men* (Nashville: Abingdon, 1997), 142–44.

2. Center for the Prevention of Sexual and Domestic Violence, 936 N. 34th St., Seattle, WA 98103.

3. James Poling and Marie Fortune, "Calling to Accountability: The Church's Response to Abusers," in *Violence against Women and Children,* ed. Adams and Fortune, 458.

4. Personal correspondence with Linda Crockett.

5. *Broken Vows,* a video on prevention of domestic violence (Seattle: Center for the Prevention of Sexual and Domestic Violence, 1995).

6. Patricia Hill Collins, *Black Feminist Thought: Knowledge, Consciousness, and the Politics of Empowerment* (New York: Routledge, 1990).

7. For further discussion of the issues of this section, see James Newton Poling, *Deliver Us from Evil: Resisting Racial and Gender Oppression* (Minneapolis: Fortress, 1996), 136–48.

8. Kelly Brown Douglas, *The Black Christ* (Maryknoll, N.Y.: Orbis, 1994), 15.

9. Ibid., 17.

10. Riggins Earl Jr., *Dark Symbols, Obscure Signs: God, Self, and Community in the Slave Mind* (Maryknoll, N.Y.: Orbis, 1993), 52.

11. Jacquelyn Grant, "Come to My Help, Lord," in *Reconstructing the Christ Symbol: Essays in Feminist Christology,* ed. Maryanne Stevens (New York: Paulist, 1993), 54–71. See also Jacquelyn Grant, *White Women's Christ and Black Women's Jesus: Feminist Christology and Womanist Response* (Atlanta: Scholars Press, 1989).

12. Delores Williams, *Sisters in the Wilderness: The Challenge of Womanist God-Talk* (Maryknoll, N.Y.: Orbis, 1993), 164.

13. Hazel Carby, *Reconstructing Womanhood: The Emergence of the Afro-American Woman Novelist* (New York: Oxford University Press, 1987), 25.

14. Rita Nakashima Brock, "Losing Your Innocence but Not Your Hope," in *Reconstructing the Christ Symbol,* ed. Stevens, 30–53. See also Rita Nakashima Brock, *Journeys by Heart: A Christology of Erotic Power* (New York: Crossroad, 1988).

15. Gerda Lerner, *The Creation of Feminist Consciousness: From the Middle Ages to 1870* (New York: Oxford University Press, 1993).

16. See James Newton Poling, *The Abuse of Power: A Theological Problem* (Nashville: Abingdon, 1991).

17. See Poling, *Deliver Us from Evil,* 148–55.

18. John Dominic Crossan, *Jesus: A Revolutionary Biography* (San Francisco: Harper, 1994); Burton L. Mack, *The Lost Gospel: The Book of Q and Christian Origins* (San Francisco: Harper,

1993); William Herzog II, *Parables as Subversive Speech: Jesus as Pedagogue of the Oppressed* (Louisville, Ky.: Westminster/John Knox, 1994).

19. The Westminster Confession of Faith (1647), *The Book of Confessions* (Louisville, Ky.: Presbyterian Church [U.S.A.]), 6.010.

20. Itumeleng T. Mosala, *Biblical Hermeneutics and Black Theology in South Africa* (Grand Rapids, Mich.: Eerdmans, 1989); Cain Hope Felder, ed., *Stony the Road We Trod: African American Biblical Interpretation* (Minneapolis: Fortress, 1991); Elisabeth Schüssler Fiorenza, *Bread Not Stone: The Challenge of Feminist Biblical Interpretation* (Boston: Beacon, 1984).

21. Clarice J. Martin, "Black Theodicy and Black Women's Spiritual Autobiography," in *A Troubling in My Soul: Womanist Perspectives on Evil and Suffering,* ed. Emilie M. Townes (Maryknoll, N.Y.: Orbis, 1993), 25.

22. Martin here quotes from Roger Lunden, Anthony Thistleton, and Clarence Walhout, *The Responsibility of Hermeneutics* (Grand Rapids, Mich.: Eerdmans, 1985), x, xi.

23. On responses to sexual and domestic violence, see the following: Carole Warshaw and Anne L. Ganley, *Improving the Health Care Response to Domestic Violence: A Resource Manual for Health Care Providers* (San Francisco: Family Violence Prevention Fund, 1995); Adams, *Woman-Battering*; Michael Paymar, *Violent No More: Helping Men End Domestic Violence* (Alameda, Calif.: Hunter House, 1993); Jeffrey L. Edleson and Richard M. Tolman, *Intervention for Men Who Batter: An Ecological Approach* (Newbury Park, Calif.: Sage, 1992).

24. Marie Fortune, *Violence in the Family: A Workshop Curriculum for Clergy and Other Helpers* (Cleveland: Pilgrim Press, 1992), 18–22.

25. See Catherine Clark Kroeger, "Let's Look Again at the Biblical Concept of Submission," in *Violence against Women and Children*, ed. Adams and Fortune, 135–40,

26. Poling, *Abuse of Power*, 35–48.

27. See Keene, "Structures of Forgiveness," 121–34; and Fortune, "Forgiveness: The Last Step," 201–6.

28. See Joanne Carlson Brown and Rebecca Parker, "For God So Loved the World?"; Emilie Townes, "Washed in the Grace of God"; Rita Nakashima Brock, "Ending Innocence and Nurturing Willfulness"; and Marie Fortune, "The Transformation of Suffering"; all in *Violence against Women and Children*, ed. Adams and Fortune.

29. Dawn Bradley Berry, *The Domestic Violence Sourcebook* (Chicago: Contemporary Books, 1995). See also statistics collected by the Center for the Prevention of Sexual and Domestic Violence, Seattle, Washington.

30. See Williams, *Sisters in the Wilderness*.

7. Preaching in a Violent Situation

1. Mitchell, *Black Preaching,* 20–21.

2. Paul Brown, *In and for the World: Bringing the Contemporary into Christian Worship* (Minneapolis: Fortress Press, 1992).

3. Toinette M. Eugene, "'Swing Low, Sweet Chariot!': A Womanist Response to Sexual Violence and Abuse," *Daughters of Sarah* 20, no. 3 (summer 1994): 10.

4. See Williams, *Sisters in the Wilderness,* 60–82.

5. Asante, *Afrocentric Idea,* 17.

6. Warren A. Stewart, *Interpreting God's Word in Black Preaching* (Valley Forge, Pa.: Judson Press, 1984), 45.

7. Samuel D. Proctor, *"How Shall They Hear?": Effective Preaching for Vital Faith* (Valley Forge, Pa.: Judson Press, 1992), 12.

8. Ibid., 85.

9. Garner C. Taylor, *How Shall They Preach?* (Elgin Ill.: Progressive Baptist Publishing House, 1977), 78–81).

10. Edward Gilbreath, "The Pulpit King: The Passion and Eloquence of Gardner Taylor, a Legend among Preachers," *Christianity Today* (11 Dec. 1995): 27.

11. Ibid., 28.

12. Cannon, *Katie's Canon,* 119–20.

13. Karen Baker-Fletcher, *A Singing Something: Womanist Reflections on Anna Julia Cooper* (New York: Crossroad, 1994).

14. Frances E. Wood, "'Take My Yoke upon You': The Role of the Church in the Oppression of African-American Women," in *A Troubling in My Soul,* ed. Townes, 40.

15. For further discussion of this idea, see Toinette M. Eugene, "Faithful Responses to Human Sexuality: Issues Facing the Church Today," *The Chicago Theological Seminary Register* 81, no. 2 (spring 1991): 1–7.

8. Preaching as Nonviolent Resistance

1. See Athanasius' text "On the Incarnation," in *The Nicene and Post-Nicene Fathers,* vol. 4, ed. Archibald Robertson (Edinburgh: T. & T. Clark, 1987), 31–68.

2. I encourage you to read any texts by these insightful and innovate Christian theologians. I have found extremely helpful Rebecca Chopp's books *Saving Work: Feminist Practices of Theological Education* (Louisville, Ky.: Westminster John Knox Press, 1995) and *The Power to Speak: Feminism, Language and God* (New York: Crossroad, 1991). See also Carter Heyward's work, and Dorothee Soelle, *Suffering,* trans. Everett R. Kalin (Philadelphia: Fortress Press, 1975).

3. For a fuller discussion of the concept of wounding as knowledge, see Rowan Williams, *The Wound of Knowledge* (Cambridge, Mass.: Cowley Publications, 1990). Although this book primarily focuses on the spirituality of Saint John of the Cross, the concept is rooted in the early monastics' experience of spiritual knowledge as a wounding or deep penetration of the heart and soul as well as the body. This concept of wounding was not about literally matching in one's own body the wounds of Christ, but about attending the deeper process of transformational encounter among human woundedness, evil, divine love, and justice in body, soul, mind, and spirit.

4. Owen Chadwick, comp. and ed., *Western Asceticism, Library of Christian Classics*, ed. Ichthus (Philadelphia: Westminster Press, 1958), 38.

5. For a wonderful contemporary look at this process, see Roberta Bondi, *To Love as God Loves* (Philadelphia: Fortress Press, 1987).

6. The Taize community in France is an ecumenical, monastic community of renewal. It has created music for liturgies that are easy to learn and eloquent. The song "Stay with Me" is one of their most popular.

7. Chadwick, *Western Asceticism*, 83.

8. Of course, there are a number of feminist texts that address such conflicting messages. I offer the following three as examples from different emphases within feminist theory and practice. From a linguistic and cultural-symbolic perspective: Luce Irigaray, *Speculum of the Other Woman,* trans. Gillian C. Gill (Ithaca, N.Y.: Cornell University Press, 1985). From a psychoanalytic and literary perspective: Jane Gallop, *Thinking through the Body* (New York: Columbia University Press, 1988). And from an experiential, media, and cultural-studies perspective: Susan Bordo, *Unbearable Weight: Feminism, Western Culture and the Body* (Berkeley: University of California Press, 1993).

9. Chadwick, *Western Asceticism,* 98

10. For a thorough analysis of the Christian tradition's history and theology of patriarchal suspicion of and abuse toward women, see Joanne Carlson Brown and Carole R. Bohn, *Christianity, Patriarchy, and Abuse: A Feminist Critique* (New York: Pilgrim Press, 1989).

11. See J. Flanagan, "The Critical Incident Technique," *Psychological Bulletin* 51, no. 4 (July 1954): 327–58; and J. Duley, "Cross Cultural Field Study," *Implementing Field Experience Education, New Directions for Higher Education* 6 (summer 1974): 13–22.

12. I would recommend joining the National Society for Experiential Education. Their head-quarters is at the following address: 3509 Haworth Drive, Suite 207, Raleigh, NC 27609; phone: (919) 787-3262; fax: (919) 787-3381.

9. Preaching about Sexual and Domestic Violence

1. I refer here to the work of Emmanuel Levinas, who argues that for those who stand within the Judeo-Christian tradition, ethics precedes ontology. We exist and exist fully only in our open-ness to the mystery of the other. In the neighbor's face (*visage*), we experience an absolute obli-gation toward compassion and justice. See Emmanuel Levinas, "God and Philosophy," in *The Levinas Reader,* ed. Sean Hand (Oxford: Basil Blackwell, 1989), 182.

2. This risk begins, in Levinas's terms, when a "face confounds the intentionality that aims at it," when all of our attempts to control, manipulate, or understand the other as an object begin to give way to an openness to the other as truly *other.* We experience the radical vulnerability of the other, and thus the beginning of responsibility for his or her welfare. Emmanuel Levinas, "Meaning and Sense," in *Collected Philosophical Papers*, trans. Alphonso Lingis (The Hague: Martinus Nijhoff, 1987), 97.

3. According to Levinas, seeing the face calls us into a new relationship, but we must respond to that face in order to practice the truth. In doing so, we risk leaving the relative safety of treat-ing the other as an object of analysis and/or manipulation. This is a real *leaving*, for it requires abandoning the very forms of reason endemic to Western culture itself. See especially Levinas, *Totality and Infinity*, trans. Alphonso Lingis (Pittsburgh: Duquesne University Press, 1969), 43.

4. This journey is likely to lead first of all into a "liberal" phase, in which one focuses on the differences between genders, therapeutic language, and a concern for abuse as a misuse of power. From there, one may proceed deeper into a more profoundly unsettling phase, in which one begins to see social constructions of gender and sexuality as fundamentally dominative in their present form. This invites the use of more politically oriented language and less-therapeutic lan-guage and encourages one to locate the seat of abuse less in willful abuses of power than in male sexual identity itself. For an excellent comparison of liberal and more-radical perspectives, see Adams, "Feminist Theology of Religion and State," 15–35.

5. This is not unlike the disorientation that occurs in therapy, though it more closely resem-bles the culturally based "liminality" described by Victor Turner, in which "'the patterned arrange-ments of role-sets, status-sets, and status sequences' consciously recognized and regularly opera-tive in a given society" are exposed to one's consciousness as arbitrary and laden with invested power. During this period of time, what Turner calls "communitas" is experienced. A new vision of society emerges—one of "free and equal comrades." During this "passage," the roles, rela-tionships, and positions of one's lived world are reconstructed. New rituals, symbols, and metaphors are seized upon to mark this passage and to secure its permanence (Victor Turner, *Dramas, Fields, and Metaphors* [Ithaca, N.Y.: Cornell University Press, 1974], 237–40).

6. Given the prevailing construction of male sexual identity, it can be very problematic for men to hear the testimonies of women survivors of battering and incest. According to Carol J. Adams, it is possible for "women's words about sexual victimization [to] become oral pornogra-phy," which "may help to account for the reason so many instances of sexual abuse by clergy and therapists occur against women who have reported to them instances of sexual victimization" (Adams, "Feminist Theology of Religion and State," 19).

7. I especially recommend Adams, *Woman Battering*; Marie M. Fortune, *Family Violence: a Workshop Manual for Clergy and Other Service Providers* (Rockville, Md.: National Clearing-house on Domestic Violence, 1981); Marie M. Fortune, *Love Does No Harm: Sexual Ethics for the Rest of Us,* with a Foreword by Joycelyn Elders (New York: Continuum Press, 1995); and Glaz and Moessner, eds., *Women in Travail.* See also Jeanne Stevenson Moessner, ed., *Through the Eyes*

of Women: Insights for Pastoral Care (Minneapolis: Augsburg Fortress, 1996); Marie Fortune, *Keeping the Faith: Questions and Answers for the Abused Woman* (San Francisco: Harper & Row, 1987); Rita-Lou Clarke, *Pastoral Care for Battered Women* (Philadelphia: Westminster Press, 1987); Linda H. Hollies, ed., *Womanistcare Volume 1* (Evanston, Ill.: Garrett Evangelical Theological Seminary, 1992); Riet Bons-Storm, *The Incredible Woman: Listening to Women's Silences in Pastoral Care and Counseling* (Nashville: Abingdon Press, 1996); Riet Bons-Storm, *Restoring the Soul of a Church: Healing Congregations Wounded by Clergy Sexual Misconduct* (Bethesda, Md.: Alban Institute, in association with the Interfaith Sexual Trauma Institute, 1995); Kali Tal, *Worlds of Hurt: Reading the Literatures of Trauma* (Cambridge: Cambridge University Press, 1996); *Domestic and Sexual Violence Data Collection.*

8. See Mark I. Wallace, *Fragments of the Spirit: Nature, Violence, and the Renewal of Creation* (New York: Continuum Press, 1996), 111. In this book, Wallace provides an excellent critique of René Girard's overly optimistic appraisal of the biblical tradition's relationship to violence. Wallace points out many of the aspects of violence that are part of the tradition.

9. For more on problems with both traditional and contemporary interpretations of atonement, see Brown and Parker, "For God So Loved the World?" 36–59.

10. Marjorie Procter-Smith, "'Reorganizing Victimization': The Intersection between Liturgy and Domestic Violence," in *Violence against Women and Children*, ed. Adams and Fortune, 432.

11. See also Anna Case Winters, *God's Power: Traditional Understandings and Contemporary Challenges* (Louisville, Ky.: Westminster/John Knox Press, 1990).

12. For more on this, see John S. McClure, "The Other Side of Sermon Illustration," *Journal for Preachers* (Lent 1989): 2–4.

13. For more on preaching as a "holding" environment, see J. Randall Nichols, *The Restoring Word: Preaching as Pastoral Communication* (San Francisco: Harper & Row, 1987), 81. When I say "holding" and use the word "hold," I do not mean something sentimental like "hugging," or something broadly empathic that implies that the preacher understands or can feel fully another's experience. Rather, I mean that we are able to reach out with prudence and trustworthiness and hold important or difficult things that are given to us—in the same way that a trustworthy parent might hold onto a precious object for a child, or a trustworthy friend might hold onto a painful worry for a friend.

14. For more on preaching and lamentation, see Mary Cathering Hilkert, "Grace at the Edges: Preaching and Lament," in *Preaching and the Sacramental Imagination* (New York: Continuum Press, 1997), 108–27.

15. Marvin Ellison, *Erotic Justice: A Liberating Ethic of Sexuality* (Louisville, Ky.: Westminster John Knox Press, 1996), 108.

16. John McClure, *The Roundtable Pulpit: Where Leadership and Preaching Meet* (Nashville: Abingdon Press, 1996). See also Lucy Atkinson Rose, *Sharing the Word: Preaching in the Roundtable Church* (Louisville, Ky.: Westminster John Knox Press, 1997).

17. For more on inductive method, see Fred B. Craddock, *Overhearing the Gospel* (Nashville: Abingdon Press, 1978); and Fred B. Craddock, *As One without Authority,* 3d ed. (Nashville: Abingdon Press, 1983).

18. For further examples of this language beyond those provided here, see McClure, *Roundtable Pulpit.*

19. Adams, "Feminist Theology of Religion and the State," 24.

20. From a sermon on 2 Cor. 4:13–5:1 preached by Marian McClure on 5 May 1994 at James Lees Memorial Presbyterian Church in Louisville, Kentucky. This story is paraphrased from a sermon by Susan Hagood Lee, "Witness to Christ: Witness to Pain; One Woman's Journey through Wife Battering," in *Sermons Seldom Heard: Women Proclaim Their Lives,* ed. Annie Lally Milhaven (New York: Crossroad, 1991), 14–15.

11. Wings of Eagles and Holes in the Earth

1. Howard Thurman, *For the Inward Journey* (San Diego: Harcourt Brace Jovanovich, 1984), 139.

15. If It Had Not Been for God on Our Side

1. "The Seventh-Day Adventist Statement on Family Violence" was adopted by the Annual Council of General Conference of Seventh-Day Adventists in October 1996 and prepared in a brochure by the Department of Family Ministries, General Conference of Seventh-Day Adventists, 12501 Old Columbia Pike, Silver Spring, MD 20904, USA.

2. The author acknowledges use of excerpts to describe a community response as published in *A Community Checklist: Important Steps to End Violence against Women* (Washington, D.C.: U.S. Department of Justice, 1996). This document includes contributions from the Advisory Council on Violence against Women.